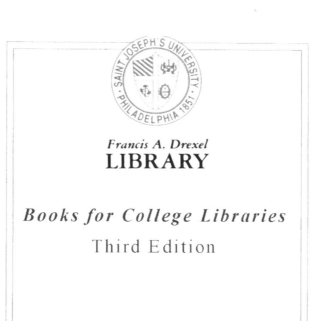

Multinationals, Unions, and Labor Relations in Industrialized Countries

CORNELL INTERNATIONAL INDUSTRIAL AND LABOR RELATIONS REPORTS

Industrial Wages in Chile, by Peter Gregory. 128 pp. $5.50 cloth; $3.00 paper.

Elites, Intellectuals, and Consensus: A Study of the Social Question and the Industrial Relations System in Chile, by James O. Morris. 312 pp. $6.00 cloth.

Poor Countries and Authoritarian Rule, by Maurice F. Neufeld. 256 pp. $5.00 cloth.

CORNELL STUDIES IN INDUSTRIAL AND LABOR RELATIONS

Value Judgments in Arbitration: A Case Study of Saul Wallen, by Brook I. Landis. 200 pp. $10.00 cloth.

Competition and Collective Bargaining in the Needle Trades, 1910-1967, by Jesse T. Carpenter. 936 pp. $17.50 cloth.

The Public Employment Service in Transition, 1933-1968: Evolution of a Placement Service into a Manpower Agency, by Leonard P. Adams. 264 pp. $3.50 paper.

Fringe Benefits: Wages or Social Obligation? by Donna Allen. 288 pp. $4.00 paper.

Procedures and Policies of the New York State Labor Relations Board, by Kurt L. Hanslowe. 224 pp. $4.00 cloth.

Hawthorne Revisited: Management and the Worker, Its Critics, and Developments in Human Relations in Industry, by Henry A. Landsberger. 128 pp. $1.75 paper.

The Labor Injunction in New York City, 1935-1950, by Jacob Seidenberg. 192 pp. $1.00 paper.

Cornell International Industrial and Labor Relations Reports and Cornell Studies in Industrial and Labor Relations are research monographs published by the New York State School of Industrial and Labor Relations. Only those books still in print are listed.

CORNELL INTERNATIONAL INDUSTRIAL
AND LABOR RELATIONS REPORT NUMBER 9

Multinationals, Unions, and Labor Relations in Industrialized Countries

Robert F. Banks and Jack Stieber

editors

NEW YORK STATE SCHOOL OF
INDUSTRIAL & LABOR RELATIONS
CORNELL UNIVERSITY

1977

Library of Congress Catalog Number: 77-4463

ISBN: 0-87546-064-X

ISSN: 0070-0029

Price: $10.00

ORDER FROM

Publications Division
New York State School of
Industrial and Labor Relations
Cornell University, Box 1000
Ithaca, New·York 14853

Library of Congress Cataloging in Publication Data

Main entry under title:

Multinationals, unions, and labor relations in industrialized countries.

  (Cornell international industrial and labor relations report; no. 9)
  1. Industrial relations—Congresses. 2. International business enterprises—Congresses. 3. Collective bargaining—International business enterprises—Congresses. I. Banks, Robert F., 1936-   II. Stieber, Jack, 1919-   III. Series: Cornell international industrial and labor relations reports; no. 9.
HD6971.M79   331   77-4463
ISBN 0-87546-064-X

PRINTED IN THE UNITED STATES OF AMERICA BY
HOFFMAN PRINTING

Contents

Preface

On November 10-13, 1974, the Conference on Industrial Relations Problems Raised by Multinationals in Advanced Industrial Societies was held at the Kellogg Center, Michigan State University, East Lansing, Michigan. The conference was designed to provide a common framework with respect to the economic, social, political, and technological conditions within which industrial relations problems of multinationals occur. The sixty-one conference participants represented unions, managements, governments, and academic institutions in the United States and other advanced industrial nations, all host countries of multinational corporations.

A planning committee composed of Oliver Clarke, Organization for Economic Cooperation and Development; Robert Copp, Ford Motor Company; Paul A. Heise, United States Department of Labor; Everett Kassalow, University of Wisconsin; Duane Kujawa, Florida International University; and Herman Rebhan, the United Automobile Workers (now an official of the International Metalworkers' Federation) assisted the editors, who also organized the conference, in developing topics worthy of exploration and suggesting names of possible participants.

The conference and publication of the proceedings were financed by generous contributions from the Bureau of International Labor Affairs, United States Department of Labor, and from Ford Foundation funds administered by the Center for International Studies and Programs at Michigan State University. Points of view and opinions presented at the conference and included in this volume do not necessarily represent the position or policy of the Department of Labor, Michigan State University, or the publisher.

An international conference and the publication of its proceedings are major undertakings and, as a result, we owe thanks for assistance and support supplied by many individuals. Special thanks go to Deans Ralph Smuckler and Gwen Andrew, respectively of Michigan State University's Center for International Studies and Programs and College of Social Science for the support, both financial and otherwise, they gave to this project. The conference planning committee gave excellent advice on conference topics and the names of possible participants. Professor Robert J. Flanagan of the Graduate School of Business, University of Chicago, supplied a useful report on the conference in his capacity as the Department of Labor's designated rapporteur; Ms. Charlotte Gold and Ms. Elaine

Gruenfeld of the New York State School of Industrial and Labor Relations provided valuable editorial advice and assistance in preparing the manuscript for publication. Ms. Margaret Pegg and the staff at the Kellogg Center are owed many thanks for putting on an exceptionally well-run conference. We also wish to express our appreciation to those on the secretarial staffs of the Michigan State University School of Labor and Industrial Relations and James Madison College, who typed the many drafts of the conference papers and the final manuscript. Special thanks for secretarial assistance and the organization of conference arrangements go to Ms. Kathleen Jackson and Ms. Shirley Kirkland. Finally, we must express our deep appreciation to all the conference participants, whose contributions made the conference an informative and enjoyable enterprise. Further, we note their good cheer and cooperation in working with us during the inevitably long period of time required to prepare the conference proceedings for the publication.

ROBERT F. BANKS, *Dean*
James Madison College
Michigan State University

JACK STIEBER, *Director*
School of Labor and Industrial Relations
Michigan State University

JOEL SEGALL, *Deputy Under Secretary*
for International Affairs
United States Department of Labor

INTRODUCTION
Robert F. Banks and Jack Stieber

The interdependence of nations is a powerful fact of life in the world economy of the 1970s, and the activities of multinational corporations (MNCs) are an important aspect of economic relations between nations. Although business firms with headquarters in one country and production or distribution facilities abroad have existed for some 150 years, the large increase in the number of multinationals and the growth of their share of world output since the early 1960s has greatly expanded their importance and visibility in both industrialized and developing countries. In addition, MNC foreign investment activities have shifted away from their earlier emphasis on vertical production integration to the horizontal extension of production and markets for manufactured goods across national boundaries. Further, while U.S.-owned MNCs still dominate the world economy, they must now compete with growing numbers of multinationals based in Western Europe and Japan. Finally, although in absolute terms the amount of foreign investment in the United States is still small in comparison to the extent of American investment abroad, it has grown rapidly since the early 1960s. This fact has caused concern in the United States, especially since the early 1970s with regard to petrodollar investments by members of the Organization of Petroleum Exporting Countries (OPEC).

The rise of multinational corporations has generated considerable controversy, particularly regarding their multifaceted impact on both home (or source) countries, where the corporation headquarters are, and host countries, where subsidiaries have been established. Some issues recurrently debated—often with considerable heat and limited illumination—in

Robert F. Banks is professor and dean, James Madison College, Michigan State University, East Lansing. Jack Stieber is professor of economics and director of the School of Labor and Industrial Relations at Michigan State University.

1

business, labor, and national and international government circles include the role of multinationals in creating or eliminating jobs in source and host economies, the effect of multinationals on the international balance of payments, the effect of transfer pricing practices on national tax policy, and the impact of multinationals on national politics and economic policies, especially with regard to their supposed challenge to the sovereignty of nation states.[1]

The Michigan State University conference, which was restricted to the industrial relations problems of multinationals in advanced industrialized countries, did not attempt to reach a consensus on any issue. Its purpose was to bring together knowledgeable representatives from unions, multinational companies, and universities in industrialized countries to exchange information and ideas on relevant industrial relations issues.

The three main topics explored at the conference were (1) the locus of industrial relations decision making in multinationals, (2) the impact of multinationals and unions on home and host country industrial relations systems, and (3) the response of organized labor to the MNC challenge, including union attitudes, policy alternatives, and tactics and strategies used in combatting the impact of multinationals. This introduction presents brief summaries of the conference papers and informal discussions on these key issues. At various points we will make reference to other published material dealing with these issues, particularly works that have appeared since November 1974 when the conference was held.[2]

Locus of Industrial Relations
Decision Making in Multinationals

The controversy over whether industrial relations decisions in multinationals are made by home company executives in New York, London, Tokyo, Amsterdam, Frankfurt, and elsewhere or by local plant managements is a recurrent theme whenever union and management representatives meet at conferences and symposia. Unions generally charge that industrial relations issues, as well as other major decisions, are decided or dictated by the parent company, usually in another country. Managements respond that such centralized decision making is not only

---

1. Oliver Clarke, "The Multinational Enterprise, the State, and International Organizations: Industrial Relations, Employment, and Other Problems," in *International Labor and the Multinational Enterprise*, ed. Duane Kujawa (New York: Praeger, 1975), pp. 6-7.

2. In preparing this introduction the authors gratefully acknowledge their reference to the report submitted by the U.S. Department of Labor conference rapporteur, Dr. Robert J. Flanagan, associate professor of labor economics at the Graduate School of Business, University of Chicago. "Summary and Evaluation: Conference on Industrial Relations Problems Raised by Multinationals in Advanced Industrial Societies, Michigan State University, November 10-13, 1974," February 1975, mimeographed.

impractical but also poor managerial practice. For example, Robert Copp's paper vigorously asserts that authority for industrial relations decision making in the Ford Motor Company resides with the firm's subsidiary managers.[3]

Critics from the unions, however, suggest that on occasion multinational managements use the existence of such supposed decentralized decision making as a defense against local union demands when, in fact, corporate action is possible and, in many other cases, has been initiated to solve problems arising in national subsidiaries. Other participants argue that because local industrial relations managers work within the framework of a companywide industrial relations policy it is incorrect to claim that MNC headquarters exercise a benign influence on the industrial relations practices of subsidiaries.[4]

Part of the problem resides in differing definitions of the term *industrial relations*. Thus, Copp's paper distinguishes between investment decisions regarding plant location and production deployment and the effects of such decisions on manpower. The former, in Copp's view, are outside the scope of industrial relations while the latter are appropriate subjects for consultation and bargaining with unions. This view was held by most of the management representatives. Ben Sharman's argument reflects the typical union view that this is a false distinction, for investment decisions and their consequences are inseparable. It makes no sense to the unions to bargain over the effects of investment decisions when it is too late to affect the basic decisions concerning where plants are to be located and how production is to be allocated.[5]

Academicians, such as B. C. Roberts and David H. Blake, have approached the problem from another angle. They have tried to identify criteria that determine the degree of centralization or decentralization of decision making on industrial relations issues in MNCs. The following hypotheses have fairly widespread support:

1. Corporate philosophy and style affect management's approach to decision making. Some companies, usually those inexperienced in mul-

---

3. For a similar statement concerning the policy of General Motors, see Frank W. Angle, "The Conduct of Labor Relations in General Motors' Overseas Operations," in *International Labor*, ed. Kujawa, pp. 138-46. For additional evidence that the determination of employment conditions is essentially a matter of local decision making, see the recent surveys by the International Labor Office, *Social and Labour Practices of Some European-based Multinationals in the Metal Trades* (Geneva: ILO, 1976), p. 114, and *Multinationals in Western Europe: The Industrial Relations Experience* (Geneva: ILO, 1976), pp. 53-54.

4. The ILO survey, *Social and Labour Practices of European-based Multinationals* (p. 76), observes that "it is hardly conceivable that a certain company spirit . . . [i.e.] unwritten rules of behavior and generally accepted standards . . . should not affect managerial decision-making in labor relations and personnel policy."

5. For further evidence of the significance of centralized investment decisions in multinationals, see ILO, *Multinationals: The Industrial Relations Experience*, pp. 15-17.

tinational operations, are inclined to be ethnocentric while others are polycentric in their industrial relations orientation. The former are likely to try to export home country practices; the latter to follow prevailing practices and leave decision making to local executives.

2. Membership in employer associations in host countries promotes decentralization.

3. Extensive legal regulation of industrial relations, as in West Germany, requires MNCs to grant greater local autonomy in decision making.

4. The further removed a host country's culture and customs from those of the home country, the greater the need for decentralization in decision making.

5. The more integrated are production processes, the greater the inducement to centralize decision making in the home office of the company.

6. The higher the ratio of foreign to home country employment, the greater the tendency to decentralize industrial relations decision making.

7. Because of financial and planning considerations, issues such as pension plans and wage payment systems are frequently subject to headquarters' control.

8. There appears to be more centralization of decision making in new subsidiaries than in those acquired through purchase or take-over of existing companies.

9. Crisis situations, such as strikes, lead to greater involvement of headquarters staff even in relatively decentralized MNCs.

A 1975 survey of 168 MNCs, conducted by the Conference Board, found that American MNCs exercised more centralized control of labor relations policies than MNCs based elsewhere.[6] The same survey found that MNCs that already had been targets of multinational union actions—one-quarter of the total—tended to be more centralized than nontarget firms. One wonders whether there is a cause-and-effect relationship and if so in which direction it operates. Do centralized labor relations policies cause MNCs to become union targets, or does joint union action lead a firm to follow a more centralized policy? Two examples presented in the Conference Board survey suggest the former. Thus the director of labor relations for a U.S.-owned food company that gives its local management wide latitude in determining policy said, "Our firm believes in decentralization and consequently has not been a target of coordinated union campaigns." A U.S.-owned machinery and chemical MNC ascribed the failure of the strong union representing its employees to cross national boundaries to the fact that "each plant management . . . has total autonomy as to labor relations."

---

6. *The Multinational Union Challenges the Multinational Company* (New York: The Conference Board, 1975), pp. 14-15. The survey included 134 corporations with headquarters in the United States and 34 with headquarters in other countries.

Because a very high proportion of multinationals are based in the United States, any discussion of MNC industrial relations policies tends to focus on U.S. companies. It is necessary, however, to remember that MNCs based in other industrialized nations are growing rapidly and that foreign investment in the United States has about doubled during the last decade. Thus questions raised about industrial relations problems of MNCs have relevance not only for the United States. The paper by Michael J. Jedel and Duane Kujawa and a later monograph by the same authors are among the few studies of the manner in which foreign MNCs conduct their industrial relations in the United States.[7]

The Jedel-Kujawa study, though limited by the low response rate to their questionnaires, the small number of unionized firms in the sample, and the fact that their data were gathered entirely from management representatives, indicates that there is little difference between U.S.-owned MNCs operating abroad and foreign-owned MNCs in the United States in the locus of decision making in industrial relations. Like their U.S. counterparts, foreign-owned companies claimed minimal involvement in industrial relations decision making in their U.S. subsidiaries. The U.S. operations of these companies were reported to be completely autonomous on such issues as union security, participation in employer associations, composition of management negotiating teams, and whether bargaining should be on a local or national basis. This apparently high degree of decentralization was found despite a somewhat greater tendency for foreign multinationals to use home country staff in top-level industrial relations positions than U.S. multinationals operating abroad. This characteristic may be a function of the relative newness of such operations in the United States rather than the result of a deliberate policy regarding staffing of industrial relations offices.

Listening to the conference participants and reading case studies of industrial relations in MNCs leads us to the conclusion that, although unions may inveigh against decision making by headquarters executives, they are less interested in where the decision is made than in the nature of the decision. An unpalatable decision made by management is not more acceptable because it originates with local management, and a beneficial action dictated by central corporate headquarters is not less welcome because of its origin. This explains why international union federations try to influence headquarters labor relations executives to overrule a local management decision on some occasions, while criticizing them for interfering with local management at other times.

This pragmatic approach by unions has its counterpart in MNC

---

7. Michael J. Jedel and Duane Kujawa, "Management and Employment Practices of Foreign Direct Investors in the United States" (Atlanta: Georgia State University, 1976), mimeographed.

managements. Some situations will cause even the most decentralized corporate management to become involved in local decision making. Strikes that affect MNC plants outside the country of occurrence are only the most obvious example. Plant shutdowns, large-scale dismissals, and the introduction of pension schemes creating long-term obligations are cited in an International Labor Organization report as other issues that may involve MNC headquarters in local decisions.[8] In addition, home offices exert influence through the selection and training of local top management who make most of the industrial relations decisions.

The pragmatic approach taken by unions and managements to decision making in industrial relations should not deter scholars from research on criteria affecting the degree of centralization and decentralization in MNCs. The trigger point for involvement of central headquarters in decisions on labor issues will vary among companies. Understanding how different factors affect decisions to intervene will add to our understanding of MNC behavior on industrial relations issues. Such research, however, is not likely to explain union-management differences on the question of centralization and decentralization, which derive more from self-interest than from any overall philosophy.

Impact of Multinationals and Unions on Home and Host Country Industrial Relations Systems

The growth of multinational corporations across national boundaries and the increased communication and interaction among unions from different countries obviously offers opportunities for the introduction of industrial relations policies and practices on a worldwide basis. To what extent have MNCs and unions taken advantage of these opportunities to influence the characteristics of industrial relations systems in home and host countries?

It follows from the positions taken on the issue of centralization versus decentralization of MNC decision making that union representatives, who believe that decisions on industrial relations matters are often made or controlled by home offices, see MNCs as extending home country policies and practices to their subsidiaries and branches abroad. Employers, on the other hand, who stress the decentralized nature and conduct of industrial relations with local management making virtually all decisions, possibly after consulting headquarters, see conformity to host country policies and practices rather than innovation as the norm. There is less debate over the role of unions in facilitating innovation because they are not in a position to effectuate change unilaterally but must depend on economic power to influence MNC managements or political power to affect government

---

8. See ILO, *Multinationals: The Industrial Relations Experience*, pp. 26-32.

policies or statutes in the area of industrial relations. Unions also must be able to persuade their counterparts in other countries that it is in their interest to borrow standards and practices from abroad before acting to effectuate such transfers.

True to the above scenario, Nat Weinberg's paper argues that MNCs have, and use, the power to transmit standards and policies from home to host countries and to follow practices abroad that are prohibited at home, such as racial and sex discrimination, with only one objective in mind—to promote or maximize their economic interests. Among the practices cited by Weinberg and others as characterizing U.S. MNC behavior are a preference for company rather than employer association bargaining, layoffs based solely on economic needs, resistance to unionization, opposition to the introduction or extension of worker participation, fixed-term as opposed to open-end contracts, changes in wage payment systems, productivity bargaining, job evaluation and merit rating, and dealing with a single union rather than many unions.[9]

Not all of the MNC innovations are undesirable or disadvantageous to workers and unions. Indeed, some have become accepted and widely adopted by domestic companies and even by unions in host countries. This points up an apparent inconsistency in the position of those who favor conformity to host country practices and at the same time advocate transnational bargaining by MNCs and unions. As pointed out by John A. Belford, such bargaining could take place only outside the jurisdiction of employer associations and this would be contrary to the norm in many host countries.

Roger Blanpain's paper concludes that the industrial relations impact of multinationals in the United Kingdom and Belgium has been minimal. A specific evaluation of their impact on such issues as union recognition, membership in employer associations, job security, productivity bargaining, relative wages, and the duration and nature of collective agreements identifies some MNC innovations, but the general picture shows conformity with local practices.[10] The argument that MNCs generally prefer to bargain on a company basis is questioned in the Blanpain study, and management participants argued that most multinationals have a variable policy on the issue of employer association membership with affiliation decisions being made by host country managers.[11]

9. For further examples of some of these practices, see ILO, *Multinationals: The Industrial Relations Experience*, pp. 26-39.

10. Blanpain does suggest that multinational policies and actions have contributed to the general Western European movement toward decentralized bargaining.

11. The ILO Survey, *Social and Labour Practices of European-based Multinationals* (p. 74), reports that most MNC subsidiaries studied were members of the appropriate employer association. It also noted, however, that as a result of "such active participation in national employers' organizations the companies unanimously report that, in applying directives or

In situations in which multinationals influenced local practices un-
favorably, U.S.-owned MNCs were most often cited in examples. But they
are by no means the only or even the worst offenders of local mores or
cultures. Kazutoshi Koshiro gives examples of Japanese MNC behavior in
Southeast Asian countries that rival or exceed even the most egregious mistakes made by U.S. companies. On balance, he believes that American
MNCs in Japan have adapted better to local customs than Japanese MNCs
operating overseas. In general, the wider the cultural gap between countries, the more difficult the problems of adaptation. This explains some of
Japan's problems operating in nations with vastly different cultures and
norms for corporate behavior: paternalism, consensus decision making,
payment by seniority rather than performance, and other practices foreign
to Western nations pose special problems for Japanese MNCs. The
relationship between cultural gap and industrial relations problems also
may explain why Western-based MNCs have greater difficulty adapting in
underdeveloped countries than in industrialized nations that share many
of the same values and have considerable similarity in governmental forms,
degree of unionization, and aspirations of people. Despite the fact that this
conference was supposed to deal only with MNCs in industrialized countries, the worst examples of MNC behavior almost always were drawn from
operations in developing countries.

Though unions have played a less active role than managements in the
transmission of industrial relations policies and practices, there are examples of worker benefits crossing national boundaries. The extended
vacations pioneered in the United States by the steelworkers' union are, according to Weinberg, an adaptation of the "long service leaves" in
Australia, and the payment of vacation bonuses, only beginning to be mentioned in the United States, has its genesis in Western Europe where such
extra payments are common practice. European unions have also borrowed from the United States: wage increases tied to cost of living, annual
productivity increases, increased relief time in the automobile industry, the
forty-hour workweek, supplementary unemployment benefits, and concern with the quality of working life. This borrowing among unions cannot be traced directly to MNCs. It is rather a natural result of increased communication through international secretariats; interaction in
organizations like the ILO, the Organization for Economic Cooperation
and Development (OECD), and the European Economic Community

---

recommendations resulting from such membership, they have not encountered any problems
attributable to the international links of a company. First, they appear to wield sufficient influence in the organizations to prevent the emergence of policies detrimental to their own interests. Secondly, they appear to have ample leeway in their labour relations policies and practices as a result of being free from interference from headquarters, in accommodating
themselves to local patterns. Thirdly, they generally are able to offer better employment conditions than local industry."

(EEC); and visits of union officials to each other's countries as fraternal delegates to exchange views on common problems. The existence and growth of MNCs and the common interests of unions representing workers in the same multinational, however, have undoubtedly facilitated and accelerated the pursuit of new benefits and common objectives in collective bargaining.

It is inevitable that discussions focused on innovation and change will produce examples where MNCs and, to a lesser extent, unions fostered such developments. The general conclusion of most conference participants, however, was that the overall impact of MNCs on industrial relations practices in industrialized nations has been small, that adaptation to local and national norms is more characteristic than aggressive innovation and change, and that the more experience an MNC gains in overseas operations, the less inclined it is to try to force home office policies and practices upon host country management. This corresponds with the tenor of discussions at other conferences and in the literature on industrial relations policies of multinationals.[12]

Bargaining Experience with MNCs

These general conclusions about multinationals were further confirmed in the reports on actual bargaining experience with foreign-based multinationals operating in the United States, the United Kingdom, and West Germany. In the United Kingdom, union experience with several U.S. and Canadian companies compares favorably with relationships with British companies of similar size and product. Though resistance to unionization was encountered in a few companies, after recognition they were highly cooperative both in negotiations and in consultation on future plans. According to A. M. Evans of the Transport and General Workers' Union, those MNCs in the United Kingdom with which he had experience had adapted to the local environment when faced with a strong union, although most sought to establish companywide industrial relations policies with emphasis on wage structure reform, usually involving changes from piece work to day wage systems.[13] Evans had some reservations about whether MNC behavior would be the same with weak unions but offered no examples to support this view.

Walter Schlotfeldt, a West German management participant, indicated that once MNCs understood the dual system characterizing industrial relations in that country—negotiating through employer associations

---

12. For a similar conclusion based on a general survey of MNC management opinions, see ILO, *Multinationals: The Industrial Relations Experience*, p. 69.

13. The ILO survey, *Multinationals: The Industrial Relations Experience* (p. 32), notes that it is "fairly common . . . for [multinational] subsidiaries to introduce large or small parts of their own (home country) job evaluation; job rating and other wage system practices."

with unions on wages and working conditions and consultation with works councils on other matters—they behaved no differently from domestic companies.

Similarly, Joseph Kirk, a United Steelworkers of America representative in the South, testified to the adaptability of MNCs to community patterns.[14] Kirk gave an interesting example of a union using a "big stick" to bring a foreign MNC operating in the United States into line. The United Steelworkers union, engaged in a bitter strike for union recognition against a West German MNC, called on the German Confederation of Trade Unions (DGB) for help. The DGB put pressure on the parent company by threatening to withdraw financial support being provided the company through the union's banking subsidiary, if it did not rein in its U.S. plant. The strike ended and a bargaining relationship was established. This example shows that pressure brought to bear by home country forces is not limited to MNCs but also can be exercised by unions.

In their general comparison of attitudes and opinions of managers of foreign-owned MNCs in the United States and persons occupying similar positions in domestic companies, Jedel and Kujawa also found more similarities than differences on a wide variety of issues, with both groups agreeing that there should not be significant variations in industrial relations practices. In another study based on personal interviews, the same authors did find a few important differences between foreign-owned and U.S.-owned companies in the United States: newer foreign firms tended less frequently to be unionized; Japanese-owned companies, though willing to accept unions when legally required to do so, felt that the presence of a union "complicated" employee relations; and U.S. workers in foreign firms felt that there was a greater emphasis on productivity and product quality in foreign-owned enterprises. On the specific issue of collective bargaining, however, negotiation patterns in foreign firms were similar to those in similarly situated U.S.-owned enterprises.[15] Conference discussions among the larger group of practitioners also elicited no evidence to challenge the general conclusion that adaptation to national and community standards in union relations and negotiations was much more common than bucking the tide by MNCs operating in industrialized countries.

Organized Labor's Response to the Multinational Challenge

Typically, organized labor has viewed the emergence of the mul-

---

14. Joseph Kirk gave an oral presentation at the conference. Because there was not a written version, his talk could not be included among the papers in this volume.

15. Jedel and Kujawa, "Management and Employment Practices," pp. ii-ix.

tinational enterprise as an extension of the historical spread toward widening product markets, which raises two potential threats to union members and their organizations.[16] The first potential threat is to the job security of union members, especially in source countries as multinationals produce abroad what could have been produced at home, thus eliminating current jobs or not creating new employment opportunities. The second is to union bargaining power in both source and host countries as a result of MNC abilities to shift production between countries during strikes, thus reducing the cost of the dispute to the affected company.

Traditionally, unions have chosen between collective bargaining and legislative enactment to further their general objectives. Such choices or mixture of choices have varied between labor movements and over time within national movements. In responding to the multinational challenge these same alternatives have been used by organized labor with the particular strategy mix selected dependent on the character of trade union structure and bargaining relationships, ideology, the specific nature of the threats posed by multinationals, and the extent of political support for labor and union influence over the general economic environment.[17] In general, two varieties of collective bargaining have been identified: (1) direct bargaining with MNC headquarters and (2) coordinated international (transnational) collective bargaining. Alternatively, two types of legislative approach can be noted: (1) protective national legislation and (2) international codes of conduct (fair labor standards) for MNCs.

A common assertion is that MNCs enjoy significant advantages over unions in combating threats posed by organized labor. Weinberg cites the following as typical multinational advantages: centralized decision-making structures, substantial political influence in host countries, effective international communication systems, the resources to collect information on national social and labor legislation and labor contract provisions and practices, the ability to use local employer association membership as a shield against companywide union demands, the manipulation of production and investment location decisions to thwart union international bargaining initiatives, and the capacity to act unilaterally on industrial relations issues.

Union participants also note the various difficulties confronting unions in developing coordinated international strategies to combat multinationals. These difficulties include the lack of strong centralized decision-making authority within most labor movements, financial weaknesses that impede communication and information flows,

---

16. Flanagan, "Summary and Evaluation," pp. 7-8.
17. Robert W. Cox, "Labor and the Multinationals," *Foreign Affairs* 54, no. 2 (January 1976): 355-59.

ideological and religious differences among labor groups, variations in national bargaining objectives and practices, and the lack of wage parity, harmonization of working conditions, and common contract expiration dates across national boundaries.

While acknowledging these limitations on union bargaining power, several conference participants argued that both national and international labor organizations have had a significant impact on multinational operations and that this is likely to increase. Further it is suggested that multinational managements rarely make production or investment decisions wholly on the basis of industrial relations considerations and that since existing investments cannot be easily abandoned—at least not in the short run—multinational industrial relations options are significantly limited.

Union Ideologies and Policies toward MNCs

Unions everywhere are deeply concerned over the growth and proliferation of MNCs. Their shared concern, however, does not necessarily lead them to pursue or support similar policies or approaches in dealing with the phenomenon. Everett Kassalow's paper shows that the greatest differences among unions are to be found in the positions of international, regional, and national federations, especially between those that represent the "free unions" and those that speak for communist-oriented unions and the World Confederation of Labour (WCL), which is made up of socialist-oriented Christian trade unions. Even within federations and countries, there are differences in the way unions approach the MNC problem.

The views of the International Confederation of Free Trade Unions (ICFTU) and its autonomous trade union secretariats are very similar. The International Metalworkers' Federation (IMF) is the largest and most active secretariat engaged in countering MNC threats to its member unions and workers. The IMF has established worldwide company councils of union leaders from different countries in which particular MNCs operate. These councils exchange data on MNC subsidiaries operating in their countries, attempt to coordinate collective bargaining in different plants of an MNC, and through the secretariat staff, seek support from unions dealing with the same MNC in cases of strikes and other crisis situations. Other secretariats try to achieve much the same objectives with regard to MNCs in their jurisdictions.[18]

On another level, the IMF favors an international code of conduct to

_____
18. The International Federation of Chemical and General Workers' Unions, the International Union of Food and Allied Workers, and the International Federation of Commercial, Clerical and Technical Workers also have been particularly active in the struggle against multinationals.

regulate the MNCs. Such a code is also supported by the ICFTU, which, although critical of MNCs, is not ideologically opposed to their existence. In the United States, the AFL-CIO generally supports the activities of the international trade secretariats and favors the idea of international regulation of MNCs. But because it is disappointed with the lack of progress made in these efforts, the AFL-CIO has placed greater emphasis on national regulation of MNCs. This reflects the great concern of U.S. unions, which is not shared by unions in most other countries, over the extent to which the growth of MNCs has led to the loss of jobs for their members. This concern is to some extent shared by Swedish trade unions, which have acted to regulate the export of capital to protect jobs at home.

Contrast these views and approaches with those of the communist-led World Federation of Trade Unions (WFTU) and the WCL. To the WFTU, multinationals are just another manifestation of the contradictions of "world monopoly capitalism." It is critical of the international codes of conduct proposed by the free trade union federations as based on an "illusion about changing the nature of capitalism." As for the worldwide councils organized by the IMF and other secretariats, the WFTU is opposed to "multinational union" negotiations with the MNCs. It regards such councils as limitations on autonomous national unions and stresses the development of "national norms" and international cooperation among national unions through exchange of data. This is in sharp contrast to the IMF, which sees national unions, acting alone, as not capable of coping with powerful multinationals and, therefore, on occasion favors joint action even at the cost of limiting the autonomy of member unions.

Support for the WFTU position is found among national communist-led unions. The French General Confederation of Labor (CGT) scorns "trade union counter-power" and codes of conduct for MNCs as merely "making acceptable capitalist relations of production and the new forms of exploitation." This view is shared by other communist-influenced union leaders in Italy and Great Britain.

Just as communist unions and leaders support the WFTU position, so do the so-called free national and individual trade union bodies generally espouse the approach of the ICFTU and its secretariats. The British Trades Union Congress (TUC) favors "coordinated countervailing force" against MNCs, international regulation of MNCs, and, ultimately, bargaining on an international level. Kassalow regards this commitment to transnational bargaining as less than total and cautions that not all TUC affiliates would support its statements on international union cooperation and regulation of MNCs.

Another illustration of the conflict between free and communist-led unions is provided by the contrasting positions on worker participation in management. Western European unions have long supported and many have achieved some form of worker participation in management decision making. Some also regard such participation as a useful way of influencing the behavior of MNCs. Communist unions oppose worker participation as "dust in the eyes of the workers." They favor requiring management to provide information and even to consult with workers but oppose involving employees in management decisions as a vehicle for making them share responsibility for decisions that have as their ultimate objective the increase of profits.

The WCL, although critical of Soviet-style socialism, has a position on MNCs that to some extent includes the views of both the communist-led and the free trade unions. The WCL sees the MNCs as a "channel of imperialism" and an impediment to national "planification." Nonetheless, it favors a "minimum code," enforceable by the United Nations, to regulate MNCs. On multinational collective bargaining, the WCL believes that it is "not desirable" unless it results from a real "balance of forces and does not take place in a 'vacuum.'"

Reflecting their different level of economic development, Asian affiliates of the ICFTU have a more favorable attitude toward MNCs than the parent organization. Thus, the principal officer of the Singapore National Trades Union Congress warns the ICFTU not to be too "protectionist" in prohibiting the export of capital by MNCs and sees multinationals, effectively controlled, as a source of investment and vehicles for the transfer of technology to the third world. The Asian ICFTU seeks more direct investment by MNCs in the less developed countries while controlling them through a "code of conduct."

In what may lead to the most direct action taken to regulate MNCs in any country, Japan has formed a tripartite committee made up of union, management, and government representatives to examine the policies of Japanese-owned MNCs abroad. The objective of the Liaison Council for the Study of Industrial Relations and the Multinational Enterprise is to establish a code of behavior for Japanese enterprises overseas. To appreciate the significance of this action, it is as if, in the United States, the AFL-CIO, the National Association of Manufacturers, and the federal government were to form a committee to study the operations of U.S.-owned MNCs abroad with the express purpose of developing a code of conduct to guide MNC behavior in the future.

Emilio Gabaglio of the communist-socialist-led Italian General Confederation of Labor (CGIL) agrees with Kassalow's conclusion, but cautions against overemphasizing the practical consequences of the different union positions. Recently in Western Europe, for example, political and ideological differences have not prevented some degree of unity between diverse national labor centers in Italy, Holland, France, and Belgium. This trend to common action is demonstrated in the 1974 membership enlargement of the European Trade Union Congress (ETUC), which originally was established by the European organizations affiliated to the ICFTU, to include all organizations formerly affiliated with the WCL's European organization, other autonomous national centers, and the CGIL, a WFTU affiliate.[19] This organizational transformation has been encouraged by labor's growing realization of European economic interdependence, partly a consequence of multinational activities, but is mainly the result of the growing impact of the European Community (EC). Many observers have argued that the establishment of a communitywide code of company conduct for both national and multinational enterprises and the emergence of some form of regionwide collective bargaining are likely prospects in the near future.[20]

Trade union policies and approaches to deal with the MNC phenomenon reflect the depth of concern felt by the unions toward this new challenge that threatens their existing national power bases. Despite differing ideologies, structures, and experience, all unions feel threatened by the MNCs and impelled to counter this new source of power, although they are far from united or clear on how this is to be done. Still, as may be the case in Western Europe, ideological objections to joint action may be eroded by opportunities for unions to pursue common policies to counter multinationals.

MNCs and Transnational Bargaining

Transnational collective bargaining between unions representing employees in several countries and individual MNCs has not yet occurred, and because of the previously mentioned barriers to joint union action it is not a likely prospect in the foreseeable future. This conclusion is based on discussions at the conference and is consistent with the findings and views of many surveys, studies, and informed opinions of academic scholars and union and management representatives expressed in articles, seminars, and conferences during the early 1970s.[21]

MNC employers, almost without exception, are opposed to transnational bargaining. The only break in the employer ranks in in-

19. Gabaglio also reports the likely emergence of some form of relationship with the ETUC by the communist-led French CGT.

20. For various views on this question, see Hans Günter, "Labor and Multinational Corporations in Western Europe: Some Problems and Prospects" and P.L. Dronkers, "A Multinational Organization and Industrial Relations: The Philips Case," in *International Labor*, ed. Kujawa, pp. 147-72, and B. C. Roberts, "Multinational Collective Bargaining: A European Prospect?" *British Journal of Industrial Relations* 11, no. 1 (March 1973): 1-19.

21. Occasionally unions in host and source countries have made representations to individual MNC headquarters concerning future production or investment plans or specific labor conflicts in subsidiaries, but management has never viewed these meetings as formal negotiating sessions, and they have had mixed results.

dustrialized countries recently reported by the ILO came from the Fiat
Company, which favored transnational bargaining "tending to standar-
dize the regulations in the metal industries covering individual employer-
worker relations and their collective aspect, provided national bargaining
defines their technical and economic content." The Fiat reply was directed
particularly to multinationals in the European Community.

Unions, although much more favorable in their attitudes toward
transnational bargaining, are by no means of one mind regarding its
desirability. Questionnaire surveys and interviews conducted by the ILO
indicate much greater support for international cooperation among unions, exchange of information and data, and opportunities to be consulted
before decisions are made affecting employment and production than for
full-fledged transnational collective bargaining. This may reflect the
recognition of the relatively good wages and other economic benefits
received by workers employed by the MNCs in the developed nations, as
well as the many obstacles to transnational bargaining. Sentiment for
transnational bargaining appears to be stronger in smaller countries such
as Belgium and the Netherlands, but even there it is seen as limited to the
EEC. In the United States, the AFL-CIO sees serious limitations in
transnational bargaining and the United Steelworkers was one of the unions reported by the ILO as having formed no opinion on this approach to
dealing with MNCs.[22]

Though not necessarily favoring transnational bargaining, many unions have been involved in various forms of international cooperation or
sympathetic action in support of workers in other countries. These actions
have usually been initiated or coordinated through one of the international
secretariats. The most active of the secretariats is the IMF whose auto councils are described in the paper by Burton Bendiner, coordinator of the IMF's
World Automotive Councils.

Starting in 1966 with councils for four multinational automobile
manufacturers, there are today ten world automotive councils covering all
major automobile companies. The councils have three major functions, all
designed to coordinate bargaining: communications, solidarity action,
and the holding of periodic meetings. Member unions are kept informed
about negotiations going on in other countries, union demands and
management responses, and the final terms of settlement when agreements
are reached. In strike situations, the auto council coordinator takes
whatever action is feasible to assist striking workers. In one situation, this
involved intervention by the president of the Japanese auto workers union
on behalf of striking workers of the Nissan-Mexicana plant in Mexico,
which according to the IMF led to a settlement well above management's

---

22. See ILO, *Social and Labour Practices of European-based Multinationals*, pp. 91-96.

original offer. In another situation, union representatives at the Cologne works of Ford Motor Company agreed not to accept overtime work on production shifted from the Dagenham plant in the United Kingdom, which was shut down by a strike. In no instance, however, has the IMF called a strike in any country to support a stoppage in an auto plant in another country.

The IMF believes that some of its most important and effective work has been done on behalf of unions in developing countries, which need encouragement and support from their counterparts in the more advanced nations where MNCs are based. In several instances, IMF member unions have exerted pressure or influence on a parent company in their country to intervene with its subsidiary in a developing nation. The IMF also assists unions in developing countries by organizing training programs and seminars that bring them in contact with the more experienced and powerful unions in Western Europe and the United States.

John Alan James, an international management consultant, sees little interest among either management or labor representatives in transnational bargaining if that term is defined as having as its objective legally binding negotiation of agreements across national lines. On the other hand, he regards discussions between unions and a single MNC or employer association on a wide variety of subjects as potentially useful and possible to achieve. Such discussions have already taken place in a few MNCs, most notably between the Philips Company and its unions under the auspices of the European Metalworkers Federation (EMF).[23] According to an ILO study "no real progress was achieved" after four meetings and a fifth, scheduled for May 1975, was cancelled because the EMF insisted on including in its delegation an adviser from the International Metalworkers' Federation. Philips regarded this as a violation of a previous agreement to include representatives only from member countries of the European Economic Community and refused to meet on this basis.[24]

The ILO conclusion regarding lack of progress in the Philips meetings, while perhaps true with respect to resolving specific issues or reaching concrete conclusions, may be too sweeping a judgment on the value of such meetings generally. Another ILO report concludes that, at least for the un-

---

23. Since the late 1960s, such international meetings on a variety of subjects have been held between groupings of unions and various companies, including Philips, N.V., Brown-Boveri, Nestlé, Fokker-VFW, Europanballage (Continental Can), AEG/Telefunken-Zanussi, IBM, and Ford. Multinational managements uniformly stress the informal nature of these meetings. See Günter Köpke, "Union Responses in Continental Europe," in *Bargaining without Boundaries: The Multinational Corporation and International Labor Relations*, ed. Robert J. Flanagan and Arnold R. Weber, pp. 212-15 (Chicago: University of Chicago Press, 1974) and ILO, *Multinationals: The Industrial Relations Experience*, pp. 56-60.

24. ILO, *Social and Labour Practices of European-based Multinationals*, pp. 94-95, and P. L. Dronkers, "The Philips Case," pp. 166-69.

ions, such transnational meetings have proved valuable both for informational purposes and as opportunities for the unions to raise questions
and register complaints regarding nonuniformity of working conditions
in plants of different countries.[25] Company representatives, even though
acceding to such meetings, have a more limited view of their value and
most would prefer not to have them.

It is clear from discussions at the conference as well as at similar
gatherings and from other expressions of opinion that discussion and consultation is far more acceptable to MNC managements than transnational
bargaining. Indeed, James suggests that the term "transnational bargaining" be dropped so that MNC managements would have assurance that any
agreed-upon meetings would not be transformed from discussion and informational sessions into efforts by the unions at negotiations. Even with
such assurances, however, studies in the United Kingdom and the United
States indicate that only a minority of MNC managements would be
prepared to cooperate with union requests for meetings on a regional or international basis.

National and International Efforts
to Regulate MNC Behavior

Although no papers were commissioned on national and international
efforts to regulate MNC behavior, several papers and many of the discussions referred to various proposals for legislative controls including
codes of conduct on fair labor standards and other issues. This topic has
become a subject of intense attention in various countries and a wide range
of international organizations that have developed or are working on
regulatory approaches.[26]

National legislative controls have included efforts by unions in source
countries to restrict, or at least raise the cost of, investment abroad by multinationals, thus limiting job losses at home. The major example of such
an approach is the Burke-Hartke bill proposed with the support of the
AFL-CIO in the U.S. Congress in the early 1970s. In addition, legislative

---

25. ILO, *Multinationals: The Industrial Relations Experience*, especially pp. 46-48.

26. For a discussion of such activities by the ILO, the United Nations, the Economic and
Social Council (ECOSOC), and the Conference on Trade and Development (UNCTAD), see
ILO, *International Principles and Guidelines on Social Policy for Multinational Enterprises:
Their Usefulness and Feasibility* (Geneva: ILO, 1976), pp. 3-6. In May 1976 it was reported
that the OECD had formulated a code of conduct for multinationals, including guidelines on
the disclosure of information and on various industrial relations matters. See "24 Nations Set
Up a Corporate Code," *New York Times*, May 27, 1976, pp. 1, 6-7. For a review and discussion
of various regulatory approaches for multinationals, see Paul A. Tharp, Jr., "Transnational
Enterprises and International Regulation: A Survey of Various Approaches in International
Organizations," *International Organization* 30, no. 1 (Winter 1976): 47-73, and Robert O.
Keohane and Van Doorn Ooms, "The Multinational Firm and International Regulations,"
International Organization 29, no. 1 (Winter 1975): 169-209.

proposals have been made to many national governments that would enable organized labor to combat multinationals more effectively, ensuring that they do not compete unfairly on such issues as collective bargaining rights and fair labor and social policy standards. A specific proposal discussed at the conference is to establish regulations requiring uniform accounting standards and principles for multinationals with information being provided for each national subsidiary as well as for the global operations of the MNC as a whole. A key ingredient in such an accounting framework would be the provision of data especially relevant for collective bargaining.[27]

Under the label of the "beachhead principle," Weinberg proposes national legislation that would permit foreign investments by MNCs only when these firms would agree to undertake in their foreign subsidiaries a variety of social obligations, including the payment of fair wages and provision of fair labor standards, a guarantee of collective bargaining rights, and a commitment not to discriminate against workers on the basis of race or creed. Such legislation could put teeth into the various relevant ILO recommendations, which either have been ratified only by a few countries or are ratified but not enforced and might ultimately have a liberalizing effect on the industrial relations and social policies of the various host countries.[28]

Further, labor representatives argued that because national governments have fears about putting their MNCs at a disadvantage relative to other nations and because of the absence of MNC loyalties to home countries, international regulation is imperative if multinationals are to play socially responsible roles in industrial relations. Several participants proposed a comprehensive international code of regulations for multinationals through amendments to the General Agreement on Tariffs and Trade (GATT). Such amendments could require various fair labor standards for MNCs, including wages and conditions related to productivity, the maintenance of full employment, full collective bargaining rights, compensation to workers dismissed by multinationals, and the provision of information about MNC production and investment decisions, including union opportunities to negotiate on such issues.

Conference discussions acknowledged the pressures recently generated on the issue of MNC legislative control by national governments, inter-

27. See ILO, *Social and Labour Practices of European-based Multinationals*, pp. 96-100, for union criticisms of information currently available about MNC operations.

28. The ILO report, *International Guidelines on Social Policy* (p. 20) makes a similar recommendation suggesting that "the granting of certain financial or other advantages or facilities, such as incentives and guarantees for international investment, either by a home or host country, might be made conditional upon the observance by the [multinational] enterprise concerned of specified employment policies and labour standards, irrespective of whether those standards were already embodied in the country's general legislation."

national organizations, and organized labor, but also called attention to the serious barriers to such international action as a result of national disagreements over the standards to be applied and how or to what extent they should be enforced. Many participants noted that a strategy involving protective national legislation may not be compatible with transnational bargaining; for example, policies that restrict the transfer of jobs abroad are contrary to the interests of workers in possible host countries. Several trade union representatives rejected this view and argued that a variety of national and international strategies were compatible with each other.

After reviewing the conference discussions and general literature on this subject, the following conclusions seem justified. Union efforts to get recognition for the need to control or at least constrain MNC behavior have been successful. In the future, both organized labor and governmental institutions at all levels are likely to pursue eclectic strategies to counter MNCs, ranging from national and international legislative efforts and bilateral nation-state negotiations to union transnational bargaining and information-sharing efforts.[29] Although the "free booter" era is undoubtedly over, multinationals' contributions to world economic growth and their capacity to achieve corporate objectives by adapting to a wide variety of controls, regulations, and pressures have ensured them a prominent role in the world economy.

Conclusion

The conference papers and comments provoked spirited debates, which is not surprising in view of the diverse backgrounds of the participants. It is hoped that these conference proceedings will add to the growing stock of knowledge about the impact of multinational corporations on industrial relations in the industrialized world, but obviously much more research is needed on this subject. Realistically the solutions to the many industrial relations problems identified at the conference and in the literature generally will have to be hammered out by unions and management either at the bargaining table or in various legislative forums. In closing we venture the observation that the interest and concern generated by the growth of MNCs is reminiscent of the excitement and apprehension in the 1960s over the spread of automation. Both phenomena aroused fear on the part of trade unions and a vigorous defense by the business community. Both spawned innumerable conferences, meetings, debates, scholarly and popular books and articles, investigations by government bodies, and proposals for regulation. The automation furor has pretty much subsided. Whether the same fate awaits the current speculation over the effects of the multinationals should become apparent within the next five or ten years.

---

29. See Cox, "Labor and the Multinationals," pp. 362-65.

Part I. The Multinational and Industrial Relations: A Global View

LABOR AND MULTINATIONALS
Leonard Woodcock

The impact of multinational corporations on employment in the United States has been widely debated in recent years—to no decisive conclusion. It is clear that a growing share of U.S. imports involves sales by foreign subsidiaries to the controlling corporations in the United States at internal transfer prices, rather than at prices determined on a competitive world market. It is also clear that production jobs in labor-intensive industries are being transferred abroad to lower wage areas, particularly to developing countries where dictatorial regimes prohibit free trade union organization and strikes. While production jobs are transferred abroad, the centralization of managerial decision making and research and development at corporate headquarters increases the number of managerial, professional, and clerical jobs. Thus, aggregate employment data mask the structural unemployment that has been created. In this way, with the emphasis placed on estimating the overall impact of MNCs on employment, the adverse structural effects of foreign investment by these corporations are being neglected.

The key managerial decision affecting employment opportunities and job security is the investment decision, which is typically made at the multinationals' headquarters. Although the industrial relations managers of foreign subsidiaries are usually given broad responsibilities in collective bargaining, the basic policies concerning labor relations are centrally determined. The focus of potential conflict between these corporations and the trade union movement lies herein. This power relationship is the distinctive characteristic of multinationals that requires the trade union movement to develop a new system of industrial relations: multinational collective bargaining.

Leonard Woodcock is president of the International Union of United Automobile, Aerospace and Agricultural Implement Workers of America.

U.S. Multinationals and Western Europe

Although multinational corporations pose serious problems for American workers, the fact that a majority of the world's multinationals are American-owned and -based makes them even more threatening to Western European workers. Let me illustrate this point with several examples. A key proposal in the German Social Democratic party's legislative program, which is given top priority by the West German government and labor movement, is a bill that would extend what is called codetermination—equal representation of workers with shareholders on the supervisory boards of companies—to all companies with at least two thousand employees.[1] Equal representation currently exists only in the coal, iron, and steel industries; in others the supervisory boards are two-thirds shareholders and one-third worker representatives. These boards choose the executives who oversee the company's day-to-day operations.

American firms account for about 45 percent of all foreign investment in West Germany. Some fifty U.S. multinational corporations that would be affected by the proposed law have challenged its legality, contending that such a change would violate the rights guaranteed them by the 1954 German-American trade treaty. They have asked the State Department to intervene on their behalf. Past complaints by the American Chamber of Commerce in West Germany have been denounced by both government and party leaders as interference in domestic German affairs.

I need not emphasize, surely, the socially destructive aspects of this action. It is as if a foreign multinational in the U.S. were to lead the pack in seeking legal ways to disobey the Equal Pay Act (EPA) or the National Labor Relations Act (NLRA) on the grounds that such legislation interferes with management decisions.

The activities of the Big Three auto companies in Europe further illustrate the problems created by the multinationals' investment decisions and labor policies. These three companies have virtually taken over the British auto industry, leaving only one independent British auto company—British Leyland Motor Corporation. During the Arab oil embargo in the winter of 1974 when the British coal miners struck and Britain went on a three-day workweek, the London *Economist* carried the headline, "When will Detroit start closing Britain down?" The article began with these words: "When will Detroit start closing Vauxhall, Ford or Chrysler factories in Britain? Soon, say persistent reports from Detroit. And for good."[2] In June 1974 Chrysler (U.K.) management warned union officials that the company would close its plants permanently if there were

---

1. A new codetermination law was approved by the West German parliament in March 1976.—editors

2. *Economist* 250, no. 6809 (February 23, 1974): 94.

another strike.

Now it is true that since 1968 there have been frequent strikes in British auto plants over wage issues. In contrast to the United States where the entire auto industry is organized by one union and collective bargaining agreements are legal contracts enforceable in the courts, in Britain the workers in one auto plant are represented by as many as nineteen unions and agreements are voluntary and legally unenforceable. The British auto companies historically paid workers on a piece rate basis and Leyland continues to do so. After Ford and General Motors (Vauxhall) replaced piece rates by the measured-day work system, Ford and Vauxhall workers, once the highest paid in the auto industry, fell behind the workers at British Leyland's plants.

In 1971 workers struck Ford for ten weeks; it was the longest major official strike in the United Kingdom since the General Strike of 1926. The workers were demanding wage parity with workers in the Chrysler Rootes plant in Coventry. Ford's handling of this dispute illustrates the critical characteristics that distinguish multinationals from national corporations. In the third week of the strike, Ford announced that it had ruled out England as the site for a new engine plant; shortly afterward Henry Ford II, president of the company, made well-publicized declarations in Manila and Tokyo that the manufacture of components in Britain for Ford's assembly plants in Asia would be discontinued and that operations in the United Kingdom would be redirected to serve only the British market.

Ford then came to Britain where he met with Prime Minister Heath to warn him, in person, of his intent to invest no further in Britain. It so happened that, quite by coincidence, I was in London shortly thereafter to preside over a meeting of the World Automotive Councils of the International Metalworkers' Federation (IMF). Joined by Jack Jones, president of the huge Transport and General Workers' Union, and Hugh Scanlon, president of the slightly smaller Amalgamated Union of Engineering Workers—both of which organize Ford workers—I went to see Mr. Heath.

We told him that we felt it shameful for a British prime minister to allow himself to be lectured to by a foreign millionaire; that to permit himself to be linked to the chief of a multinational *against* his own people was terribly wrong. We then joined the workers on their picket line to demonstrate our total solidarity with them. Shortly after that, German Ford workers flew into London with an even more concrete offering of solidarity—a promise to help with strike benefits and not to scab.

Given this example of international labor solidarity and the determined attitude of British workers not to be beaten, Ford finally settled the strike to the general satisfaction of labor. But I fear that Ford has had the last word on this, for it has since announced its intent to place sizable investments in

Spain to produce cars for the European Economic Community (EEC). In Spain, of course, there are no meddlesome trade unions to interfere in the board rooms or to interrupt production; there are civil guards to maintain order and civil laws to prohibit strikes.

Since the war, most of Ford's and GM's expansion has taken place on the Continent, centered in West Germany. Although it is good managerial tactics to blame labor problems, this shift is probably more attributable to the desire to get behind the Common Market tariff barriers and to reap savings in transport costs. The general director of GM in Europe recently admitted that the factory price of a British car is 17 percent cheaper than a comparable German car, while Ford's managing director in the United Kingdom puts the difference at 20 to 30 percent. British wages are lower, and British steel carries a 35 percent subsidy. Moreover, British workers can still be drawn into auto plants in large numbers. On the Continent, the overwhelming majority of auto workers are temporary migrants.

Shifting new investment to the Continent reduces the rate of increase of productivity in the British plants, thereby diminishing the incentive for the companies to grant wage increases. Consequently, British auto workers' wage increases have failed to keep pace with recent inflation, and their dissatisfaction has led to frequent work stoppages. These factors plus the lagging state of the British car market may induce the multinationals to transfer further new investment away from Britain creating a vicious circle.

Playing off the workers in one country against those of another is a standard practice of multinationals. For example, when Ford first established its plant at Genk, then an underdeveloped region of Belgium with a permanent labor surplus, the union leadership accepted worse working conditions than in Ford's nearby plants in Antwerp and Cologne (including a longer workweek for the same weekly wage). Then Ford transferred some assembly operations from Britain and all the truck production from Cologne to Genk. Later that year (1968) during a strike at Genk for working conditions equal to those at the Ford Antwerp assembly plant, the management threatened to transfer production to other countries.

One scholar explained the impact of U.S. investments in Europe in the following manner:

> From the point of view of the companies involved, integration means looking at their subsidiaries in different countries, not as separate operations, but increasingly as part of the same continental operations, regarding the different countries increasingly as provinces in the same country and planning, investing, manufacturing and marketing on an EEC or even Europe-wide basis. From the point of view of any one European country, integration means that companies can increasingly switch new investment, employment, and exports from one country to another.[3]

---

3. Y. S. Hu, *The Impact of U.S. Investment in Europe: A Case Study of the Automotive and Computer Industries* (New York: Praeger, 1973), p. 168.

Ford now has a policy of standardization and interchangeability of parts and dual sourcing in purchases of parts from outside suppliers. Cars are designed so that parts from West Germany can be used in Ford's British assembly plants and vice versa, and Ford of Europe has at least two sources—one on the Continent and one in Britain—for most of the components of its common car models. This puts the company in a position to switch suppliers during strikes.

MNCs and Host Governments

Threats posed by multinational corporations to job security are compounded by the policies of individual governments, which attempt to lure foreign companies to underdeveloped regions by offering low-interest financing, tax holidays, and other inducements. While there is some public awareness in the United States of this problem as it pertains to runaway American plants and industries relocating in Latin America and Southeast Asia, it is less well known that various subsidies have been offered to multinational corporations by several Common Market countries to induce them to open plants in particular locations. After the failure of the French in the early 1960s to persuade the EEC countries to adopt a common policy toward foreign investment, these incentives were sometimes offered on a competitive basis. Major investments by GM in Belgium and Ford in France, for example, were financed wholly or largely by European capital on a subsidized basis. It was by this means that President George Pompidou of France induced Henry Ford to locate a plant to produce automatic transmissions for all of Ford of Europe's cars in Bordeaux, the center of an underdeveloped agricultural region with a labor surplus. Parenthetically, we should note that while European governments are subsidizing employment-creating investments as part of their national plans to develop lagging regions, the U.S. government is subsidizing foreign investment by U.S.-based corporations through loopholes deliberately built into the tax structure, such as the tax deferral and credit on profits generated abroad.

Development of Transnational Bargaining

Since the mid-1960s, consciousness has been growing in trade union movements of the need for workers to unite across national boundaries in order to deal effectively with multinational corporations. But the stage has not yet been reached at which transnational collective bargaining is possible. The sole exception is in the UAW contracts covering both American and Canadian workers in the auto industry, and this is possible because all the workers belong to one union.

In laying the foundations for transnational collective bargaining, the

UAW has led the way through the formation of World Automotive Councils affiliated to the International Metalworkers' Federation, a trade secretariat. The auto industry is particularly adaptable to international organization; in 1973 almost 87 percent of the entire world output of autos was produced by only nine multinational companies.

There are now nine World Automotive Councils, one each for GM, Ford, Chrysler, Renault-Peugeot, Toyota-Nissan, Fiat-Citroën, Volkswagen-Daimler Benz, British Leyland Motor, and Volvo-Saab. Other world councils within the framework of the IMF cover the agricultural implements industry and the electrical-electronics industries. At present, the principal activity of the world councils is to hold periodic conferences bringing together trade union representatives from each company's subsidiaries. The purpose of these meetings is to exchange information and views, and to adopt a common strategy with respect to certain goals. The basic goal is harmonization of working conditions: line speeds, relief periods, holiday pay, annual leave, voluntary overtime, health and safety, and fringe benefits, including pensions. Most recently, another important issue has been raised—job environment and monotony.

Harmonization of working conditions is intended to discourage multinational corporations from transferring operations from one country to another in order to lower costs at the expense of workers by offering poorer working conditions. My basic message to the companies has always been—by all means, compete to make better, safer, more economical products. But the companies cannot compete by paying their workers less, or speeding them up more, or endangering their health and safety. On such questions, all workers must be treated equally, according to the highest possible standard.

Sharing information is an important function of the world councils. Member unions notify the coordinator's office in Geneva of all strikes and developments in current collective bargaining negotiations. In turn, the coordinator informs the council members, alerting them to the possibility that the company will attempt to transfer production. During the 1971 strike at Ford of Britain, the German workers at the Ford plant in Cologne pledged to refuse overtime work on parts normally made in the struck English plants.

Barriers to Transnational Bargaining

International solidarity of labor, however, is sometimes difficult to maintain when the multinational integration and interdependence of production creates conflicts of interest among workers. In September 1974 a strike by 1,800 workers at two British Ford plants created parts shortages that resulted in the layoff of over 15,000 auto workers in England and the closing of Ford's West German plant at Saarlouis, affecting another 4,500 workers.

Besides conflicts of interest, obstacles to effective international union cooperation include linguistic and cultural differences, which are greater for workers than for business executives, and institutional differences in collective bargaining approaches reflecting differences in trade union organization and philosophies. In addition, some countries, the United States among them, have laws that prohibit secondary boycotts, including strikes in sympathy with workers abroad.

The basis for union organization varies across countries. In Britain workers are organized in craft unions on a geographical basis. On the Continent unions have political or religious affiliations; thus, there are Social Democratic, Communist, and Christian trade unions. In France and Italy, the two largest unions, the CGT and the CGIL, are communist-controlled and affiliated with the Russian-dominated World Federation of Trade Unions. These unions are not affiliated with the IMF, which is allied with the International Confederation of Free Trade Unions; consequently, most French and Italian auto workers, even the unionized ones, are outside the IMF structure.

All this goes to say that trade unionists are highly conscious that collective bargaining alone cannot solve all the problems faced by workers in their jobs and communities. In today's interdependent world, not even national governments, acting individually, can cope adequately with the problems raised by international flows of capital, goods, and services, and the international migration of labor.

It is necessary, therefore, to expand the domain of international law to cover the activities of multinational corporations. International standards of accounting and reporting must be imposed and enforced by corresponding modifications of each country's internal revenue laws and regulations. Public disclosure of agreements between governments and multinational corporations must be required, to discourage the practice of attracting foreign investment at the expense of labor standards. International occupational health and safety standards must be adopted and made a precondition for every foreign investment. The General Agreement on Tariffs and Trade (GATT) must be amended to incorporate the obligation to adhere to fair labor standards:

• Employers must strive to achieve and maintain full employment.
• Employers must recognize the freedom of association of workers and the right of collective bargaining.
• Employers must recognize the right to strike.
• Employers must offer full compensation to workers who become unemployed because of international competition until they are reincorporated into the production process. This compensation should include

retraining and moving to other places of residence.

• Employers contemplating major production and investment decisions, especially transfer abroad of plants, which affect the welfare of their workers, must provide the unions concerned with full information and negotiate with them in a sense of social responsibility toward their employees, the community, and the country where they are operating.

There is a hiatus in the institutions governing our international economy that must be filled by establishing minimum codes of corporate behavior and responsibility. If GATT is not the vehicle for such reforms, then we must find another or we must create one. Humanity has long passed the age when great chartered companies could sail out on their own, conquering lands and exploiting helpless natives. Companies, workers, and entire societies *must* reach agreements within broadly defined international standards.

Comment
Robert Copp

In his paper on labor and multinationals, Leonard Woodcock made several significant misstatements of fact and unsupportable implications about Ford Motor Company, its officers, and its subsidiaries. Normally the company does not attempt to correct such misstatements when they occur at trade union conferences or in publications, and some of them by now unfortunately are ineradicably imbedded in the literature. This, however, is not a trade union conference, and because of my active participation in its planning I believe that my remaining silent would be irresponsible, lending a credibility to these misstatements that they do not deserve.

The following quotations are taken from the text of Woodcock's address.

> After Ford and General Motors (Vauxhall) replaced piece rates by the measured-day work system, Ford and Vauxhall workers, once the highest paid in the auto industry, fell behind the workers at British Leyland's plants.

Ford Motor Company began car assembly in Britain in 1911. It has never used a piece work pay system there.

> In the third week of the strike, Ford announced that it had ruled out England as the site for a new engine plant; shortly afterward Henry Ford II, the president of the company, made well-publicized declarations in Manila and Tokyo that the manufacture of components in Britain for Ford's assembly plants in Asia would be discontinued and that operations in the United Kingdom would be redirected to serve only the British market.

In his visit in the Asia-Pacific region in February and March 1971, Ford several times remarked publicly about what managements of Ford assembly companies had told him about the unreliability of components shipments by Ford Motor Company Limited in Britain. He said nothing about discontinuing in Britain the manufacture of components for assembly in the region and likewise said nothing about restricting operations in Britain to serve only the British market.

Robert Copp, overseas liaison manager, labor relations staff, Ford Motor Company, made these comments at a conference session on the day following Leonard Woodcock's address. Copp had requested an opportunity to present this statement immediately after the Woodcock address, but at the suggestion of the conference convenors agreed to make his remarks at a plenary session. Woodcock was not at the session. Following Copp's remarks, Nat Weinberg, a former UAW official, made the following statement for the record: "Mr. Copp has made a lot of statements, most of which are just assertions in refutation of assertions made by Leonard Woodcock. Mr. Woodcock did not come here with a speech which cited all the evidence in support of his remarks. I think it has to be clearly understood that if Mr. Woodcock were here, he would have the opportunity to cite the evidence upon which his assertions were based and confront Mr. Copp's assertions with that evidence."

> Ford then came to Britain where he met with Prime Minister Heath to warn him, in person, of his intent to invest no further in Britain.

Ford is a long-time personal friend of Edward Heath, then prime minister. In 1971, long before the strike against Ford, he had made plans for a regular business visit to Britain, including a luncheon with Heath. Neither during that luncheon nor on any other occasion did he warn Heath of his intention to invest no further in Britain. Pressed by the news media for a comment after the luncheon, he did comment publicly that given the labor situation then facing Ford and its suppliers in Britain, he would find it difficult to persuade the board of directors of Ford Motor Company to commit significant new investment funds in Britain.

> But I fear that Ford has had the last word on this, for it has since announced its intent to place sizable investments in Spain to produce cars for the European Economic Community.

The Ford investment in Spain has nothing to do with the labor situation in Britain or with labor costs there or elsewhere. It represents a long-considered decision to reenter the Spanish market as a significant competitor there. Some of the production of the Spanish plants will be exported.

> Since the war, most of Ford's and GM's expansion has taken place on the Continent, centered in Germany. Although it is good managerial tactics to blame labor problems, this shift is probably more attributable to the desire to get behind the Common Market tariff barriers and to reap savings in transport costs.

Neither Ford Motor Company nor any of its subsidiaries has ever attributed its German investment to labor relations elsewhere, and Ford knows of no basis for Woodcock's inference. Ford management would not regard it as "good managerial tactics to blame labor problems."

> The general director of GM in Europe recently admitted that the factory price of a British car is 17 percent cheaper than a comparable German car, while Ford's managing director in Britain puts the difference at 20 to 30 percent.

Ford Motor Company Limited is unable to ascertain the basis for the statement attributed to its managing director and, in the absence of more specific information about Woodcock's source for this statement, cannot affirm it or otherwise correct it.

> Shifting new investment to the Continent reduces the rate of increase of productivity in the British plants, thereby diminishing the incentive for the companies to grant wage increases. Consequently, British auto workers' wage increases have failed to keep pace with recent inflation, and their dissatisfaction has led to frequent work stoppages. These factors plus the lagging state of the British car market may induce the multinationals to transfer further new investment away from Britain creating a vicious circle.

Between November 1972 and July 25, 1974, Ford of Britain's wages and other economic conditions of employment were subject to controls promulgated under the counterinflation program. Ford of Britain was the first automobile company in Britain—and one of the first large employers—to grant the maximum cost-of-living (threshold) allowance permitted by state III of the counterinflation program.

In a marked departure from its usual policies, Ford of Britain offered on September 20, 1974, to revise its Conditions of Employment Agreement nearly six months early and in the ensuing negotiations settled, on October 19, for a wage increase of about 22 percent for most employees.

As far as Ford of Britain is concerned, there is no lagging market. The managing director said in a management meeting on September 9, 1974, that Ford dealers in Britain could sell every unit that the company could build, and more.

> Later that year (1968) during a strike at Genk for working conditions equal to those at the Ford Antwerp assembly plant, the management threatened to transfer production to other countries.

During this strike against Ford's Genk operations in Belgium, no representative of the management threatened to transfer production to other countries.

> Ford now has a policy of standardization and interchangeability of parts and dual sourcing in purchases of parts from outside suppliers. Cars are designed so that parts from Germany can be used in Ford's British assembly plants and vice versa, and Ford of Europe has at least two sources—one on the Continent and one in Britain—for most of the components of its common car models. This puts the company in a position to switch suppliers during strikes.

Ford companies in Europe do not have a dual sourcing policy, and we are unable to ascertain the basis for Woodcock's erroneous assertion. Indeed, these remarks are inconsistent with Woodcock's earlier correct statement that a September 1974 strike in Ford of Britain's stamping plants caused shortages of single-sourced components that resulted in a suspension of production at Ford plants in Saarlouis, West Germany.

THE MULTINATIONAL
CORPORATION:
SHADOW AND SUBSTANCE

Charles H. Smith, Jr.

We are in danger of being seriously misled by a term of convenience, namely that of "multinational" corporation. Insofar as labor relations are concerned, there is really no material difference between a multinational corporation and a one-country company. MNCs are aggregations of national corporations tied together by a common ownership. Each individual corporation is incorporated under the laws of its host country and is bound by those laws, including laws and customs governing labor relations. Therefore, I see no basis for the assumption that MNCs raise special labor relations problems. But there is no question that special problems can be created *for* MNCs by a host of political interests, including those of powerful unions.

American-owned multinational corporations are under serious attack at home and abroad. They are being attacked by politicians and labor union leaders for self-serving purposes, by that particular breed of journalist and news media personality that finds it profitable to criticize the more visible elements of what the young generation calls "the establishment," and by individuals committed to the elimination of private ownership of the means of production. Such individuals can hardly be expected to be enthusiastic about evidence that proves the capitalist system is bringing an improved standard of living to people everywhere that come in contact with it, and at a far more rapid pace than systems of state ownership.

Charles H. Smith, Jr., is chairman of the board of the Chamber of Commerce of the United States, U.S. employer representative to the International Labor Organization, and president of SIFCO Industries.

A significant contradiction is formed by the two main forces attacking the multinationals: the labor unions of the industrial countries and the governments of the communist countries. The objective of the labor unions is to force multinational bargaining and, in the process, to increase their power over the economies of the free world. The objective of the communist leadership is to slow the economic growth of the free countries. So, while the labor unions of Western countries hope to increase their influence by condemning the multinationals, their partners in this attack—the communists—have the goal of undermining the economic base on which the unions are dependent.

We are entering an era in which we will no longer be able to afford the luxury of economic inefficiency indulged solely for the purpose of enhancing political illusions. We face widespread shortages of raw materials, the prospect of world famine, the specter of industrial recession, and a financial system struggling to cope with the need to recycle billions of petrodollars. The free flow of international investment and production, embodied in the operations of the multinational corporation, is our best hope for surmounting these problems.

Arguments against MNCs

Many of the arguments made against multinational corporations in their home countries are also used in reverse by their critics in host countries. For example, in the United States, the critics of MNCs claim that multinational enterprises fail to bring back to the United States a sufficiently large proportion of annual earnings; outside the United States the critics claim they take too much of their earnings out of the host country. In the United States, the critics of MNCs claim that they harm the national economy by exporting its most advanced technology and patent rights; in host countries, the same MNCs are criticized for retaining their most advanced technology at home. Again in the United States, critics, often from the unions, charge that U.S. jobs are lost because of plants built outside the borders of the United States to serve markets not only in the host country but in other countries and the home country as well; the opposite argument, that MNCs restrict the markets available to their affiliates abroad, is used by critics in the host countries.

It is very popular in some countries for critics to claim that the most important decisions are made in the home office with little regard for the objectives and problems of the host countries. The critics in the United States, on the other hand, claim that multinational enterprises frequently proceed with their plans without giving adequate consideration to the problems and objectives of the United States.

It is not necessary to pursue this point further. That critics of MNCs can take completely opposite sides of the same argument and apply them with equal vehemence against MNCs would seem to suggest that the arguments arise primarily out of emotion and ignorance, rather than from any basic problems peculiar to the MNCs.

In 1970 J. J. Servan-Schreiber's *The American Challenge* appeared, which described "the economic invasion of Europe by the United States." His book put the MNC in a glaring spotlight, but the coldly provocative statements of that time seem quite tame in comparison with the intemperate charges leveled today in various United Nations' organs and other forums against MNCs.

It does little good to chide those who view with suspicion and alarm the successes and accomplishments of international investment. Instead, we must face the gravity of the current examination and bring the facts into proper focus, working particularly hard to communicate as widely as possible the many constructive contributions of MNCs.

The U.S. Chamber of Commerce recognized several years ago that the emotional and often irrational arguments against MNCs might prevail unless the facts were available to disprove the charges. Consequently, the chamber obtained pertinent data in a survey made with the cooperation of the head offices of many of the largest U.S.-owned MNCs. The findings clearly show that the MNC is an important force for good in our world.

Host Country Attitudes

Nevertheless, confrontations between MNCs and host governments are increasing. The leverage of most host governments has increased because of their better access to knowledge about international market conditions and because of rising competition among MNCs. Consequently, host governments are now more able to increase the benefits for their economies relative to the cost of the foreign investment.

Many of these host governments have attempted to retain economic independence by seeking alternatives to direct foreign investment and by breaking up the MNC package of capital, technology, management, and market access. It has thus become incumbent on MNCs to prove the benefits they can provide for the local economy, and to establish that MNC activities are the best, if not the only, way of realizing those benefits for the host country's objectives. To provide convincing evidence, the MNC must develop effective information dissemination on the impact of its operations on the local economy.

One of the principal sources of controversy between researchers from MNCs and host countries arises because of the difference in the perspective, or standards of comparison, used by the two protagonists in establishing evidence. The corporations, and most academic observers, measure the impact starting from a hypothetical situation that would have existed without the direct foreign investment. Host country observers, on the other hand, frequently attempt to measure the impact from a hypothetical model in which the MNC is assumed to contribute the greatest possible benefit to the host economy. It is understandable that the estimated impact of direct foreign investment is usually very different when comparisons are made from these two different standards of reference.

MNCs, being susceptible to the policy initiatives of host governments, must address directly the points of misinformation, lack of information, and presumed grievances put forth by host countries. "Social or economic audits" are becoming more common requirements during the process of MNC entry, as are requirements for the inclusion of estimates of the impact on the local economy. Thus forced to disclose more, MNCs might be well advised to develop their own independent systems of reporting on the current and cumulative impacts of their operations on the host economy in a relevant and persuasive manner.

In connection with a study of MNCs by the International Labor Organization, the International Organization of Employers collected data on 400 MNCs in eighty countries. To a substantial degree, this information refutes the claims that decisions on labor relations matters are made by anonymous executives in far-away headquarters of MNCs. The survey results show that personnel recruitment and vocational training decisions of practically every company are made by the executives in the host countries; wages, fringe benefits, and other conditions of work are the result of decisions made in the host country; and the decision-making power in the case of collective bargaining, almost without exception, lies with the management in the host country.

In the great majority of multinational enterprises, trade unions operate normally and the companies are fully integrated with the custom and practice of negotiations in the countries where the subsidiaries are located. Among subsidiary managers, the ratio of source country staff to nationals is very small. Wages paid by multinationals in developing countries are similar to those paid by national companies of similar importance in the same industry. The companies surveyed also provide many social contributions, such as schools, clubs, churches, hospitals, theaters, housing programs, roads, power stations, and water and sewer works. In general, the findings of the study reflect favorably on both the economic and social responsibility of multinational corporations.

The MNC as a Catalyst of Growth

The MNC needs to be viewed in perspective. The challenge to raise to adequacy the incomes of two-thirds of the world can be met only if the world's resources are used efficiently. The chance to achieve this goal has been greatly improved by the explosive growth of multinationals since World War II, for the MNC is probably the single most important means for bringing a higher standard of living to all the world's people. As the economy of each nation becomes increasingly "internationalized" in the process of meeting demands for progress, both business and political figures will have to help fashion and adjust to new governmental and economic arrangements.

Since World War II, multinationals have grown faster than other forms of corporate activity. Their sales have increased at a compounded rate of 10 percent a year, and the book value of their investment ($160 billion in 1971) has increased fivefold since 1950. The enormous size and growing importance of MNCs is best seen in context. With world economic output estimated at around $500 billion in 1971—in terms of value added in production—MNC output comes to about one-fifth of world gross national product, not including the centrally planned economies.

The typical MNC is large in size, although they are by no means all giants. It operates in a high-technology industry with relatively few other firms, and it has affiliates spread over several countries. In 1974 the United States accounted for more than half of the MNCs larger than $1 billion in sales and for more than half of the total estimated book value of MNC investment.

Four countries—the United States, the United Kingdom, France, and West Germany—account for 80 percent of the foreign operations of MNCs. The most dramatic growth, however, has been in Japan, West Germany, and the United States, reflecting technological advances, a search for markets, an intensified search for raw materials, and shifts in the relative productive power of major industrial countries.

The MNC and the World Economy

Economist Judd Polk, formerly of the U.S. Council of the International Chamber of Commerce, pointed out that the multinational company is itself a reflection rather than a source of a new phenomenon, namely the *internationalization of production*.[1] The scientific revolution through which we are living has created for the first time the ability to treat the world as the basic economic unit in allocating resources to productive uses. There is no evidence whatever that the advance of technology is about to slow down or be reversed. On the contrary, the technology of instantaneous transmission and processing of world data is only in its infancy.

We are just beginning to become familiar with the potential of world

---

1. Judd Polk, "The World Economy," *Columbia Journal of World Business* 3, no. 1 (January-February 1968): 7-15.

communication. Corporate planners tell us that the speed of communication is likely to increase a millionfold in the next thirty years. This could mean stationary satellites beaming education by television to great areas of the earth, as is now happening in India. It could mean earth resource satellites supplying worldwide data on crops, moisture, irrigation, and expected yields, as well as on oil and mineral resources and the like, to a world-oriented environmental monitoring system. And it will mean many other advances that we cannot anticipate in detail now.

We speak glibly about the interdependent world we live in—hardly a public speech is made without such a reference. Yet with the growth of economic interdependence, our economic problems also become inextricably linked, and only a comprehensive and systematic international effort will be able to deal with them.

Even though the development of a world economic framework is probably inevitable, many current government policies are inconsistent with it. Trade-oriented balance-of-payments accounting itself fails to measure in any meaningful way the new international relations that are developing. The United Nations, for example, estimates that the production totals of foreign affiliates of MNCs reached approximately $330 billion in 1971, somewhat larger than the $310 billion total for exports of all market economies. Yet the current accounting system fails to consider the new conditions under which international production has surpassed trade as the main vehicle of international economic exchange. It tosses up deficits that have little or no meaning but fails to track international credit movements at all, and they are now of profound interest and concern.

The broad policy implications that flow from the growth of this new world economy should be clear. We need only look at the past success of the United States for guidance. During the last century, from 1872 to 1972, the U.S. economy enjoyed a fortyfold rise in its annual output. Its per capita output increased sevenfold, to about $6,500 for every man, woman, and child in the United States. This is because the United States has enjoyed an open economy free from barriers to trade and investment among the states and regions.

In the same way, the primary interest of the United States in *international* economics should be the most rational and effective allocation of world resources. It should be clear that the economic integration of the world is in our interest and that of all people because it is the route to rational world resource allocation, which is the route to maximization of world income. It is the keenest irony that the best chance to raise incomes for the poor two-thirds of the world encounters at every turn the rising suspicion of nationally oriented political, financial, business, and labor leaders.

The positive contributions of MNCs are easily demonstrable in the areas of employment, income, tax revenues and trade, not to mention the transfer of ideas, technology, new products, services, and new management methods to people in many nations far sooner than they would otherwise have been available.

Beyond the purely economic problems, some foreign governments and critics have viewed MNCs as seeking excessive political power, basing an indictment of all on the evidence of a few allegations. Some unions fear the threat of MNCs that appear able to move employment across national boundaries. The rising shortage of raw materials has dramatically strengthened the bargaining power of many countries in which MNCs are developing such resources. In Europe, especially, MNCs are under suspicion because they have easily transcended national cultural, political, and economic institutional differences that even political leaders working toward socioeconomic integration have been unable to surmount.

UN Report of Eminent Persons

The 1974 UN report of the Group of Eminent Persons on multinational corporations in world development acknowledged that the ability of MNCs to "tap financial, physical and human resources around the world and to combine them in economically feasible and commercially profitable activities, their capacity to develop new technology and skills, and their productive and managerial ability to translate resources into specific outputs have proved to be outstanding." Yet later the report suggested, "multinational corporations have developed important capacities which can be put to the service of world development."[2] It is almost as though excellence in production, marketing, management, and technology is regarded by the authors as having been harmful.

The *potential* for abuse of power seems to be a concern. The UN authors referred to the ability of MNCs to "affect patterns of consumption and the direction of innovation . . . and . . . political processes of both home and host countries." The authors expressed concern that "countries may find their national sovereignty infringed upon and their policy instruments blunted by the operations of multinational corporations."[3] Yet they also warned that however sacred and inviolable national sovereignty may be from the political point of view, few national boundaries correspond to economic demarcation lines, and they called upon nation-states to cooperate in the exchange not only of goods and services but also of finance and technology.

---

2. United Nations, Department of Economic and Social Affairs, *The Impact of Multinational Corporations on Development and on International Relations* (New York: UN, 1974), pp. 28 and 30.

3. Ibid., p. 30.

Actually, there are a number of points in the UN report with which one can agree. The one thing that comes through loud and clear is the complexity of the subject and the controversy that surrounds it. The report itself demonstrated the need for serious analysis lest myths should prove more appealing than facts and emotions stronger than reason.

Poor Public Image of MNCs

Sadly, the myths have proved more appealing. In the early 1970s, a public opinion survey in the United States revealed that two out of every three Americans favor discouraging rather than encouraging the expansion of U.S. business abroad. The majority of respondents were evidently unaware of such benefits as balance of payments and trade surpluses and domestic job market stimulation, which U.S. foreign investment brings to this country.

Jacques G. Maisonrouge, president of IBM World Trade Corporation, has called attention to a number of myths surrounding MNCs, one of which is the misconception that all multinational corporations are, ipso facto, large. The UN report dismissed from consideration all companies with less than $100 million in annual sales. Although many multinational companies are indeed large, there are hundreds of smaller firms with comprehensive organizations in many countries. This fact is documented by a report of Booz, Allen and Hamilton on the size of U.S. companies inaugurating foreign activities. Of 368 manufacturing companies starting overseas operations in 1972, 142 (more than 38 percent) had sales volumes of $99 million or less.

Furthermore, an examination of the period from 1961 to 1972, when 5,050 manufacturing firms went international for the first time, shows that 2,239 (44 percent) had sales volumes of $99 million or less. For non-manufacturing industries, the respective percentages were 32 and 36. My own company, SIFCO Industries, is a multinational with sales of less than $50 million yearly.

The growth of smaller MNCs ties in with the great growth of world trade in recent years. Total world exports have risen from $118.4 billion in 1961 to $327.8 billion in 1972 and at a compound growth rate of some 11 percent. Hence, those companies that wish to compete and grow would be wise to enter the international market.

Foreign Investment in the United States

We should not leave this subject without touching on a fairly recent source of concern—foreign investment in the United States. A number of important questions are being raised on this subject. Is the dramatic increase in Japanese investment in Hawaii disruptive enough to the local community to warrant some action by the government? How much of the timberland on the West Coast and in Alaska has been purchased by non-U.S. citizens? Is there a level of foreign investment at which the national interest might be jeopardized? Are the expressions of concern in the Midwest over reports of the foreign purchase of large agricultural tracts and transportation facilities legitimate or fanciful? Is it appropriate that foreign banks are allowed to establish branches in more than one state, contrary to the restrictions on domestic banks, and that their U.S. operations fall outside the jurisdiction of the Federal Reserve System? What about the entry of foreign brokerage houses into the new national exchange system in the spring of 1975?

The importance of devising an appropriate policy response has been underscored by the recent enormous increase in foreign government earnings from oil production, the so-called petrodollars, which now overhang world financial markets. The distinguished economist Henry Wallich estimates that oil producers are generating revenues totaling between $100 and $110 billion per year. Of this total some $40 billion is capable of being absorbed in the oil countries, leaving $60 to $70 billion annually as surplus.

The annual accumulation of $60 billion by the Organization of Petroleum Exporting Countries (OPEC) seems to have mesmerized a portion of the American public. The apples and oranges comparison of that $60 billion to what it could potentially buy in the United States in inappropriate. These funds should not, in any regard, be considered as a maneuverable mass ready to shift one way or the other for purely speculative or political reasons. As Wallich pointed out, "There are *many* individual OPEC governments involved and there is no evidence that they are taking unnecessary risks with their funds. Rather, these countries are likely to distribute their funds over a wide range of investment, always mindful of the need for security and stability." Certainly the experience in 1974 indicates that the OPEC countries, as would any investor, will attempt to maximize the return on their invested funds consistent with the degree of risk involved. Consequently, we must expect that they will continue to act in an economically rational manner.

There are many potential outlets for Arab investment in the United States. Real estate, direct investment in industry, bank deposits, Treasury bills, equity purchases, and commodities are a few. Their holdings in these areas are unknown, but government sources are likely to keep a close watch on them in the future.

The real problem is not the leverage that might result from massive investments of petrodollars in the United States. Instead, we need to concern ourselves about how we can encourage the OPEC countries to make long-term investments in our country and elsewhere rather than limiting the disposition of their surplus funds to short-term bank deposits.

In order to encourage long-term investments by the oil-producing nations, we must be sure they are not dissuaded from investing by fears of exchange losses, stock market slumps, or confiscation of their foreign holdings. We cannot prevent stock market slumps, and exchange rates can be guaranteed only by iron-nerved currency dealers. But we can mitigate the danger of large internationally held short-term balances by avoiding undue restrictions on Arab investment in our own country.

Recycling is a thoroughly international problem; trying to act alone in this process is tantamount to disaster. The world must find a responsible alternative to the destructive harassment of MNCs that is being proposed in many arenas. Before we can do that in a rational, dispassionate manner, we must conquer our irrational fears of the MNC. Those fears are largely fears of the unknown, and the best antidote to them is understanding. This paper is an attempt to make a small contribution to the growth of such understanding.

Part II. Multinational Management's Conduct of Industrial Relations

LOCUS OF INDUSTRIAL RELATIONS DECISION MAKING IN MULTINATIONALS
Robert Copp

This paper (1) defines a "problem" for trade union critics about the locus of decision making in industrial relations, (2) specifies the Ford Motor Company's definition of industrial relations questions, and (3) describes, with reference to several illustrations, some aspects of Ford's industrial relations decision-making processes. Its central argument is that the authority to make industrial relations decisions in the Ford Motor Company, a multinational, is held by managers at the locus where collective bargaining or other relationships with employees take place. Thus, trade union criticism about remoteness and elusiveness of management authority in industrial relations matters in this company lacks validity.

The Problem as Seen by Trade Union Critics

The International Labor Organization has noted:

Trade unions are concerned that, in the case of a multinational's subsidiary, the locus of managerial decision making, particularly as regards matters arising in collective bargaining, is not always where the confrontations between management and trade unions take place. Rather, it is contended, the relevant decisions are made at the headquarters of the multinational, beyond the reach of the trade union concerned. It is argued that not infrequently, when demands, claims, or grievances are submitted to local management, the reply is that such a matter can only be decided at headquarters. This means that trade union negotiators do not have the opportunity of personally presenting their case to those who ultimately make the decisions. Trade unions feel that it is of the highest importance to them

Robert Copp is the overseas liaison manager, labor relations staff, Ford Motor Company.

to have access to the source of decisions on industrial relations and related issues.[1]

An example of this trade union view was expressed by Clyde L. Cameron, the Australian minister for labor, in discussing a strike against a large car assembly plant of the Ford Motor Company of Australia Limited in 1973. After allowing that, having been away in Geneva, he did not know all the facts in the strike, already in its thirty-eighth calendar day, he said:

> What I do know is that here you have some Australian workers fighting to get a better level of wages and working conditions than they have got. They are fighting a multinational corporation with headquarters in New York. That headquarters is deciding industrial [relations] policy. I don't like a situation in which Australian workers have to fight an industrial contest against somebody whose decisions are being made in the boardrooms of New York. This is something which is very bad. It is a foreign company; it is owned by foreigners; its policy is being made by foreigners; and Australian workers have become the meat in the sandwich.[2]

Industrial Relations Questions

Broadly defined, industrial relations questions generally involve remuneration and conditions of employment, including employee benefit plans, recruitment and training of employees, recognition of trade unions or other employee representatives, establishment of collective bargaining and grievance procedures, and resolution of disputes that might arise concerning these matters.

Management decisions about new or redeployed production facilities are not, as such, industrial relations questions. The effects or impact of those decisions on employees, however, are the concern of management industrial relations executives, and in most firms these effects are an appropriate subject for consultation and bargaining with recognized representatives of designated groups of employees.

Attempts by trade union bodies, mostly at the international level, to involve themselves in multinational firms' basic investment decisions, rather than in the consequences of those decisions for trade union members, generally have prompted management to deny these organizations a role in these general decisions, and thus have provoked most of the trade union criticism about the locus of decision making.

---

1. Working paper for Meeting on the Relationship between Multinational Corporations and Social Policy, International Labor Organization, Geneva, October 26-November 2, 1972, reprinted in *Multinational Enterprises and Social Policy*, ILO Studies and Reports, n.s., no. 79 (1973), p. 91.

2. Cameron during a television interview broadcast from London to Australia, June 23, 1973, transcribed by Ford Motor Company of Australia Limited. The minister, a former trade union official, probably did not represent his government's position, since no other government official expressed this point of view to the company in Australia.

Management representatives appreciate that this view is not accepted by most international trade union bodies. A 1972 Organization for Economic Cooperation and Development meeting of management specialists concluded with the following comment by one of its members:

> It seems inherent in the logic of the situation that unions, which consistently try to widen the scope of collective bargaining within national industrial relations systems, should be driven to try to influence decisions at the multinational level which have important consequences for them and their members, rather than content themselves with negotiations within their own country on the local consequences of such decisions. In short, the companies' wish to define certain decisions as industrial relations matters and other decisions as outside the scope of industrial relations, will never be accepted by the unions.[3]

Accepted by the unions or not, the prevailing and current management position is to consider basic investment and production deployment decisions as outside the scope of industrial relations matters appropriate for consultation or bargaining.

The Industrial Relations Decision Process at Ford

At the Ford Motor Company, the allocation of responsibility and authority for industrial relations within the parent company and in the worldwide organization is not based on the naked power inherently available at any given organizational level. Rather, the objective is to grant authority to that level of the organization best suited to achieving specific goals.[4]

Every Ford subsidiary has a senior executive, with an appropriate staff, responsible for the industrial relations or the employee relations function. In every case, this executive reports to the managing director of the subsidiary. The corporate staff and the national company management expect that this person will be a qualified and experienced professional capable of (1) reporting and interpreting employee attitudes, aspirations, and performance; (2) participating actively in the formulation of the local management's business objectives; and (3) interpreting those objectives to employees and to their designated representatives.

The primary responsibility of this local staff is to develop and administer an industrial relations program appropriate to the national setting in which the subsidiary operates. Indeed, this staff, along with the managing director and the board of the subsidiary, is the principal management deci-

---

3. Kenneth F. Walker (final rapporteur), *Labor Problems in Multinational Firms: Report on a Meeting of Management Experts*, Paris, June 21-23, 1972 (Paris: Organization for Economic Cooperation and Development, 1972), p. 11.

4. Adapted from informal remarks by Malcolm L. Denise, vice-president—labor relations, Ford Motor Company, at a luncheon for International Metalworkers' Federation World Automotive Councils, Dearborn, Michigan, June 3, 1966.

sion maker in industrial relations matters. This allocation of primary responsibility in industrial relations matters to national subsidiaries is typical of the multinational automobile employers based in the United States and of multinational employers generally.[5]

As senior members of management, industrial relations executives also study, evaluate, and report to their other management colleagues the effects of management decisions on employees. In investment or production deployment decisions, for example, the industrial relations considerations, including forecasts of the possible settlement of matters appropriate for local negotiation, very early become involved in the decision-making process.

Industrial relations professionals are selected and trained according to principles broadly accepted throughout the corporation. Most recruits study and test these principles in assignments at one or more Ford locations before returning to their home companies. This results in similar and predictable approaches to industrial relations in national subsidiaries. As the illustrations in the next section demonstrate, however, this does not produce a sterile uniformity in company industrial relations policies.

Predictable and similar approaches to industrial relations are also encouraged by the consultant role played by the corporate staff. Local national managements, faced with a novel question, frequently seek the assistance of the corporate staff in identifying where else within the Ford organization there might be some experience and expertise to deal with that question. In some cases, for example in the development of funded benefit programs, the corporate staff has by now dealt with enough national company proposals that it has developed an expertise of its own.

Illustrations from Ford Experience

The 1973 dispute at the Ford Motor Company in Australia initially involved demands for additional pay and a second tea break in the shift. On both matters the local management, without any "guidance" or "advice" from the corporate staff, had reached a settlement that was accepted by employees in eight plants and by most employees in the ninth plant, a large car assembly plant.

The local management, at least initially supported by trade union officials with whom it had negotiated the settlement, took the position that an agreement had been reached and generally accepted, that the strike was unauthorized, and that the strikers' complaints would be considered only after there was a resumption of normal working in accordance with the

5. Walker, *Labor Problems in Multinational Firms*, p. 5, and Duane A. Kujawa, *International Labor Relations Management in the Automobile Industry: A Comparative Study of Chrysler, Ford, and General Motors* (New York: Praeger, 1971).

settlement accepted by most of the other employees involved. Eventually the dispute was settled when Ford of Australia and the unions agreed that a wage issue should be arbitrated by the president of the Australian Conciliation and Arbitration Commission.

All of these actions—the original negotiations, the management position in the face of the wildcat strike, and the negotiation of the eventual settlement formula—were taken by the Ford of Australia management without any direction or guidance from the corporate staff. The role of the corporate staff was limited to understanding the issues in the strike and to reporting and interpreting these issues to corporate management.

In 1963 Ford-Werke Aktiengesellschaft in West Germany decided to join appropriate regional metal industry employer associations and to adhere to collective labor agreements negotiated by those associations. Previously, Ford of West Germany had negotiated works agreements with its employee-elected works councils, not because of any corporate policy about whether to join employer associations, but because the director of industrial relations and his staff (all German nationals) believed this arrangement was then in the best interests of the German company.

Before making its decision, the German management requested a two-week visit of an experienced labor relations executive from the corporate labor relations staff to assist in outlining a comprehensive study of Ford of West Germany's collective bargaining relationships. After the completion of a study outline, Ford of West Germany prepared the study, which resulted in a recommendation, approved by the Ford of West Germany management board, to join appropriate regional employer associations. Ford of West Germany sought a further review of the study by the corporate labor relations staff to assure that the study had adequately considered all of the alternatives. The corporate staff reviewed the study in November 1962, found it to be comprehensive and thorough, and left it to the German management to decide whether and when to join the appropriate employer associations.

In 1968 Ford Motor Company Limited in Britain recognized a staff association (trade union) to represent its foremen and general foremen. Ford of Britain appreciated the position of Ford Motor Company in the United States that union representation for its supervisors was neither in their interest nor the company's and that, in the United States, the management adamantly would resist such representation. Again, however, as with employer association membership, there was no corporate worldwide policy about trade union recognition.

After several years of discussions with the petitioning union and after a careful study of what further steps the Ford of Britain management might take to assure good relations with its supervisors without the intervention of a union to represent them, the management finally decided to extend recognition in a carefully drafted procedure agreement.[6]

Again, the Ford of Britain decision to extend recognition, which was a marked departure from the position of the parent company in the United States, was made by the management of that subsidiary. The role of the corporate labor relations staff involved, first, assuring that the local management had carefully studied the question and, second, interpreting to corporate management the setting that had prompted such a prudent local decision.

Conclusions

Based on the experience of one large multinational employer, it is clear that local managements in the subsidiaries can and do have the authority to develop and administer industrial relations policies appropriate to the national settings in which the subisdiaries operate. The role of the corporate staff involves (1) supporting the provision, in each subsidiary, of a competent, professional industrial relations organization that fully comprehends the needs and problems of a particular business, (2) assuring that thorough study of industrial relations questions supports prudent decisions of managements in the subsidiaries, and (3) reporting and interpreting those decisions to corporate management.

---

6. In the United Kingdom there is no provision for representation elections, no tidy definition of bargaining units, and no certification of a representative chosen by a majority of the represented employees. Instead, employers extend recognition in a variety of ways, ranging from informal to quite structured, when they deem it in their best interest.

Comment
B. C. Roberts

The locus of decision making in a multinational enterprise is clearly an issue of critical concern to managements, trade unions, and governments. Inevitably, multinational enterprise decisions will both reflect and influence economic, social, political, and cultural differences in their home and host countries, and so far as these decisions come into conflict with expectations and aspirations they are bound to evoke a vigorous response from those affected.

To understand the impact of multinational decision making, we must explore three questions.

1. What is the nature of the decisions that have to be made in the conduct of industrial relations in a multinational enterprise at the corporate headquarters or at some other locus in the international structure of its organization?

2. What determines the locus of these decisions?

3. What is the significance of the locus of decisions to unions and governments in both home and host countries?

In the light of these questions Robert Copp's paper gives an extremely interesting account of the principles and policies of decision making in industrial relations matters in a multinational enterprise—the Ford Motor Company. In defining industrial relations, Copp acknowledges a sharp difference of view between management and unions as to the scope of this definition. He accepts that the consequences of decisions of investment and the deployment of production facilities are bound to be the subject of consultation and negotiation, but he insists that the decisions themselves are outside the scope of industrial relations matters, and thus inappropriate for consultation or bargaining.

I agree with Copp that multinational and, indeed, national enterprises are generally reluctant to consult and negotiate on investment decisions. The extent to which unions have established a right to negotiate or to be consulted on these matters is contentious in all countries. In fact, it is precisely this situation that has led European unions to press their governments to compel both domestic- and foreign-owned corporations to provide advance information about their plans. The closure of plants and transfer of production facilities from one country to another is the primary factor in the belief of unions that multinational enterprises are fundamentally a different species from national enterprises and, therefore, must be

---

B. C. Roberts is professor of industrial relations at the London School of Economics and Political Science.

regulated by an extension of national or international law, or by the internationalizing of the bargaining process. Therefore, while understanding Copp's desire to limit his paper to his definition of industrial relations questions, we must recognize that the issues go far wider.

Major investment decisions are of major concern to the corporate headquarters of a company, and in most cases corporate headquarters will have the first and the last word. Still, although the power of corporate headquarters may be virtually absolute in the long run, it may be far less than unions often suggest in the short run. Once a company has made an investment it may be locked in. Companies have often taken immense losses before pulling out, finally deciding that the loss is killing them. Before that point is reached, of course, they may have rechanneled their investment to other areas. In these decisions multinationals behave much like national firms.

The 1974 survey made by the International Organization of Employers of 400 multinational enterprises provides some interesting information on the relationship of headquarters to subsidiary units on such issues as capital expenditure on existing plants and on the establishment and closure of plants.[1] The picture that emerges is one of collaboration through an extensive and complex process of consultation between parent and subsidiary. Considerable variations in degree of local financial autonomy exist, ranging from the requirement that headquarters approve any expenditure above $50,000 to an occasional audit of local expenditure decisions. Similar variation prevails in relation to closing down a particular activity.

There is evidence that technological, cultural, and ideological factors play an important role in determining the locus of decision making between headquarters and subsidiary managements. Companies with a high capital-to-labor ratio (such as chemical processing, oil production and refining, and manufacturing companies) tend to have a greater headquarters' influence than labor-intensive companies, especially in the early years of an expansion overseas. The degree of interdependence in the production process between countries is also of considerable importance. When subsidiaries in overseas countries are dependent on a single source of supply, corporate headquarters will inevitably be drawn into industrial relations decisions that may crucially affect various subsidiaries and the ultimate profitability of the corporation as a whole.

Nevertheless, all the evidence suggests that Copp is right to stress the extent to which there is local autonomy in industrial relations questions as he defines them. It would be surprising if this were not the case. Multinationals are well aware that there are significant differences between countries in their industrial relations systems, that they must respect these

---

1. International Organization of Employers, *Multinational Enterprises: The Reality of Their Social Policies and Practices* (Geneva: IOE, 1974).

differences to avoid serious conflicts and difficulties, and that they must employ indigenous managers who have local understanding and knowledge to be primarily responsible for the conduct of most industrial relations issues. The international employers' organization survey reported that in fields of personnel recruitment, dismissals, and vocational training, practically every company delegated all decisions to its subsidiaries. On such matters as wages, fringe benefits, and other conditions of work the same delegation generally existed, with the exception of company pensions, which were often subject to the control of headquarters.

A recent survey of some thirty British-owned multinationals found similar results.[2] Only three companies said that their headquarters staff were frequently involved in the preparation for negotiations, collective bargaining, and the settlement of disputes; 80 percent of the companies responding were rarely or never involved in these matters. The situation was the reverse, however, where changes in pensions were concerned.

The pharmaceutical firms in the sample showed greater headquarters concern and involvement in the establishment of employment conditions than other types of companies. This may be related to the nature of the product, which involves a great deal of research, a high degree of transmitted know-how, and relatively large numbers of professional and technical personnel who maintain a close contact with company headquarters.

The role of the industrial relations and personnel management staff, described by Copp as that of consultants and catalysts, seems to me to be somewhat like that of the British monarch: they expect to be informed, they may warn and counsel but not dictate, and in the last resort they may dissolve the local board and appoint a new managing director. What they cannot do is govern directly themselves.

There are, however, differences among companies, related to size, technology, structure, product, and cultural origins, that influence the relative roles of management in the home and host countries. These differences were evident in the survey of British-owned multinationals, which was deliberately designed to enable comparisons with the results obtained by David Blake in his survey of U.S.-owned multinationals.[3] Blake found that U.S. multinational headquarters became significantly involved in the industrial relations areas of greater conflict—collective bargaining and strike settlements—and that the degree of involvement was related to

2. B. C. Roberts and Jonathan May, "The Response of Multinational Enterprises to International Trade Union Pressures," *British Journal of Industrial Relations* 12, no. 3 (November 1974): 403-17.

3. David Blake, "Cross-national Cooperative Strategies: Union Response to the MNCs," *Multinational Corporations and Labour Unions,* selected papers from a symposium in Nijmegen, Netherlands, May 1973.

the degree of the enterprise's multinationality. We found the opposite. Moreover, on all counts British-owned multinationals showed a lower level of headquarters involvement than U.S.-owned multinationals. What accounts for these differences? First, it seems to be more common for U.S. companies operating abroad to establish new wholly owned subsidiaries. In joint ventures or the purchase of already established local companies, the cultural influence of the headquarters may be less, even though it could have a considerable impact. Another important factor is the insistence of U.S. companies on a much greater flow of information from their subsidiary units: they use the telephone, telex, and airplane much more than do companies based in the United Kingdom or in other European countries. The flow of information is necessarily persuasive and influential. The influence, of course, is by no means entirely one way, but it is highly significant and beneficial to efficiency.

A further factor of considerable influence is the tighter financial control U.S. companies impose on their subsidiaries: rigorous profit planning, control of payrolls through headcount limitations, inventory controls, capital budgeting, and similar techniques setting parameters within which the management of subsidiaries are allowed to manage.

In general, U.S.-owned corporations have more thoroughly worked out and professionally managed industrial relations policies in their headquarters company than do British and other European companies. This difference is due to the U.S. industrial relations system and to the legal, economic, social, and political context in which it exists. In the United States, for example, a multinational company is perceived by the Department of Justice and the Internal Revenue Service, which reflect the attitudes of the Congress and public policy, as simply an extension of the U.S. company across an international boundary little different from the boundary between Michigan and Ohio.

The fact that some U.S.-owned companies (such as IBM, Mars, Kodak, and Procter and Gamble) have forced company philosophies based upon an American cultural foundation on their subsidiaries everywhere has tended to give the false impression that all U.S. multinationals are alike in this respect. Yet it is inevitable that multinational companies should have exported an element of their industrial cultures. In addition, it is significant that all these companies have modified their basic policies to come to terms with requirements of national environments. Moreover, it is by no means only American-owned companies that have developed philosophies owing a great deal to their home environment. Some other companies are Philips, Brown Boveri, Sulzers, Michelin, Lockums, Ohlsen and Bookers.

Finally, the perception of multinational enterprises as an expression of economic and cultural imperialism has led trade unions in home and host countries to seek to regulate multinationals' activities by extending collective bargaining across national frontiers via the intervention of national governments and international agencies. These responses have important implications for the future because international regulation is bound to create uniformity of policy, just as within the nation-state the demand for equality of treatment has resulted in the adoption of uniform employment policies. It will, of course, be a long time before there is anything approaching parity of pay, but it is possible to conceive, especially in areas such as Europe, of broadly similar conditions of employment. If, on the other hand, the pressure of unions to regulate multinationals through national legislation succeeds in restricting their activities in home and host countries, that would create an obstacle to the internationalizing of industrial relations.

INDUSTRIAL RELATIONS PROFILES OF FOREIGN-OWNED MANUFACTURERS IN THE UNITED STATES

Michael J. Jedel and Duane Kujawa

Industrial relations problems generated by the unique phenomenon of the multinational enterprise are not especially new. One set deals with operating practices in host countries, another with alleged job losses and employment adjustment effects in source countries. With respect to the industrialized nations, problems in the former set are frequently associated with U.S. direct investments in Europe and Canada; correspondingly, those in the latter with the U.S. environment. Considerable research has already been done on these problems.

Between 1963 and 1972 there was an expansion of foreign investment *into* the United States, especially in the manufacturing (80.9 percent increase) and petroleum sectors (131.1 percent increase). Some research has been done on this phenomenon, too, but mainly on investment rationales and general economic and commercial considerations; none has focused on the industrial relations effects, possibly because much of the investment is so recent and major personnel problems of generalizable significance have not as yet made headlines.

There is, however, a growing concern over the industrial relations prac-

Michael J. Jedel is associate professor in the Department of Management at Georgia State University. Duane Kujawa is professor of international business in the School of Business and Organizational Sciences at Florida International University.

The authors gratefully acknowledge the financial support given this research by Georgia State University's School of Business Administration, Institute of International Business, and Chair of Private Enterprise, Department of Management.

tices of foreign direct investors in the United States. The director of the U.S. Federal Mediation and Conciliation Service, for instance, reportedly questioned "whether foreign investors will insist on bringing their own management practices—forged under entirely different labor-management climates—to U.S. bargaining tables and whether American managements of foreign-owned plants will be influenced by the industrial relations policies of the owner's home country." [1] Early indications are that foreign management practices are likely to affect the entire spectrum of U.S. union-management relations. There is the allegation, for example, that Georgetown Steel Company in South Carolina, a subsidiary of the German Korf Industries, "embarked on a bitter campaign to resist union organization." [2] Sony Corporation (Japan) has stated "on the record" that there will be no layoffs at its U.S. plant. The International Association of Machinists, according to one report, "is upset by Japanese plants . . . in California, because the Americans [employed there] are getting lesser skilled work while the Japanese retain the skilled jobs at home." Another question has been raised: Will the Japanese passion for "face-saving" be translated by expatriate management in the United States into a preference for grievances being presented as group charges, a practice wholly incompatible with U.S. industrial relations? [3]

Concern also has surfaced in the United States regarding the competitive effects of direct foreign manufacturing investment. The dichotomy between the costs and benefits of such investment appears extreme. On the one hand, a U.S. congressman in a recent House speech noted that "if, as in the past, . . . foreign owned business gets a subsidy from its government, it is not fair and open competition. Able to sustain losses indefinitely, that company can undersell the American company, and eventually, force it to close shop. With the competition out of the way, the foreign owned plant controls the market and can peg the price of its product as high as it wants." [4] On the other hand, a recent study of the impact of transplanted Japanese management practices on productivity concludes that Japanese

---

1. "Wary about Importing Foreign Work Rules," *Business Week*, no. 2299 (September 29, 1973): 6.

2. Ibid. The union recognition question also reportedly resulted in a long and severe struggle between the Belgian Bekaert Steel Wire Company (Georgia) and the International Union of Electrical, Radio and Machine Workers. See Jeffrey S. Arpan, "Foreign Manufacturing Firms in the U.S.: A Study of Their Impact on Three Small Southern Communities," *Atlanta Economic Review* 24 (March-April, 1974): 6-7. This study also reports that the Bekaert management tried to implement the "paternalistic attitude employed by the parent" but found it difficult to do so because of union opposition (p. 6).

3. "Wary about Importing Foreign Work Rules," p. 6.

4. Report of the Task Force on Foreign Investment in the United States, Chamber of Commerce of the United States, September 1973," reprinted in U.S., Congress, House of Representatives, Committee on Foreign Affairs, *Foreign Investment in the United States*, Hearings before the Subcommittee on Foreign Economic Policy, 93d Cong., 2d sess., 1974, pp. 9-10.

companies in the United States "are outperforming American companies in the same industries." [5] Mainly because of the former kinds of allegations there has been serious support for more restrictive public policies controlling foreign investment in the United States. To this end, several bills have been introduced in the Congress, the most severe of which would limit foreign ownership of any United States corporation to 5 percent.[6] Subsequently, the U.S. Congress enacted the Foreign Investment Study Act of 1974, calling for data collection and analysis of the impact of foreign investment on employment and personnel practices and directing the Commerce and Treasury Departments specifically to study and analyze "the effect of foreign direct investment in terms of employment opportunities and practices and the activities and influence of foreign and American management executives employed by foreign firms."[7]

As of April 1975 the research required by the act had yet to be begun, but Commerce Department officials estimated the research task and the subsequent report would be completed before the mid-1976 target deadline. It appeared unlikely that systematic, empirical information and analyses of the industrial relations practices of foreign investors in the United States would be reported in the interim. Thus the present study was undertaken, admittedly on a very modest scale, to profile (1) the current industrial relations practices of foreign investors in the United States and (2) the attitudes and opinions of industrial relations management at these companies. Between June and October 1974 a survey was conducted through the mail. Two questionnaires were used, one for each part of the study.[8]

Both questionnaires were mailed to the 1,020 foreign-owned firms (those with 50 percent or more non-U.S. ownership) in U.S. manufacturing, mining, and petroleum industries identified in a list developed by Jeffrey S. Arpan and David A. Ricks.[9] Each envelope was marked "Forward to Senior Industrial Relations or Personnel Executive at this Location." The population was reduced to 901 because of companies that had gone out of

5. Richard Tanner Johnson and William G. Ouchi, "Made in America (under Japanese Management)," *Harvard Business Review* 52 (September-October 1974): 61.

6. "Senate Bill to Watch Foreign Investments in U.S. Congress Goes Too Far, SEC Says," *Wall Street Journal* (eastern edition), March 6, 1975, p. 11.

7. U.S., Congress, *An Act to Authorize the Secretary of Commerce and the Secretary of the Treasury to Conduct a Study of Foreign Direct and Portfolio Investment in the United States, and for Other Purposes,* S. 2824, 93d Cong., 2d sess., 1974, pp. 2 and 4. (The act was signed into law in October 1974.)

8. Copies of the questionnaires and additional study data may be obtained from either of the authors. The authors acknowledge that field interviews would have been preferable to a mail-out survey; however, this was beyond the resource constraints affecting the research.

9. The list of foreign-owned companies used was a preliminary one developed by Arpan and Ricks. The final, revised list is contained in their *Directory of Foreign Manufacturers in the United States* (Atlanta: Publishing Services Division, Office of Services, School of Business Administration, Georgia State University, 1975).

business, moved leaving no identifiable forwarding address, were no longer foreign-owned, were never foreign-owned, or were not engaged in manufacturing or processing in any way.

Practices of Industrial Relations Executives
of Foreign-owned Firms

Ninety-one completed questionnaires on the subject of practices were returned, a response rate of 10.1 percent. These returns were analyzed with respect to geographical distribution, industrial sector, and nationality of parent company (see table 1). Because the data presented in this section are not proper for rigorous statistical analysis, tests of representativeness of the sample respondents are omitted here. No major differences in representativeness between the samples obtained in the two parts of the study, however, were apparent.

TABLE 1

NATIONALITY OF PARENT COMPANY

Country	Number of Firms	Percent of Total
United Kingdom	22	24.2
West Germany	22	24.2
Canada	15	16.5
Japan	7	7.7
Switzerland	7	7.7
Sweden	6	6.6
France	4	4.4
Netherlands	4	4.4
Belgium	2	2.2
Austria	1	1.1
Italy	1	1.1
TOTAL	91	100.1[a]

a. Total does not equal 100 percent because of rounding.

Other data in the practices questionnaire included such information as nationalities and supervisory relationships of industrial relations executives, extent and year of foreign ownership, reasons for facility acquisition, work force and unionization characteristics, sales volume, employee benefits, lost time, employment process features, extent of production integration, and industrial relations changes and problems that have arisen as a result of the foreign ownership. Some interesting although not definitive findings resulted from the analysis of these data.

Commencement Date of U.S. Operations and Total Employment. Of seventy-nine firms responding to a question about the original date of foreign ownership, thirteen had Canadian parent companies, twenty-two German, and seventeen British; the rest were a varied mixture. Overall, 44.3 percent of the firms became foreign-owned before 1965, with larger proportions of Canadian (69.2 percent) and British (52.9 percent) companies belonging to this older ownership category. Conversely, ownership by West German nationals was more recent, with 68.2 percent between 1968 and 1972.

There was no clear relation between age of foreign ownership and employment size.[10] Thus the assumption that older firms would be the larger employers, as a result of adding to their work forces as they became more settled in the foreign environment, is not supportable. This finding appears noteworthy. It is possible that the small and well-established firms may be less innovative in industrial relations practices. Rather than developing on-site industrial relations talent and encouraging unique approaches to labor relations, they may rely more heavily on parent-company involvement.

Sales and Book Value. Seventy-five firms responded to this question. A majority (forty-three) reported sales of under $10 million, with the $1 million to $10 million category the modal one. British (70 percent), Canadian (64 percent), and German (59 percent) firms were concentrated at the lower end of the spectrum. Seventeen firms reported sales over $50 million. Nine were either British, Canadian, or German; the others were accounted for by four other nationalities: the Netherlands (three), Japan (two), Sweden (two), and Switzerland (one). These data do not warrant a conclusion that foreign ownership from any particular nationality has been clustered at the higher end of the spectrum; on the contrary, large firms appear dispersed.

Very little exporting of manufactured items for sale outside the United States was noted. The survey revealed that 42 percent of the respondents did not sell any items abroad; another 42 percent sold less than 10 percent of their total volume outside the United States, and only 9.9 percent had more than 25 percent of total sales abroad. A mere 3.7 percent indicated that a majority of their sales were in non-U.S. markets. This pattern of manufactured items being sold overwhelmingly in the United States was one reason for the parent firms' undertaking U.S. operations.

Information on the ratio of sales volume to number of production

---

10. Sizable majorities of firms in both the "before 1965" and the "after 1965" groups had total work forces of under 1,000. Most older Canadian and British firms were smaller employers. Only four British firms employed in excess of 1,000; of the Canadian companies nine employed fewer than 100 persons and none claimed more than 1,000. All seven respondents with employment greater than 1,000 had been foreign-owned for over ten years.

employees per firm revealed that about half the companies had ratios of under $109,000 per worker. One-third of the firms had ratios as high as $300,000 per worker. High sales ratios usually correlated with high investment per worker.[11] The larger the sales and investment per worker, the more leverage employees have vis-à-vis management. Management preference for innovation in employment practices thus would probably be heightened in such situations.[12]

Extent of Production Integration. This factor was considered important because greater reliance on supplies from other countries for parts, subassemblies, or further processing operations might increase parent company involvement in local industrial relations practices, since greater interdependence means greater costs when industrial relations problems occur in any one subsidiary.

The findings showed that more than 47 percent of the firms received processed or semi-manufactured parts from plants in other countries. For German- and Canadian-owned firms, the figures were 63.6 percent and 53.3 percent respectively. More than 30 percent of all firms reported that their U.S. subsidiaries received entire subassemblies from foreign plants.

The data also suggested that the extent of production integration was substantial. Almost 80 percent of the respondents received more than one-fourth of their parts from non-U.S. plants, and over 40 percent received more than half. In addition, more than half of those responding that their firms received subassemblies indicated that the amount received from abroad was above 50 percent.

The overwhelming majority of firms (85 percent) indicated that production did not leave the United States for additional processing. This was true for all parent nationalities, supporting the idea that these firms are in the United States to serve the American market. Although they might receive parts from abroad, their production remains here for internal distribution.

Nationality of Key Officials. The senior industrial relations executive was asked to indicate his or her nationality on the questionnaire. Approximately 25 percent were the same as the parent firm; 70 percent were Americans; and 5 percent were from other foreign nations. It is of particular interest that almost 30 percent of these firms did *not* have U.S. nationals managing employee relations. With slight variations this nationality pattern was the same in individual country company groups. This contrasts with informa-

---

11. This is especially true since high sales mean high inventories, and inventory (including the value of inventory in process) is a form of investment.

12. Two of the four Japanese respondents reported sales per production employee ratios greater than $500,000. These fragmentary data suggest support for the oft-heard statements that Japanese managers are more innovative than others. This suggestion, however, is not supported by the results of the attitudinal portion of this survey.

tion that Ford Motor Company recruits local nationals for its top employee relations positions in its foreign subsidiaries and has been successful in twenty-eight of thirty countries.[13]

Information was also obtained on the title and nationality of the person to whom the senior industrial relations executive reported. In fifty-five of the firms the executive reported to someone in the U.S. company and in thirty-six to someone in the parent company. The 40 percent reporting to a parent-company official (usually the parent president or a managing director) attest to the potential direct foreign ownership influence on U.S. industrial relations practices. In 56 percent of all firms, these officials were foreign nationals, generally from the parent company's country, although they might be considered U.S. company executives rather than parent-company officials. The chief negotiator was identified in 87 percent of the cases as in-house; a few firms used an outside lawyer.[14]

Since Japanese management practices often are singled out for special attention, it is appropriate to examine the seven Japanese firms in our sample. In all but one case the top industrial relations executive was a U.S. citizen; in this one case he was a non-Japanese foreigner. In six companies, however, the industrial relations executive reported to a Japanese: four employed by the U.S. operation and two employed by the parent. Thus the Japanese firms have the capability of exerting direct pressure on industrial relations practices through the higher level official.

Factors Responsible for Commencing Operations in the United States. Asked why their foreign parent had commenced U.S. operations, respondents first noted all relevant factors from a list of twelve potential key factors and then rank ordered those items checked. The factors cited most frequently as most important to the decision and the number of firms that so ranked that factor appear in table 2. Disregarding rank order, desirable geographical location and proximity to established markets were the factors most often cited—sixty-two and fifty-seven times respectively. Together these two factors accounted for almost 40 percent of the frequency distribution of citations of key factors, demonstrating the interest of the foreign parents to enter or expand their share of the American market.

Unionization and Bargaining Structure. Of the ninety-one firms returning questionnaires thirty-five were unionized. Only among Canadian firms were a majority unionized, perhaps because the Canadian firms are older or more geographically concentrated near U.S. population centers

---

13. Robert Copp, "The Labor Affairs Function in a Multinational Firm," *Proceedings of the Industrial Relations Research Association, 1973 Spring Meeting*, p. 455.

14. Thirty-two firms identified their chief negotiator in the survey. In twenty-two cases, the negotiator was pinpointed as the top (U.S.) plant or company industrial relations executive; in six cases, as top line management; and in four cases, as an outside lawyer.

TABLE 2

FACTORS IN COMMENCING U.S. OPERATIONS

Factor	Number of Times Ranked Most Important
Proximity to established markets	30
Desirable geographical location	20
(New) U.S. marketing opportunity	11
Bought out former customer or supplier	8
Transportation facilities	7

that are highly unionized. The relatively low degree of unionization among West German firms (only six of the sixteen) may be a result of the newness of West German ownership interests in the United States.

Bargaining units tended to be broad in the responding firms, and union shop provisions were included in more than 70 percent of the contracts. Further, all but four of the firms bargained independently and locally. The data indicated that foreign-owned firms were adopting the typical U.S. plant-level approach to bargaining rather than the industrywide structure typical in Europe.

Subjects in Collective Bargaining Agreements. A comparison of the inclusion of certain employee-related subjects in respondents' collective bargaining agreements and in U.S. national manufacturing firms appears in table 3.

TABLE 3

INCLUSION OF SUBJECTS IN COLLECTIVE BARGAINING AGREEMENTS
(In percentage)

Subject	Foreign-owned Firms Including Subject in Contract	U.S. Firms Including Subject in Contract [a]
Seniority	100.0	94.5
Grievance process	97.1	99.6
Dues checkoff	94.3	
Management rights	91.4	63.1
Overtime	91.4	
Arbitration	77.1	94
No strike-no lockout	77.1	
Union security	71.4	
Discipline	68.6	
Subcontracting	51.4	37.8

a. U.S. Bureau of Labor Statistics, *Major Characteristics of Collective Bargaining Agreements*, Bulletin 1425-1 to 14, 1964 to 1974.

With the exception of arbitration, the subjects cited generally appear at least as frequently in the union contracts of the foreign-owned U.S. firms as they do in domestic companies. Because arbitration of rights is primarily a U.S. phenomenon, the disparity with respect to its inclusion is not surprising. Grievance arbitration simply may not yet have been introduced in these foreign-owned firms.

Also of interest is the relative frequency with which the no strike-no lockout and grievance arbitration clauses appear in the same contract. In U.S. industrial relations practices, they are well-established quid pro quos. Not so in foreign-owned firms. In only twenty-two of the thirty-five contracts (62.9 percent) did both clauses appear. The relative labor peace to which U.S. firms have become accustomed while contracts are in effect may not be as widespread in these foreign-owned firms. It is likely, however, that the U.S. industrial relations approach will predominate and the relative frequency of these two clauses in contracts soon will conform to the American experience.

Payment Systems and Benefits for Production Workers. Eighty-four of ninety-one firms paid production workers on an hourly basis, six had salaried production workers, and one had a piece rate system. Those offering salaries include three British companies and one Canadian, one French, and one Swedish. It is somewhat surprising to find so few salaried workers, given the move toward salaried pay systems for production workers in the United Kingdom, the Netherlands, and other parts of Europe.

Information collected on the number of companies providing various kinds of benefits indicates that industrial relations practices of U.S.- and foreign-owned firms are similar in the relative frequency with which benefit topics are included although not necessarily in the level of the benefit.[15]

Some variations by nationality appear when overtime is examined. Overtime was mandatory in ten Canadian firms, voluntary in three; it was voluntary in more British and West German firms (thirteen of each) than mandatory (nine of each). The Canadian firms' position may arise from the fact that unionization, or in general the proximity to U.S. customs and practices, requires adopting the position prevalent among unionized U.S. firms—that seniority shall be the appropriate basis for assigning overtime. To what extent the other foreign-owned firms will be able to maintain their contrary stance remains to be seen.

---

15. Benefits examined included paid vacations, holidays, funeral leave, sick leave and personal leave, group health insurance, life insurance, retirement plans, layoff compensation, and cost-of-living increases. Comparative data for U.S.-owned firms were taken from U.S. Bureau of Labor Statistics, *Major Characteristics of Collective Bargaining Agreements*, Bulletin 1425-1 to 14, 1964 to 1972.

Hiring Decisions, Discipline, Work Rules, Layoff Procedures, and Performance Evaluation. Some interesting differences by nationality of ownership occur on the subject of who makes the firm's hiring decision. Of the ninety firms responding to this question, the line manager alone made the decision in 48 percent of the cases, and jointly with personnel staff in another 17 percent. In the Canadian firms, the local personnel official had decision power more frequently (63 percent of responses) than in the British (48 percent) or West German (32 percent) firms.

For a number of other practices, the major distinguishing characteristic appeared to be unionization. A unionized firm, for example, regardless of nationality of ownership, typically had formal written disciplinary procedures, work rules, and layoff procedures; performance evaluation was rarely used. Nonunionized firms did not have written policies on discipline, work rules, or layoff procedures, and performance evaluation was more common.

Most unionized firms weighted seniority heavily in determining layoffs, whereas nonunionized firms gave managerial judgments on comparative abilities more weight. Practices in these areas appeared to conform to the U.S. experience.

Worker Participation in Decision Making. Works councils, relatively common in Europe, give employees an opportunity for extensive participation on some issues of concern to the union and the work force. The survey results suggest such practices are not common here. No firm indicated that its workers' participation in decision making was extensive, although 76 percent acknowledged that workers played at least a minimal role in major firm decisions.

Foreign Ownership Influence. Respondents were asked to identify which industrial relations policies and practices were influenced as a result of their non-U.S. ownership.[16] Benefits appear to have been most significantly influenced (29 percent of the firms cited this area), but there is evidence that other practices have been affected, or at least are *perceived* to have been affected, in some instances.

Problems Resulting from Foreign Ownership. There were very few responses to the final question about industrial relations problems that had arisen or were foreseen as a result of the non-U.S. ownership. "Heightened concern for job" was cited most often (six times); "developing a collective bargaining stance," and "increased turnover" next (four each); "excessive number of grievances" was cited three times.

---

16. Respondents were queried specifically on strike experiences, man-days lost, and incidence of wildcat strikes as related to foreign influence. Seventeen strikes were reported, all of short duration, but no useful data resulted.

Additional research could further probe and substantiate the relationships suggested from this survey concerning the industrial relations practices of foreign-owned firms operating in the United States.

Attitudes of Industrial Relations Management

A comparison of the attitudes and opinions of managers concerned with industrial relations in U.S.- and foreign-owned firms was expected to be useful in two major ways: (1) to the extent that corporate behavior follows managerial perceptions and values, the recording of attitudinal differences between managers in the two groups might well precede actual behavioral differences, and (2) the profiling of the attitudinal patterns might be useful as a reference point for subsequent studies, especially those of differences in managerial styles of foreign and U.S. investors and their impact at the workplace. The managers of the foreign-owned firms were asked to record their reactions to statements on various industrial relations practices; their responses were then compared to those provided by key industrial relations officials of U.S.-owned companies who also participated in the survey. The ultimate objective was to isolate differences and similarities between the two sets of respondents.

Limitations in this approach should be noted. First, there are many elements besides management values and opinions that influence corporate industrial relations behavior including the economic, technological, and legal environments. (In fact, this research tried to identify some of these elements and record their importance.) Second, there is the question whether similar levels of management responded in both groups; analysis of the returns indicates that they did. In the foreign-owned companies, respondents were invariably either the top industrial relations executives or senior line managers; in the U.S.-owned companies, respondents were generally the top industrial relations executives or members of the industrial relations staff (there were no responses from senior line managers). Thus, the foreign respondents may be more pragmatic and less sophisticated about the complexities of industrial relations, but they may also be more involved in the decision making in their respective firms. Finally, it is possible for individual statements to be worded so as to elicit certain responses, and thus it can be doubted whether respondents really said what they believed. Since both sets of respondents reacted to the *same* statements, however, any bias should not create *differences* between the two groups. In addition, in an effort to encourage forthright and honest responses, the cover letter accompanying the survey instrument stated that all returns would be handled anonymously.

Seventy-one completed attitude questionnaires were returned, representing a response rate of nearly 8 percent. For a control group the questionnaire was sent to 298 U.S.-owned manufacturing or processing firms listed in the 1973 *Membership Directory Handbook* of the Industrial Relations Research Association. A total of seventy-two responses (24.2 percent) was received from this group. Responses from both groups were requested on a five-point scale as follows: 1. disagree, 2. tend to disagree, 3. undecided, 4. tend to agree, and 5. agree.

Representativeness of Respondents of Foreign-owned Companies

The representativeness of the respondent set of foreign-owned companies was tested against the population of all foreign-owned companies (in manufacturing) in terms of parent-company nationality, geographical location within the United States, distribution by industry within manufacturing, and length of time in the United States. Appropriate tests indicate that the findings here and in subsequent sections are statistically significant, despite the relatively low response rates.[17]

The difference in the parent-company nationality distributions was found to be significant at the .10 level, the Dutch providing 44.5 percent of the variance. The difference in geographical location was highly significant (.01 level). The Southeast accounted for 62.7 percent of the variance; the number of responses from firms in Georgia and South Carolina was much greater than expected, probably because it was obvious that the questionnaire originated from Georgia State University. Neither the difference in industry classification nor in length of time in the United States was significant at the .10 level. Since foreign direct investment in Georgia and South Carolina is relatively recent, and since there are no differences either in industry classification or in length of time in the United States, it is unclear just how the difference in geographical location may have affected the survey results.

It also would have been useful to test the survey respondents against the population of foreign-owned firms in terms of size distribution and extent of unionization, but the characteristics of the population regarding these parameters are unknown and cannot even be sensibly estimated.

---

17. The nonparametric Kolmogorov-Smirnov two-sample test was used exclusively in this part. This test requires a sample size of at least forty from each population. Thus response *rate* is not crucial to a determination of statistical significance. See Sidney Siegel, *Non-parametric Statistics for the Behavioral Sciences* (New York: McGraw-Hill, 1956), pp. 127-36. Also, with small samples (for example the four or five responses used when specific nationalities are discussed), the chi-square approximation of the Kolmogorov-Smirnov statistic can be used, but it will result in a more conservative test of the null hypothesis. See ibid., pp. 134-35, and L. A. Goodman, "Kolmogorov-Smirnov Tests for Psychological Research," *Psychological Bulletin* 51 (1954): 160-68. Finally, the ordinal nature of the response data and the inappropriateness of any normal distribution assumption when value judgments are being offered dictated the use of a nonparametric testing technique rather than the more powerful and robust *t*-test.

Characteristics of Respondents

Comparisons were made between respondents from foreign-owned and U.S.-owned companies regarding geographical location within the United States, distribution by industry within manufacturing, employment levels, and extent of unionization. Respondents were found significantly different (.001 level) regarding geographical location. This was somewhat expected since the control set was selected from the membership list of the Industrial Relations Research Association, which has especially strong appeal in the Midwest. But, as with foreign-owned companies alone, it is unclear just what bias location difference should have on the survey results. There was no difference (.10 level) in terms of industry classification, but analysis showed that (each at .001 level) the U.S.-owned companies had larger work forces and were more unionized than foreign-owned companies. The importance of these differences is noted in the analyses that follow.

Survey Response Data and Analyses

Management Style and Worker Participation in Decision Making. All respondents were asked to rate themselves on a five-point integer scale ranging from individual decision making (1) to group decision making (5). The results are shown in table 4. There was no difference (.10 level) between industrial relations management at U.S.-owned and foreign-owned companies in autocratic or participative decision-making preferences. All respondents leaned slightly toward the autocratic side. The Germans, however, were found to be significantly (.02 level) more autocratic than the respondents in U.S.-owned firms, but not different (.10 level) from German and U.S. nationals in German-owned firms. Perhaps one important conclusion from this is that future union or worker complaints about alien management styles of foreign investors—at least in terms of shared or not-shared decision making—are likely to be unfounded, except in the case of the Germans. Another implication is that there are not likely to be any special innovations in the United States by foreign investors regarding worker participation.

Officials were also queried specifically concerning worker participation in management decision making. The respondents in U.S.- and foreign-owned firms both tended to disagree that "workers should have extensive participation in management decision making" (2.211 and 1.871 mean responses respectively). When the statement is softened, however, to the other extreme "workers should have minimal participation," U.S.-owned firms still slightly tended to disagree (2.917 mean response), while foreign-owned companies shifted and tended to agree (3.574 mean response) with the statement. The difference between the two is significant at the .05 level.

TABLE 4

RESPONSES ON MANAGEMENT STYLE

Ownership	Number of Responses	Mean Response	Is There a Difference Between U.S. and Others?		Nationality of Respondents (Number)			
			Decision	Significance Level	U.S.	Same as Parent	Other Non-U.S.	Unknown
United States	71	2.937	—	—	—	—	—	—
All foreign	70	2.700	No	.10	54	12	3	1
United Kingdom	19	2.868	No	.10	17	2	0	0
West Germany	18	2.250	Yes	.02	12	6	0	0
Canada	11	2.500	No	.10	5	3	2	1
Switzerland	6	3.417	No	.10	6	0	0	0
Netherlands	5	2.900	No	.10	5	0	0	0
Japan	4	3.625	No	.10	4	0	0	0

NOTE: Kolmogorov-Smirnov two-sample test used to determine significance for "all foreign." Chi-square approximation of Kolmogorov-Smirnov statistic used for specific nationalities (e.g., British).

By nationality, the British (3.833 mean response) and Germans (3.944 mean response) stand out at the .10 and .01 levels respectively. German national respondents disagreed significantly more (1.833 mean response) than did U.S. nationals at German-owned firms (4.083 mean response). In fact, the latter tended to agree with the statement. One might speculate that these positions originate in the movement in Great Britain toward more participation and the more traditional practice in Germany regarding codetermination. The statement that "there is no place for worker participation in management decision making" found the respondents on both sides of the "undecided" fence—those at U.S.-owned firms tended to agree; those at foreign-owned firms tended to disagree. There was, however, no significant (.10 level) difference between them. Both sets of respondents agreed (4.68 mean U.S. response; 4.45 mean foreign response) that workers have a right to basic economic information on the enterprise. The particular intent of this statement was to see if the informational function of the works councils in Germany, the Netherlands, and Belgium might possibly become a new union role in the United States. Any conclusion is obscured, however, by the mean response from U.S.-owned companies. Perhaps the "good faith bargaining" provisions of the U.S. National Labor Relations Act and management disclosures to the investment community regarding future profits and the like have had some impact on U.S. managements' thinking on the disclosure question.

The survey data on worker participation indicate that foreign investors will not be great innovators, although they appear somewhat more willing to allow some form of shared decision making. The British and German managers, especially German nationals, are more willing than the other groups.

Differences in Industrial Relations Problems and Practices. On the question of possible differences between U.S.- and foreign-owned firms in industrial relations problems and practices, both sets of respondents agreed there should be no real differences but those in foreign-owned firms agreed significantly (.05 level) more so, with only the British responding somewhat differently (see table 5).[18] On the question that foreign-owned firms should be innovators in industrial relations and employment practices, both sets of respondents "tended to disagree," with no significant difference between them. The British disagreement was significantly (.05 level) more strong, however, than that of the U.S.-owned firms. These responses may indicate that foreign investors in the United States, especially the British, are quite concerned that they not appear different from American firms in industrial relations matters.

18. It is actually not clear in this statement whether "should" is meant in the positive or normative sense. The authors intended the former. The responses to the next statement on innovators indicated the respondents viewed "should" in the positive sense, too.

TABLE 5

RESPONSE ON INDUSTRIAL RELATIONS IN U.S.-OWNED FIRMS AND FOREIGN-OWNED FIRMS

Statement	U.S.-OWNED FIRMS		FOREIGN-OWNED FIRMS			IS THERE A DIFFERENCE BETWEEN UNITED STATES AND OTHERS?	
	Number of Responses	Mean Response	Number of Responses	Mean Response	Parent Nationality	Decision	Significance Level
There should be no real difference between U.S.-owned firms and foreign-owned firms in terms of industrial relations practices and problems.	72	3.598	69	4.188	All firms	Yes	.05
			19	4.211	British	Yes	.10
On the average, I would expect foreign-owned firms in the U.S. to be innovators in industrial relations and employment practices.	72	2.444	69	2.217	All firms	No	.10
			19	1.737	British	Yes	.05

NOTE: Kolmogorov-Smirnov two-sample test was used to determine significance for "all firms." Chi-square approximation of Kolmogorov-Smirnov statistic was used for specific nationalities (e.g., British).

Work Force Management. Statements on work force management covered three areas: voluntary overtime, salary status, and one aspect of job performance. The statements and responses are shown in table 6.

The U.S.-owned firms tended to react negatively to the idea of voluntary overtime; the Canadians disagreed (.10 level) less intensely. The Germans tended to agree (.02 level) with the concept, and the Japanese agreed quite strongly (.02 level). This strong evidence suggests that foreign-owned firms are not prepared to defend the mandatory overtime concept traditionally favored by U.S.-owned companies.

Responses to the statement on salary status for production workers "making sense" were surprising. The expectation was that, given developments in their parent countries, the British-owned and Dutch-owned companies in the United States would view salary status in a favorable light. But foreign-owned firms, *including* the British, disagreed with the idea to an even greater extent (.025 level) than their U.S.-owned counterparts.

Both U.S.- and foreign-owned firms agreed they are interested in solving the problems workers have after hours that affect job performance.

Grievances and Discipline. Both sets of respondents tended to disagree (2.875 mean U.S. response; 2.870 mean foreign response) with the proposition that a formal, written grievance procedure was "the best way to handle employee complaints and problems," but they both tended to agree (3.403 mean U.S. response; 3.343 mean foreign response), with the same idea regarding employee discipline problems. No doubt the importance of formalized procedures regarding discipline has been more universally recognized. Both sets also tended to agree (3.236 mean U.S. response; 3.116 mean foreign response) on the use of arbitrators to settle employee grievances.

Fringe Benefits. Respondents tended to disagree with the idea that a male worker should have paid leave when his wife has a baby, except for the Germans and the Japanese who separately tended to agree with the idea (.10 level). Both sets also tended to disagree with the concept of a "thirteenth month" or year-end bonus, except for German national respondents at German-owned companies, who agreed with the idea (3.667 mean response) and differed significantly (.05 level) from U.S. nationals (2.167 mean response). The idea of a "vacation bonus" was rejected by both U.S.- and foreign-owned firms, undoubtedly because of cost considerations. Thus, innovative breakthroughs in fringe benefits offered by foreign-owned firms do not appear likely.

Employment Security. Regarding employment security, responses by U.S.- and foreign-owned companies were as follows: (1) both tended to agree

TABLE 6

RESPONSES ON MANAGEMENT OF WORK FORCE

Statement	U.S.-owned Firms		Foreign-owned Firms			Is There a Difference Between United States and Others?	
	Number of Responses	Mean Response	Number of Responses	Mean Response	Parent Nationality	Decision	Significance Level
Overtime work should be handled on a voluntary basis.	72	2.139	69	2.986	All firms	Yes	.05
			18	3.222	German	Yes	.02
			10	2.700	Canadian	Yes	.10
			4	4.500	Japanese	Yes	.02
Putting hourly paid production workers on "salary status" makes sense to me.	72	2.972	70	2.414	All firms	Yes	.025
			18	2.278	British	Yes	.10
We're only interested in how workers perform on the job. If they have problems after work hours, that's their business.	72	2.083	69	2.348	All firms	No	.10

NOTE: Kolmogorov-Smirnov two-sample test was used to determine significance for "all firms." Chi-square approximation of Kolmogorov-Smirnov statistic was used for specific nationalities.

(2.306 and 2.493 mean responses respectively) that layoffs need not be avoided at all costs; (2) both tended to disagree (1.806 and 1.943 mean responses respectively) with the notion of permanent employment; and (3) both were really undecided (2.986 and 2.985 mean responses respectively) if they would hire new workers when others go on strike (in the absence of a union agreement).

The first two items were included because of the alleged inclination of foreign investors, especially the Japanese, to provide continuous and permanent employment. Apparently, this inclination does not hold true for those operating in the United States. The last item is certainly a drastic action. The predominance of the "undecided" responses from both respondent groups probably indicates that action in each instance would depend on careful examination of all variables, options, and possible consequences.

Employee Development and Training. Responses regarding performance evaluation and employee development are interesting. Both U.S.- and foreign-owned companies tended to disagree with the ideas that performance evaluation makes little sense for production workers and that training programs should relate specifically to current, job-related needs; both tended to agree that training programs should aim beyond present work needs to develop new skills and talents. For each statement, respondents from companies owned by a single nationality reversed these trends significantly (see table 7).

The foreign-owned companies tended in the "right" direction, although not significantly relative to the U.S.-owned companies in their responses regarding training—if the "right" direction is that which indicates that foreign investors should upgrade skill levels and expand human capital in their U.S. locations. Based on these data, it would clearly be inappropriate to conclude that workers at foreign-owned plants would benefit from their companies' expanding investment in human capital any more than workers at U.S.-owned plants. It might be argued, however, that foreign investors (especially recent investors) are more technologically advanced than their U.S. competitors, and thus must expand workers' skills to meet present job needs—needs which U.S.-owned firms have not yet even identified. This inference is compromised, however, by the fact that there was no significant (.10 level) difference between the respondent sets in terms of industry classification. The question of differentials in technology levels and investments in human capital between foreign- and U.S.-owned firms within the same industry still needs to be researched.

Promotion. The data in table 8 show response trends concerning promotions. Both U.S.- and foreign-owned firms tended to disagree that

TABLE 7

RESPONSES ON EMPLOYEE EVALUATION, DEVELOPMENT, AND TRAINING

Statement	U.S.-OWNED FIRMS		FOREIGN-OWNED FIRMS			IS THERE A DIFFERENCE BETWEEN UNITED STATES AND OTHERS?	
	Number of Responses	Mean Response	Number of Responses	Mean Response	Parent Nationality	Decision	Significance Level
Periodic, formal employee performance evaluation makes little sense for production workers.	72	2.278	70	1.957	All firms	No	.10
			6	1.167	Dutch	Yes	.10
Employee training programs at my company should be limited only to those which improve skills directly related to the employee's present work needs.	72	1.972	70	2.529	All firms	No	.10
			18	2.889	German	Yes	.10
Our employee training programs should go beyond just what's needed on the present job and should be aimed at the development of skills and talents needed for advancement.	72	4.333	70	4.014	All firms	No	.10
			11	3.636	Canadian	Yes	.10

NOTE: Kolmogorov-Smirnov two-sample test was used to determine significance for "all firms." Chi-square approximation of Kolmogorov-Smirnov statistic was used for specific nationalities.

upward advancement was limited or that seniority should be the main factor in determining promotions, but were nearly undecided regarding employees' desires for promotion into management. Again, for two of the three statements there is at least one set within the foreign-owned that reverses the trend significantly (see table 8).

Because the questionnaire clearly emphasized production workers, and because the U.S.-owned firms were significantly more unionized than the foreign firms, it is surprising that American firms reacted so negatively to the emphasis on seniority regarding promotion. Perhaps "promotion" was interpreted to mean promotion out of the production ranks; yet these same firms also tended to disagree that their workers even wanted to move up into management positions.

Worker Motivation and Fulfillment. Worker productivity is usually directly related to worker motivation. Good pay and self-fulfillment are usually viewed as correlating positively with high productivity. Concerning this relationship respondents at both U.S.- and foreign-owned companies tended to disagree that good pay is the best worker motivator; were nearly undecided about providing challenges outside of the shop for production workers; and tended to disagree that self-fulfillment for production workers was a myth. On the first and last questions, however, the British-, German-, and Dutch-owned firms reported somewhat different opinions (see table 9).

Conclusions on the actions of foreign investors regarding worker motivation are unclear, at best. On the one hand these firms, except for those of British and German parentage, rejected high wages as the best motivator. On the other hand they agreed, except for the Dutch, that self-fulfillment is a realistic objective for production workers. They were all undecided about the desirability of providing workers with challenging outlets outside the plant. One point is clear, however. Given (1) the large number of variables other than pay that affect motivation and hence productivity, (2) the numerous avenues open for realizing self-fulfillment that were not investigated, and (3) the indicated variations by nationality of ownership on the few statements listed, considerable research remains to be done in this general area.

Unions. The survey sought some information on how foreign investors viewed U.S. unions. Responses indicate that U.S.- and foreign-owned firms tended to agree across the board with all three of these statements: the union shop idea is unfair (3.833 and 3.957 mean responses respectively); efficiency goes down when workers are unionized (3.444 and 3.515); and the management preference is not even to deal with a union (3.944 and 4.382). Apparently, unions can expect no different treatment from foreign investors than they receive from U.S.-owned firms.

TABLE 8

RESPONSES ON PROMOTION

Statement	U.S.-OWNED FIRMS		FOREIGN-OWNED FIRMS			IS THERE A DIFFERENCE BETWEEN UNITED STATES AND OTHERS?	
	Number of Responses	Mean Response	Number of Responses	Mean Response	Parent Nationality	Decision	Significance Level
Upward advancement for workers at my company is rather limited.	72	2.111	70	2.571	All firms	No	.10
			18	2.778	British	Yes	.10
			18	2.889	German	Yes	.10
Seniority should be the main factor in determining promotion.	72	1.506	69	1.623	All firms	No	.10
On the average, workers at my company want eventually to be promoted into supervision or management.	72	2.833	68	2.971	All firms	No	.10
			4	3.750	Japanese	Yes	.10

NOTE: Kolmogorov-Smirnov two-sample test was used to determine significance for "all firms." Chi-square approximation of Kolmogorov-Smirnov statistic was used for specific nationalities.

TABLE 9

RESPONSES ON WORKER MOTIVATION AND FULFILLMENT

Statement	U.S.-OWNED FIRMS		FOREIGN-OWNED FIRMS			IS THERE A DIFFERENCE BETWEEN UNITED STATES AND OTHERS?	
	Number of Responses	Mean Response	Number of Responses	Mean Response	Parent Nationality	Decision	Significance Level
The best way to motivate an employee to work well is to pay him well.	72	2.125	70	2.571	All firms	No	.10
			18	3.275	British	Yes	.01
			18	3.111	German	Yes	.10
When production work is routine and boring, the employer should provide a worker with outlets— outside of the shop— which challenge his mentality and spirit.	72	2.750	70	3.014	All firms	No	.10
"Self-fulfillment" for production workers is a myth.	72	2.042	68	1.971	All firms	No	.10
			6	4.645	Dutch	Yes	.10

NOTE: Kolmogorov-Smirnov two-sample test was used to determine significance for "all firms." Chi-square approximation of Kolmogorov-Smirnov statistic was used for specific nationalities.

Equal Employment Opportunity. Several statements on equal employment opportunity were included in the survey. All firms disagreed (1.319 mean U.S. response; 1.700, foreign) that equal employment opportunity made little sense. The Canadians, however, were significantly lower (.05 level) in the intensity of their disagreement (2.000 mean response). Perhaps they view discrimination as a problem unique to the United States.

Foreign investors (2.029 mean response) tended to disagree significantly (.05 level) more intensely than U.S.-owned firms (2.694) that racial and sexual barriers to advancement existed in their companies. The Dutch disagreed (1.427) significantly (.05 level) more than the others.

One would expect reducing barriers to advancement to be more difficult in unionized firms, with their contractual seniority provisions. One would also expect larger firms to be more aware of both their discriminatory barriers and the problems inherent in reducing them. Smaller firms, which were important in the foreign investor sample, have not yet borne the brunt of enforcement activities and would be expected to have less discrimination awareness than the larger, U.S.-owned firms. Thus, U.S.-owned firms should be in less disagreement with the statement than foreign investors. The data support these expectations.

A Summary of the Attitudinal Survey

Having identified many differences of opinion on industrial relations matters between U.S.- and foreign-owned firms, it became possible to develop "nationality profiles." The profiles are extremely tenuous, however, because there is no indication of how representative each nationality sample cell is of that nationality as a whole.[19] Nationality-specific data were developed for the British, Canadians, Germans, Dutch, Japanese, and Swiss, but not for the other nationalities because of extremely small cell sizes.

Perhaps the most interesting nationality profile is of the Swiss—a nationality not even mentioned in the preceding analyses of the responses. This is because in no case was there a significant difference between the Swiss and U.S. respondents. Evidently, and not unexpectedly, the Swiss know quite well how to adapt.

Industrial relations managers in German-owned firms differed most often (eight times) with their counterparts at U.S.-owned firms. They were characterized as more autocratic, less willing to have production workers share in management decision making (although this was not true for German nationals who held management positions at these companies—they favored worker participation), more willing to have overtime handled on a

---

19. This same qualification existed, of course, in the preceding analyses, too, when responses of managers from countries of specific nationalities were discussed.

voluntary basis, more in favor of paid paternity leaves, more in favor of granting the "thirteenth-month" fringe benefit (albeit only in the case of German nationals again), less opposed to limiting training to only currently needed job-related skills, acknowledging less upward mobility for production workers, and agreeing that pay is the best way to motivate workers.

The British differed with their U.S.-owned counterparts on five points. They were very concerned neither to be innovators nor really different from U.S.-owned firms in U.S. industrial relations practices. Yet, according to the data, they were significantly different in some areas. They agreed production workers should have some participation in management decision making; the U.S. firms did not. They disagreed more strongly about putting workers on salary status. They disagreed less strongly that upward advancement for production workers is limited in their firms. Finally, they agreed slightly that good pay is the best motivator; U.S. firms did not.

The Canadians stood apart on only three points. They were less decisive than their counterparts in U.S. firms in disagreeing that overtime work should be voluntary. They were less in agreement that workers' employment and training should relate to advancement rather than just the present job. They were less in disagreement that concern about equal employment opportunity makes little sense. In each case where they differed, it was just a matter of degree; the Canadians were on the same side of the issue but were more centrist in their positions.

The Dutch differed in areas especially related to the handling of employees on the job. They felt more strongly that formal performance evaluation for production workers made good sense. They strongly agreed, while all others disagreed, that self-fulfillment for production workers was a myth. They more strongly disagreed that racial and sexual barriers to advancement existed in their companies.

Finally, the Japanese, who are generally considered the real innovators in shop-floor labor and personnel practices, were found to differ from their counterparts at U.S.-owned firms in only three instances. They strongly favored voluntary overtime, tended to agree with the ideas of paid paternity leave, and felt that their workers eventually wanted to be promoted into management. These findings indicate the Japanese may be less innovative than many expect.

A Conclusion

As already noted, most of what can be concluded from a study of this sort is tenuous at best. The study does, however, point to further research needs and will be helpful to those who wish to explore further the industrial relations policies, problems, and characteristics of direct foreign investors in the United States. The findings, coupled with the already recorded observations of those in the field, indicate that something new and different is indeed going on. More long- and short-range surveys, combined with detailed firm-specific research, are urgently required to assess clearly the impact of foreign firms on the American industrial relations system.

Comment
Richard L. Rowan

To gather the data for their analysis of industrial relations practices of foreign-owned firms in the United States, Michael J. Jedel and Duane Kujawa sent an eight-page questionnaire to 1,020 firms. This number was reduced to 901 as a usable population. A return of just over 10 percent was received (91 completed questionnaires). Only 35 of the 91 respondents indicated that they were unionized, representing slightly over 38 percent of the respondents and not quite 4 percent of the total usable sample. These facts concern me greatly. The data and methodology are simply not sufficient to support generalizations regarding industrial relations practices. Indeed, Jedel and Kujawa themselves acknowledge much of this and consider their results inconclusive.

What, then, are the most suggestive aspects of the practices section of their study? For one, they suggest that small foreign-owned firms that have been operating in the United States for a fairly long period of time are less likely to be innovative in industrial relations practices than large firms that have entered in recent years. I think that this can be taken for granted. Certainly, one would expect greater parent-company involvement as problems arise in the smaller, older, established firms than in the case of larger, newer firms. Smaller firms are also more likely to be unorganized, and therefore to be dealing with rather routine personnel problems rather than complex industrial relations activities. As a result they would have less room for creative or innovative practices.

One of Jedel and Kujawa's most interesting findings is that among the firms they examined the extent of production integration is substantial: "Almost 80 percent of the respondents received more than one-fourth of their parts from non-U.S. plants." This, coupled with the finding that foreign firms are producing in the United States for predominantly U.S. markets, raises a significant question pertaining to multinational industrial relations. If a firm decides to integrate production and rely solely on parts manufactured by a single source in the world, does this make the firm more vulnerable to the pressures for international collective bargaining? The findings might suggest that international collective bargaining would be an appropriate mechanism by which a firm could ensure continued production over an extended period. This is a matter that will probably receive serious attention from both companies and unions in the future.

Richard L. Rowan is professor of industry and codirector of the Industrial Research Unit at the Wharton School, University of Pennsylvania.

With regard to the structure of bargaining, the authors found "that foreign-owned firms were adopting the typical U.S. plant-level approach to bargaining rather than the industrywide structure typical in Europe." This is a bothersome statement particularly when we bear in mind that so few unionized companies responded to the questionnaire. In addition, I am not sure what is meant by a "typical U.S. plant-level approach to bargaining." I assume that they have not confused this with companywide bargaining in American industry; but if they have not, the statement is even more confusing.

The authors find that the subjects covered in collective bargaining agreements are about the same in foreign-owned and U.S.-owned firms, with the exception of an apparent reluctance on the part of foreign-owned firms to include no-strike, no-lockout provisions, which the authors find to be a common U.S. practice. This finding suggests that labor peace may not be expected in the foreign-owned firms to the same extent as in the American firms. Personally, I would be surprised at any significant difference with regard to this matter, but further research would have to be done in order to substantiate any hypothesis.

Those who tend to worry about foreign firms importing "adverse practices" in the industrial relations area focus mainly on the subject of participative management. Interestingly enough, the paper suggests that worker involvement, via works councils and other forms of employee participation, in what might be looked upon by Americans as managerial decisions has not yet been brought into the United States.

The second part of the Jedel-Kujawa paper deals with an attitudinal survey of industrial relations practitioners from a selected number of both U.S.- and foreign-owned firms operating in the United States. This questionnaire was sent to the same 1,020 foreign-owned firms as the practices questionnaire (reduced to 901); only 71 completed questionnaires were returned (about 8 percent). Only 31 of the respondents (less than half) were unionized, representing slightly more than 3 percent of the total usable population. The questionnaire was also sent to 298 U.S.-owned companies, with a return of 72 responses (about 24 percent). Of the 72 respondents, 61 were unionized (84 percent), representing about 20 percent of the total population. The statistical analysis seems to suggest that the two sets of respondents were significantly different regarding geographic location, employment size, and extent of unionization. The authors have taken note of these differences and commented on them where appropriate, but it seems to me that they are of such a magnitude as to cause one to view the findings with a certain amount of skepticism. It also should be noted that the authors have not clearly defined whose attitudes they are recording: top management, middle management, and line management responses are all lumped together.

The authors did not find very many differences between the attitudes of U.S.- and foreign-owned company industrial relations managers with regard to such matters as fringe benefits, management style, worker participation, innovations, grievances, wage increases, unions, and employment security. This is not surprising; companies entering a host country would be expected to adapt rather quickly to the existing institutional framework under which they must operate. The authors corroborate the finding that among foreign investors in the United States, the British in particular, are anxious not to stand out in industrial relations matters. It would be interesting to know to what extent this attitude is based on British management observations of American firms in Britain that have attempted to introduce innovations into the British industrial relations system.

The attitude concerning worker participation is a very interesting one; the authors seem to think that their data suggest that worker participation will not be transported into the United States by foreign investors, even though foreign investors are "somewhat more willing to allow some form of shared decision making." This will come as a great source of consolation to the American managers who are more uncertain about the probability of such changes coming about.

I was particularly surprised that U.S.- and foreign-owned respondents agreed that "the union shop idea is unfair; efficiency goes down when workers are unionized; and the management preference is not even to deal with a union." This suggests that the desire for unilateral, managerial determination of wages, hours, and working conditions is more universal than I had imagined. It is not surprising that management worldwide would prefer not to deal with a union. But once the union-management relationship has been established—through certification in the United States or otherwise in other parts of the world—it would seem likely that management would prefer a form of union security, perhaps a union shop, that results in the most efficient plant operation.

Another interesting area of agreement among the respondents was employment security, including layoffs and lifetime commitments. Traditionally, job security has been a much more important matter in the European industrial relations context than in the United States, and I would have expected foreign firms, especially British and German, to be more sensitive in this area. Jedel and Kujawa suggest, however, that when operating in the United States foreign-owned firms adopt American attitudes in this area.

In regard to equal employment opportunity, the authors expected the U.S. companies to understand the concept of affirmative action as including some kind of outreach program. They were surprised that the American managers did not indicate this on the questionnaire, instead of merely responding that they would hire from those who come forward on a nondiscriminatory basis. Such a response, however, could be expected because of the way their statement was phrased: "New production workers should be selected by choosing the best people from among those who come forward to seek employment irrespective of race, creed, color, or sex." Anyone reading that statement probably would tend to agree with it. It does not call for any further elaboration. It cannot be implied that simply because a company agreed with the statement, it does not understand its obligation under the Civil Rights Act of 1964 to develop affirmative action programs. The complexity of racial discrimination in employment in the United States would probably result in a difference in attitude on the part of foreign and American managers operating in this country.

The authors did find some fundamental disagreements among the respondents. One important disagreement, classified under work force management, involved attitudes on overtime and salary status. Foreign-owned company managers appeared to be more accepting of the principle of voluntary overtime than U.S. managers, who have relied on compulsory overtime to meet production deadlines. It would be interesting to know what experience firms have had operating under the two concepts. It was also found that managers in foreign-owned firms were more reluctant than those in U.S. firms to accept salary status for production workers. Implications of this are interesting. American unions, beginning with the United Auto Workers, have begun to move toward the idea of salaried blue-collar production workers, and I thought this was the case in some of the other advanced industrial societies. One can expect to see continued drives in this direction as unions organize white-collar workers. In my judgment, the hourly system of pay may very well be considered a relic of the past within our lifetime.

Having been somewhat critical of the method used by the authors, it is incumbent upon me to suggest what I might have done given the same topic to explore. I probably would not have attempted to study *attitudes* without the assistance of a trained industrial psychologist, although I agree that they are important—to the extent that they are translated into practice—and thus worthy of study.

If I had set out to study industrial relations *practices,* I would not have used a mailed questionnaire survey technique as the major means of eliciting information and data. I think that one would get a much better grasp of the topic by selecting a number of U.S. firms and a number of foreign-owned firms operating in the same industry in the United States and visiting with the various industrial relations managers to gather information in nonstructured interviews. It would make much more sense to compare British Petroleum with Exxon, Nestlé with General Foods, Imperial Chemicals Industries with DuPont, or Lever Brothers (Unilever) with Procter and Gamble. The comparison would then be with similar companies operating in similar markets under similar conditions. It would be my hypothesis that there are few, if any, significant differences in the practices of these industrial relations managers. If, however, differences were discovered, a much more reliable basis would be established for exploring the reasons they exist.

Comment
David H. Blake

Robert Copp has defined industrial relations issues in a very narrow way, by suggesting unions or workers have a legitimate role to play only with respect to the *effects* of production and investment decisions. Trade union leaders are not likely to accept being brought into the process only after the decision is made to haggle over how it is to be implemented. Politically and practically, this definition was not wise. Methodologically, Copp's paper is interesting, but it is exceptionally limited because it reports on the experience of the Ford Motor Company only. Thus the study is instructive and useful, but very limited.

Michael J. Jedel and Duane Kujawa's paper is methodologically the opposite of Copp's; they were looking at aggregate results on an overall basis. Their study is an intriguing and useful attempt to undertake some important research, which is obviously neither final nor definitive. Richard L. Rowan's comment indicated that he would not approach the subject as Jedel and Kujawa did, but rather via a series of comparative case studies selected with a view to obtaining a high degree of similarity among the situations examined. This is an admirable approach, though it suffers from the same problem as the Copp paper. In-depth, precise studies of specific corporations and comparisons with other corporations are useful, but aggregate research is helpful as well.

There is one substantive point I would like to mention about the Jedel and Kujawa paper, relating to the degree of production integration existing in the plants included in their research. They indicated that a significant portion of the firms studied had used components or products coming from overseas operations and they felt that this relationship might lead to a greater degree of control on the part of the parent company, given the in-

David H. Blake is professor in the Department of Political Science at the University of Pittsburgh.

tegrated nature of production. What I would find interesting is a reverse flow situation in which major components from these U.S. firms are fed into plants and facilities around the world. Here, I would suspect, the impact of a work stoppage would be even more crucial and might result in a greater degree of control on the part of company headquarters.

Research Strategies and Approaches

The question of the locus of industrial relations decision making is obviously situation specific. A trade union leader is concerned about the particular subsidiary of a particular corporation dealing with a specific issue at a particular time. But there is a role for aggregate research on this subject.

Such research can help to identify various tendencies, trends, and patterns in the behavior being studied. Even if one assumes a certain degree of "gilding the lily" and looks upon survey results with some skepticism, differences among corporate orientations toward industrial relations matters do deserve attention. B. C. Roberts and Jonathan May's research with British multinationals, for example, discovered differences with the results of my investigation of U.S. multinationals, even though both studies relied on corporate responses to questionnaires.[1] The research found statistically significant differences on the amount of headquarters involvement in subsidiary industrial relations matters: U.S.-owned corporations were significantly more likely to become involved in settlements of strikes and collective bargaining activities. In other areas, such as grievance activities, the U.S. corporate headquarters were unlikely to get involved.

There is a great deal to be learned about multinational industrial relations, and rigorous aggregate research, despite its limitations, is essential in this process. Both labor and management need to be more open in helping us investigate this area; their hesitancy to interact prevents investigation and analysis of important questions.

Some Research Questions

There are several general areas where further research and assessment need to be done. The first area is that of union reactions to and relations with foreign-owned multinationals. It is a critical counterpart to Jedel and Kujawa's examination of the corporate side of the issue.

Second, there are extensive misunderstandings about the characteristics of multinational corporations. The differences among them may well have important implications for their relations with trade unions and host

---

1. David Blake, "Cross-national Cooperative Strategies: Union Response to the MNCs," *Multinational Corporations and Labour Unions,* selected papers from a symposium in Nijmegen, Netherlands, May 1973.

governments. One can point to the extractive industries, for example, and note the significant differences between petroleum, copper, and aluminum companies as they interact with host governments. In manufacturing, there may be major differences among capital goods industries, intermediate goods industries, and consumer goods industries. Each type of industry may present different labor relations problems, and their relations with host governments may also differ. There are also differences in the service industries. A representative from the International Federation of Commercial, Clerical and Technical Employees (FIET) would probably say that they were having significant problems with U.S. banks abroad that are reluctant to recognize clerical unions.

In addition to the character of the industry and the product manufactured, technology is a crucial issue. Firm size, the degree of production integration (which Jedel and Kujawa very cleverly researched), and the age of the subsidiary are also important. Whether a subsidiary is an acquisition or a new investment is another significant factor that needs examination. Academics, trade union leaders, and business executives need to be more alert to the distinctions among the different types of multinational corporations.

A third area that needs to be examined more extensively, in a nonanecdotal fashion, concerns the question of mobility and flexibility in closing down subsidiaries. The empirical evidence on this question is very scarce. I do not know whether multinational corporations are very mobile or not. How many of these firms, in fact, have closed down production operations in one country and moved to another country—either from the source country to the host country or from one host country to another? Sufficient research on this question has not yet been done. The International Union of Electrical Workers has prepared a list of plants that were closed in the United States and those that were opened up abroad. This kind of investigation and subsequent analysis needs to be done on a more extensive basis. That multinationals have mobility may be a myth with some individual substance but without widespread generality. The corporations may be merely politicking when they threaten to move, not reinvest, or not expand investment.

In some of these issues, we also need to recognize the nature of the corporate structure. We tend to think of large social institutions, be they corporations or unions, as unified structures with a single purpose and a single control with absolute direction. My analysis of such social institutions indicates that this just is not the case. We need to be more aware of the differences that exist within corporations and unions.

A fourth important topic is the issue of MNC innovation in or conformity with local industrial relations practices. I feel that a corporation should not be multinational if it is going to conform precisely to the way things are done in host countries. If an American firm, or any multinational firm, attempts in Rome to be more Roman than the Romans, it is not bringing anything to the environment. Accepting this, the question then becomes how innovations will be introduced. I think Copp was way off base in suggesting that innovation is not the business of either union leaders or workers. Innovation is a fundamental function of multinational corporations: key questions are how it is going to be pursued and what the role of unions and workers should be in the innovation process.

A fifth area to be researched is the corporation as a responsive organism. How it handles its industrial relations depends somewhat on the power situation in which it finds itself. It responds differently to different types of environments, different types of rules and regulations, and different types of pressures. This is illustrated by the efforts of multinational corporations to adapt to very stringent governmental regulations such as those in the Soviet Union. In their home countries, they would be horrified if they had to operate under similar restrictions. But given the appropriate sorts of payoffs, the companies respond to the demands of unions and governments in order to continue to earn acceptable profits. Clearly, the corporation is a responsive institution—responsive to the exercise of pressure, power, and irresistible demands—and labor leaders are well aware of this. Nat Weinberg has argued that there are no management prerogatives, except what labor cannot take away. This concept of the corporation as a responsive organization is quite critical, for it suggests that trade unions are not as powerless as is sometimes suggested.

Sixth, the flows of information and of influence within multinationals need to be investigated. It seems important to find out the degree to which subsidiary practices, in some cases demanded by host unions, influence management decisions at headquarters. How is sensitivity to the local environment developed and managed, and how does it influence headquarters practices and orientations? I have found that the headquarters support staff is often not prepared to fill a supporting role. Thus, one may find a greater degree of resistance at the headquarters level to new and foreign practices just because of the lack of training in this area.

Seventh on the list of important foci for research is the actual comparison of company behavior. The work of John Gennard, which examined the actual behavior of multinational and nonmultinational firms with respect to pay scales and frequency and longevity of strikes, is representative of the types of aggregate research that can be undertaken and needs to be supported.[2]

Finally, to gain more understanding about the relationships between

2. John Gennard, *Multinational Corporations and British Labour: A Review of Attitudes and Responses* (London: British-North American Committee, 1972).

multinational corporations and labor unions, we need to organize the issue in a number of different ways. We have to begin to examine the relationships between corporations and workers, between corporations and unions, and between corporations and governments of the host and source countries. Picturing the MNC in the center with these various relationships fanning out, we also see the need to understand more about the relationships between the various points—workers and unions, workers and shop stewards and unions, workers and their own governments, and trade unions and their own governments.

The interaction and relationship with governments is especially critical because governments are subject to many competing and contradictory demands regarding the role of multinational corporations. The nature of trade union influence on government policies, for example, is important to investigate, as are the efforts of governmental bodies at the host state, parent state, and international levels, as well as nongovernmental organizations, to deal with the challenges and opportunities posed by international firms.

In conclusion, the evolving relationships between multinational corporations, workers, and trade unions suggest that the management of worldwide industrial relations increasingly will become centralized in corporate headquarters—especially for those large firms and their subsidiaries in the advanced industrial countries. This, ironically, will be the result of governmental actions and international trade union cooperation that will penalize multinational corporations for disparities, inequities, and mistakes in the industrial relations practices of the firm and its subsidiaries. No longer will multinational firms be able to afford to have management in one subsidiary making errors that have broader impacts for the corporation in other host countries, in the parent company, or in its worldwide operations. Whether this is good or bad, it is likely that there will be greater centralization of industrial relations and personnel practices. The corporate response that emerges will be that of *planned and coordinated diversity*. The corporation will have to develop an industrial relations and personnel system that recognizes and accommodates the different practices and customs of subsidiaries in many countries; yet this will occur within a framework established and managed by headquarters, which seeks to provide corporationwide guidelines and standards for the conduct of industrial relations. This centralization of the industrial relations function seems a likely consequence of the internationalization of industrial relations.

Comment
Ben A. Sharman

By severely limiting the definition of industrial relations, Robert Copp has managed to produce a fairly convincing argument that the locus of decision making in multinational corporations is at the local or national level. He does, however, concede that this position will never be accepted by trade union bodies, especially at the international level. I will endeavor to explain why trade union organizations cannot accept Copp's conclusions.

We in the trade union movement do not contend that industrial practices can or should be uniform in different countries. We fully realize that an individual country has its own, often extensive, laws and traditions regulating union-management relations. Each national trade union also has different priorities and practices. It seems, however, that some multinational corporations have attempted to introduce industrial relations practices into subsidiaries in other countries. Although these practices have been completely acceptable to trade unions in their home country, their implementation in other countries has often resulted in labor unrest and work stoppages.

The general practice of multinational corporations is to hire local management familiar with local conditions. Copp's claim that local managers are free to set industrial relations policy without direction from the home office is, however, a misconception. A more realistic example of procedures for industrial relations policy making within a multinational corporation was given by John A. Belford, vice-president of Massey-Ferguson, Ltd.

> The most useful form for policy that I know—certainly in the industrial relations function—is a statement of objectives and principles, objectives being the conditions we aim to achieve and principles being the basic assumptions that guide management action directed to the achievement of the objectives. Each functional policy enunciates attainable objectives, the achievement of which would serve the purpose of the corporation; and its principles aim to distill the lessons of management and research experience as a guide to management action.
>
> To be fully effective, the policy statement must meet certain standards which have been enumerated before. Among these are the following:
> 1. It must be applicable universally within the enterprise. In the international company it must be applicable in all countries.
> 2. It must be in writing. Although it has been stated that if the policy is not in writing there is no policy, I concede that in many circumstances policies can be

Ben A. Sharman is international representative of the International Association of Machinists and Aerospace Workers.

operative and, in substantial measure, effective without being in writing. However, the more complex and extensive the enterprise, the more important that its policy should be written. This is especially so in the international company.

3. It should be in broad terms permitting application to meet varying conditions and provide the framework for local tailormade practices and programs. It should not inhibit innovation and experimentation.

4. It should be justifiable on an assessment of its contribution to the basic objectives of the enterprise.

5. It should be authorized by the highest authority in the corporation.

6. It must be regarded as inviolate so far as this is within the power of management.[1]

Later in the same article Belford argued:

> Our experience in industrial relations policy convinces us in a number of ways that working to policy is good business. Sound policy orients all operating management to the defined objectives of the enterprise. It gives practical effect to the philosophy of management by objectives. Good policy provides operating management with a basis for consistency and integrity in its relations with employees, employees' representatives and government agencies. At the same time, it permits flexibility. Contrary to the opinion of some people who have not worked to written policy, policy is not restrictive. Rather, it serves to free up operating management by providing a framework within which to act promptly and decisively on problems as they arise. When policy is developed—as it should be—with the participation of operating management, it helps to build a concerted management group of all management at all locations. Finally, it provides an instrument for control at the corporate or operating-unit level— control, in the sense of measurement of results against a standard.[2]

Setting policy guidelines on industrial relations in the manner Belford has described would directly involve the head office of a multinational corporation in the decision-making process. It is inconceivable that any local manager who wishes to work outside such policy guidelines could do so without receiving permission from top-level management.

In his paper, Copp asserted that "management decisions about new or redeployed production facilities are not, as such, industrial relations questions." The trade union view is that when a collective bargaining dispute occurs and a multinational corporation threatens to move its production facilities as a means of putting pressure on the union to settle, it is automatically making a redeployment decision part of its industrial relations policy. Threats to move production to other countries have been used in Europe during contract negotiations and industrial disputes.

The International Metalworkers' Federation, an international trade

---

1. John A. Belford, "The Supranational Corporation and Labor Relations" in *Western European Labor and the American Corporation*, ed. Alfred Kamin (Washington, D.C.: Bureau of National Affairs, 1970), p. 6.

2. Ibid., p. 9.

secretariat, reported, for example, that in March 1971, Henry Ford II visited Prime Minister Edward Heath and threatened to move production from Dagenham, England, to West Germany, unless the British government could tame unions that at the time were on strike in Dagenham. It would be very difficult to convince the British trade union movement that this was not an industrial relations matter and that the top management from the source country was not involved in the decision-making process.

It would be just as difficult to convince German trade unions that codetermination is not a part of their industrial relations system. In 1974 U.S.-owned multinational corporations, through the U.S. Chamber of Commerce, protested the West German government's decision to implement codetermination in all industrial enterprises in West Germany. Surely German trade unions representing workers in these corporations considered this a direct attempt by American management to interfere with the industrial relations system of West Germany. It also is obvious that if U.S.-owned multinational corporations were exempted from codetermination, they would have an unfair competitive advantage over German-owned enterprises.

It is difficult for me as a trade union representative to see how financial decisions and industrial relations questions can be handled separately. Costs are the major part of a collective bargaining agreement; this fact cannot be avoided. It is my understanding that cost and financial decisions are made at the corporate headquarters level, and if this is true, then decision making on industrial relations matters is in the hands of top management. I presume that top management of a parent company sets financial guidelines for local management to follow in collective bargaining. If it does, the parent company would be once again involved in the decision-making process. Also, if local management is not able to reach a settlement within established guidelines, top management would have to be consulted before any decision could be made.

I will now comment on the illustrations Copp used to support his contentions. I would agree, on the basis of the facts presented, that consideration for a tea break in an Australian plant should not have been a reason for involving top management of the parent company. I suspect that the Australian minister's accusations were an expression of nationalism and dislike of foreign enterprise. When accusations of this kind are made, they confuse the real issues, and should not be included as examples of industrial relations problems between trade unions and management. It is possible that the aim of the Australian minister of labor in criticizing the Ford Company was to induce its Australian affiliate to take the dispute to the Australian Conciliation and Arbitration Commission for settlement. If this was the case, I would congratulate him on his effectiveness.

Regarding Copp's second illustration, I would like to ask whether the management board of Ford of Germany will determine whether the new codetermination policy in Germany will be adhered to or whether the U.S. Chamber of Commerce, under the instructions of U.S.-owned multinational corporations, including Ford, will be responsible for making that decision.

The third illustration, referring to Ford of Britain, is clarified by a point I made earlier. Trade union organizations do not expect industrial relations practices to be uniform in different countries, because legislation regarding trade union recognition and trade union practices differs from country to country. If American criteria had been enforced in this example, established practices in Britain would have been ignored, and I am sure that this would have resulted in serious industrial labor relations problems, including the strong possibility of a work stoppage.

In conclusion, I would contend that multinational corporations that establish industrial relations or financial policy guidelines are directly involved in the decision-making process of all subsidiaries. If local management has to consult with top management before decisions can be made outside policy guidelines, the locus of decision making is at the top management level. Even if there are no written policy guidelines for industrial relations practices, it is obvious that through the chain of command within the structure of a multinational corporation the locus of decision making will be at the top level. The only questions that arise are at what stage will top management become involved and how much flexibility will local management have.

Comment
Mokoto Kuroiwa

Before commenting on the papers of Robert Copp and Michael J. Jedel and Duane Kujawa, it is necessary to state briefly the nature of our company. Mitsubishi Aircraft International, Inc., (MAI) is a subsidiary of Mitsubishi Heavy Industries, Ltd., and Mitsubishi Corporation of Japan. MAI produces the twin-engine turboprop business aircraft called Mitsubishi MU-2, and is responsible for marketing it in the United States and worldwide. To produce this aircraft, we import one-third of the final product from Japan; the other two-thirds comprises American labor, products, and services. We have about four hundred employees, eleven of

Mokoto Kuroiwa is president of Mitsubishi Aircraft International, Inc., San Angelo, Texas.

whom are Japanese. During the early period of this project, production and marketing of the aircraft was done by an American aviation company. Our company took over this operation in 1970.

In 1972 our employees voted against representation by a labor union; accordingly we have no experience in collective bargaining with labor unions. We talk with our employees directly at the local level. The parent company has widely delegated responsibility in industrial relations to local management. After taking over the total manufacturing and marketing operation in our American company, we established good industrial relations between employees and management and, at the same time, greatly improved employee benefits.

From our own observations, through talks with our people, and from an opinion survey of all our employees conducted by a well-known independent opinion survey agency, we have found that the majority of our employees are pretty well satisfied with our improvement of their benefits and trust the top management. Making a contribution to U.S. society and industry and improving the prosperous future of our employees are two of the most important goals of our company. I believe that our management in the United States will continue to talk directly with our employees and will continue to have good relations with them.

If we should have a collective bargaining relationship, our parent company, a large organization, would probably adopt a policy similar to that of the Ford Motor Company, as described by Copp. The only difference might arise from the fact that because customs concerning industrial relations in Japan are different from those in this country, our parent company might not be able to advise local management, as the Ford Company can do with their overseas firms. Thus the locus of decision making would reside with the management in the United States.

Regarding the Jedel and Kujawa survey, I would like to point out that some differences apparent in multinational companies may be caused by factors such as company history, size, the nature of business, and other items that do not relate to the multinational operation.

In sum, I feel that while there may be some continuous problems between labor unions and corporate management, the critical problems do not exist because of the existence of multinational firms.

Comment

Laurent C. Enckell

I am pleased to have an opportunity to present a trade union view on the subject of multinationals. In our earlier discussions, I often felt as if I was sitting in on a debate among Christian Scientists on the subject of communicable diseases as there was no mention, except in the most minimal way, of the role of trade unions. I concur with Richard Rowan that a major shortcoming of the paper by Michael Jedel and Duane Kujawa is its failure to take account of probably the most relevant variable in their study—the degree of unionization within the companies surveyed.

What concerns me is that this omission is not altogether accidental. I have participated in too many discussions and have read too many articles and studies on the subject of multinationals to know that it is not an accident when the real issue is not addressed, namely: what is the role of unions vis-à-vis multinational companies? While opinions may differ as to what needs to be done to counteract the power of multinationals, it has become fairly evident that *something* needs to be done. Most of the writing and the discussions here, however, have presented a management position, which completely denies any important role for unions at the international level. This raises basic questions about the role of labor organizations in general.

This lack of emphasis on the role of trade unions is particularly relevant to Robert Copp's paper and the Jedel-Kujawa study. Copp made several references to companies that, apparently unilaterally, decided to recognize unions, or to grant or allow this or that concession. Jedel and Kujawa sought to determine what companies have introduced as industrial relations practices. It is our experience that very few companies have introduced what we could call positive industrial relations practices. Companies will indulge in whatever practices the market will bear. If they deal with strong unions, then they "decide," surprisingly, to have a very positive attitude toward them. If the unions are weak, however, then somehow the companies' policies change and industrial relations are no longer as progressive. Thus, it is pointless to avoid the issue and not talk about the power relationships that exist between organized workers and employers. Ignoring the fact does not make it disappear.

Much of the Copp paper concerns the responsibility of corporate headquarters for industrial relations in Ford's subsidiaries. I am not qualified to speak about the automobile industry, but I am surprised at some of his

Laurent C. Enckell is representative, North American regional office of the International Union of Food and Allied Workers' Association.

assertions, even though similar arguments have also come from the head-quarters management of other multinational companies. These include the views that "It's a local problem; we have absolutely nothing to do with it"; and "The responsibility lies with local management; we cannot intervene." I have often wondered if this was really an efficient way to run a company, but then this is a management problem. The point is that unions simply cannot accept such statements. If a local problem is of no concern to top management, then we will have to *make* it their concern. Do you really expect our international to answer an affiliated union, which has written to us about a problem with a multinational, that because the problem is a local one they should settle it locally and stop bothering us?

Whether a company's headquarters wants to intervene or not in a local matter is a management, not union, question. It seems to me that it is appropriate for a multinational to fire the manager of a subsidiary, if necessary. Management's responsibility, after all, is to assign people to various positions, among which are those concerned with industrial relations. If the appointed people are not managing their company properly, somebody has to be able to point out their mistakes to them. This role is sometimes performed by unions, for if it were not, it would not be done at all. Clearly a subsidiary cannot be fully autonomous. If it were, especially in an industry such as automobiles where there is so much interdependence among production units, there would, in fact, be no management. It is my opinion that multinational management often says it is not concerned with a "local" question when in fact it is.

Although Copp suggested that his description of Ford is typical of the experience of multinational companies, it certainly does not correspond to the experience the IUF has had in dealing with multinationals. In our dealings several multinationals, which stated at the outset that they would do nothing, eventually went a long way toward influencing local industrial relations practices.

Jedel and Kujawa attempted to relate the behavior of foreign-owned multinational companies in the United States to practices prevalent in the parent-company countries. This is at best a dubious relationship; wide differences can be found among multinational companies based in the same country, and some company headquarters are based in countries where industrial relations experience is all but irrelevant to corporate behavior abroad. Consider, for example, a Swiss multinational that may do only a very small part of its total business in Switzerland. It would seem that its Swiss industrial relations experience would be of no importance to its activities in foreign countries. On the other hand, consider a company such as Unilever. Do you take the Dutch or the British experience as the most relevant? And what about a multinational based in the Netherlands Antilles, such as Schlumberger; where does its experience originate?

It seems that the home base of the company is less relevant to this question than the nature of the company itself. I would suggest that useful research can be done only if one selects certain companies and tries to determine whether any sort of pattern emerges within each company. Some companies do try to transfer practices from country to country, but not necessarily those of their home country. The Nestlé company, for example, is headed by a French national, who used to be the top officer of Nestlé's subsidiary in France. There appears to be much in Nestlé's approach to industrial relations that can be traced to his experience in that country, although certainly other factors also are important.

As trade unionists, we would never analyze situations on the basis of the "nationality" of multinationals. For a long time we have accepted the idea that many multinational companies are more powerful than the countries in which they operate; it would be a contradiction to assume that countries have a determining influence on the industrial relations practices of those companies.

Part III. The Impact of Multinationals and Unions on Industrial Relations

MULTINATIONALS AND UNIONS AS INNOVATORS AND CHANGE AGENTS
Nat Weinberg

Are bargaining issues transferable between countries? What provisions in U.S. contracts, for example, have or may in the future become negotiable issues abroad, and conversely what might U.S. unions and companies borrow from agreements or laws in other countries?

In most cases, unions and MNCs have widely different, and usually conflicting, notions concerning what should or should not be transferred across national boundaries. Nevertheless, although their respective means for effecting international transfers are also vastly different, multinationals and unions are the innovators and change agents in this area.

MNC Advantages and Union Disadvantages in Transnational Industrial Relations

Corporations, multinational as well as purely national, are hierarchical, authoritarian organizations. Orders are transmitted from the top down with the confident expectation that they will be obeyed as religiously in the remotest outposts as they are in the corporation's world headquarters.[1] National boundaries present no obstacles to the transmission and execution of directives from world headquarters—except where the directives are

---

Nat Weinberg, formerly special projects director of the International Union of United Automobile, Aerospace and Agricultural Implement Workers of America, is an economic consultant, Washington, D.C.

1. There may be differences of opinion or conflicts of interest among separate national subsidiaries but these will be resolved at world headquarters with the subsidiaries being compelled to comply.

in conflict with national laws and, even then, only when the country whose laws are affected has both the will and the means to enforce them. Will alone is not enough because, with respect to many matters, MNCs have the ability to escape or evade purely national legislation. Moreover, the will to enforce may be lacking or weak because of MNC corruption of government officials or for fear of reprisals by the MNCs. Multinationals, as the record abundantly shows, are not at all hesitant to threaten relocation, gradual disinvestment, or concentration of their expansion elsewhere if a government, whether home or host, disturbs them unduly. In addition, MNCs are often able to influence the content of national legislation, including labor laws.

In sharp contrast to the MNCs, unions can transmit labor relations or labor standards innovations internationally only through the purely voluntary action of their counterparts in other countries. The board chairperson of an MNC can impose his or her will on overseas subsidiaries; there is no individual or organization with comparable power on the union side. Practices in effect elsewhere will be adopted as union objectives only if a union within the country perceives them to be both advantageous to its members and of higher priority than other indigenous goals.

Moreover, the process of international transference on the union side is hampered severely by limited facilities and opportunities for international communication. Here again, there is a striking contrast with the MNCs where contact between headquarters and foreign subsidiaries is often daily through telex, computer interlocks, and international telephone, supplemented by frequent meetings of top management personnel. For unions, communication across international borders is sporadic, mainly in the form of infrequent meetings, limited travel by representatives of national and international labor organizations, and news bulletins or magazines published by various labor groups. Travel expenses alone are a heavy burden for many national unions and, in some cases, would present an insuperable obstacle to their participation in international meetings if not for subsidies from international confederations or trade secretariats, which themselves suffer from financial anemia. Participation by local union or shop-floor representatives in international union gatherings, often crucial for an understanding of the practical significance of contract provisions, is rare because of the prohibitive cost of compensating them for lost wages.

Superior communications also give MNCs enormous advantages vis-à-vis unions in terms of the information available to each side in bargaining about changes proposed to be imported from other countries. Comparative research studies prepared infrequently by certain international trade secretariats are assembled painfully from information supplied on a purely voluntary basis (which sometimes means not supplied at all) by often untrained staff members of separate national affiliates. Inevitably, these studies provide limited information and leave important questions unanswered. As a result of their organizational structure, however, MNCs can obtain international comparisons of laws, contract provisions, and practices almost instantaneously. If the MNCs choose to distort or to misrepresent the facts, the unions with which they bargain are often helpless to refute them.

The seriousness of this situation was recognized by the United Nations Group of Eminent Persons, created to study the impact of MNCs. In connection with its recommendation for a study of methods "to ensure the participation of workers and their unions in the decision-making process of multinational corporations at the local and international level," the UN group appended a footnote stating:

> Such participation, as well as other joint negotiations referred to below, can only be effective if the means of communication at the disposal of labor are comparable to those of multinational corporations. The latter should allow the representatives of the workers reasonable leaves of absence and travel expenses appropriate to that purpose.[2]

Needless to say, MNC managements would still enjoy enormous communication advantages even if this proposal were accepted.

Problems of communication on the union side are aggravated by the ideological and religious differences that divide the labor movement both internationally and, in some important cases, within countries. Even more serious are the obstacles that these divisions place in the way of coordinated action to achieve international transfers of collective bargaining practices favorable to workers' interests.

Differences in bargaining practices and bargaining structures further impede union efforts to coordinate activities across national boundaries. In some countries, unions generally bargain with employer associations that include both national and international corporations and firms operating in loosely related branches of a broad industry, such as metalworking. This makes practically impossible international joint action by unions in relation to a single MNC belonging to an employer association. Such bargaining, which tends to be of the least-common-denominator variety tailored to the marginal firms in the association, usually involves the negotiation of minimum (rather than actual) wage rates and fringe benefits and is unlikely to yield results that conflict with the centrally determined objectives of MNCs. In addition, international union coordination with regard to in-plant problems such as relief time and safety standards is hampered by the

---

2. United Nations, Department of Economic and Social Affairs, *The Impact of Multinational Corporations on Development and on International Relations* (New York: UN, 1974), p. 77.

fact that, outside the United States and Canada, such matters are rarely the concern of national unions. Usually they are dealt with by statutorily created works councils or, as in the United Kingdom, by shop stewards' bodies representing workers belonging to several separate national unions.

MNCs, naturally, are quick to take advantage of these differences and divisions among workers to serve global corporate ends even as they capitalize on them within their home countries.[3] Hierarchically centralized international coordination and control within MNCs, accompanied by division and dispersion of power among unions, facilitate the divide-and-rule game. Through central control over international allocation of production and investment, the MNCs have a high degree of mobility while their workers are essentially immobile. Thus, the MNCs are able, and not at all hesitant, to threaten the job security of each national worker group in order to extract concessions and to impose management's version of collective bargaining.[4]

The MNCs' locational options inevitably affect the labor standards content of collective bargaining and can even result in the nullification of labor standards legislation. To cite just one example, American asbestos corporations guilty of the needless deaths of appalling numbers of workers considered moving plants to Taiwan and Korea when faced in the United States with occupational health regulations that would have somewhat reduced the slaughter.[5]

---

3. Boulwarism, for example, was possible only because the workers at the General Electric Company were divided among about a dozen unions, each based on different plants. The corporation was able to dictate contract terms by playing the separate unions off against each other until they agreed on "coordinated bargaining"—an experience that has obvious and important implications for the international scene.

4. Henry Ford II's 1971 threat to striking British Ford workers about future investment decisions was only the most publicized of many similar incidents. On October 6, 1974, the *New York Times* reported, "Because of lost production as the result of union militance, Massey-Ferguson, Ltd., the huge Canadian-owned farm machinery producer, disclosed that it would start turning out a new range of diesel engines in West Germany instead of at its British plant. The company cited 'a tragic 18 months' of labor disputes in Britain as the reason." The company doubtless expects both its British and German workers to draw the obvious conclusions from that allocation decision.

5. Paul Brodeur's *Expendable Americans* (New York: Viking Press, 1974) spells out in horrifying detail the collaboration of large and powerful corporations, doctors, and government officials in—no softer words will suffice—the knowing and deliberate murder of workers employed in handling asbestos. Ultimately, the Department of Labor, through its Occupational Safety and Health Administration (OSHA), reluctantly and halfheartedly was moved to establish protective standards. In the words of *Business Week*'s October 5, 1974, review of the book: "Despite its mandate to 'assure safe and healthful conditions for working men and women,' OSHA did little more than give lip service to the hazards of asbestos by capitulating to industry pressure and adopting an exposure level already discredited as too high to prevent the threat of asbestosis and mesothelioma." (The former is a lung disease and the latter a form of cancer, both responsible for the deaths of many asbestos workers.) Brodeur reported the response of the corporations to OSHA's feeble gesture as follows: "I had discovered that the asbestos industry was taking a hard look at the feasibility of moving some of

In general, when MNCs unilaterally select labor practices to be transferred internationally, and when they face weak unions, they will tend to select the worst rather than the best. In a competitive world economy it is difficult for any country to establish or maintain decent standards. Moreover, the affected workers, for fear of losing jobs upon which the welfare of their families depends, will submit to conditions that threaten their lives and may even support their employers in lobbying against protective measures when faced with threats of shutdowns or relocation. Thus, the international mobility of MNCs generates a kind of Gresham's Law under which bad labor standards drive out good ones.

Another important union disadvantage results from the fact that MNCs, to a very high degree, have the initiative in introducing labor relations innovations, whether in home or host countries. As long as they operate within the framework of national law (and sometimes in disregard or outright defiance of law), they are free to export their labor policies along with their capital or to import practices that they or others have succeeded in imposing elsewhere. Thus, MNCs frequently can act unilaterally while unions can introduce changes only through success in the bilateral bargaining process.[6]

These opportunities for MNC initiatives often enable MNCs to force host country unions into defensive battles, which dissipate their energies in resisting resented innovations rather than in fighting for the international transfer of practices they consider desirable.

Multinationals As Innovators and Change Agents

I turn now to the purpose for which management is likely to use its superior ability to effect international transfers of industrial relations policies and practices.[7] I will not attempt to detail all the kinds of collective

---

its plants and facilities to Taiwan and Korea, where, presumably, it could operate unhindered by occupational-safety-and-health regulations" (*New Yorker,* November 12, 1973). In other words, if asbestos firms were to be even mildly inhibited in slaughtering American workers, they would become (some already were) multinationals so that they would be free to slaughter Asians without let or hindrance.

6. In the United States an MNC taking over an existing operation in which the workers are represented by a union would have to bargain with the union on changes in wages, hours, or working conditions. But workers in most other countries do not have similar protection.

7. In discussing this subject, I do not intend to mince words; progress is not promoted by gilding over bad situations with euphemisms. Plain and strong language historically (unfortunately, not recently) has an honored place in economics. Adam Smith, for example, did not hesitate to express sweeping generalizations about "the mean rapacity . . . of merchants and manufacturers" or to describe them as "an order of men, whose interest is never exactly the same with that of the public, who have generally an interest to deceive and even oppress the public, and who accordingly have, upon many occasions, both deceived and oppressed it." (*The Wealth of Nations* [New York: Random House, Modern Library Edition, 1937], pp. 460 and 250 respectively.) The spots of the leopards Smith characterized have not changed but there is a strong tendency today to cover them with cosmetic language—a tendency to which I do not propose to fall victim.

bargaining policies and practices that MNCs may try to transmit internationally. One broad generalization, however, can be made, and actual experiences can be cited in support of it. The generalization flows from the fact that corporate managements tend to take quite literally one meaning that the *Oxford Universal Dictionary* assigns to the verb *employ*—"to use as a means or instrument."[8] The practical consequence of this, which can be stated as a generalization, is that MNC managements, to the extent they can get away with it, will tend to treat their workers not as human beings with human needs but as tools to be bought as cheaply as possible, to be used with ruthless efficiency regardless of effects on health and safety, and to be discarded when no longer needed. No one will be convicted of the murder of the asbestos workers because society, unfortunately, acquiesces in industry's use of workers as means or instruments. These are harsh words, but the history of labor relations documents their validity.

In short, MNCs can be expected to take advantage of every opportunity to keep their workers submissive and their labor costs at a minimum even if that means the application of practices in host countries abandoned under pressure or even outlawed in their home countries. One example, too well known to be denied, is the advantage that U.S.-owned (and other) MNCs take of South Africa's abominable racial policies to deny black workers wages and fringe benefits anywhere near the same as those received by white workers for comparable work—even though the law, apartheid notwithstanding, permits payment of equal wages.[9] The fact that apartheid legislation denies trade union rights to black workers, and thus facilitates the maintenance of unjustifiable racial wage differentials, undoubtedly goes a long way to explain the strong attraction that South Africa holds for MNCs.

The outlawry of legitimate unionism by the Spanish and Brazilian dictatorships also is a significant factor in the rapid growth of MNC investments in those countries. There must be deep regret in many MNC headquarters that Greece and Portugal are no longer available as happy hunting grounds for the practitioners of eighteenth-century industrial relations policies. But the aid of the CIA may be available in such situations, as it was in Chile, to restore or establish the authoritarianism that many MNCs seem to consider an important ingredient of "a favorable

8. Of course there are exceptions—"benevolent" managements that manifest some concern and consideration for their workers as human beings. But "benevolence," more often than not, can be translated as "paternalism," which is an offence to the dignity of the workers, or explained in terms of a desire to keep unions out or, if they are in, to sap their strength and militancy.

9. U.S.-owned MNCs also readily adopt in Europe the sex differentials in wages that are common on that continent even though no law prohibits the payment of equal wages to men and women for equal work and payment of unequal wages is illegal in the firms' home country.

investment climate."

In countries where unions, though legal, are weak, the nature of the collective bargaining innovations introduced by the MNCs clearly reflects that weakness. I have heard automobile unionists from U.S.-owned plants abroad describe management practices that brought vividly to mind the pre-1941 regime of Harry Bennett at the Ford Rouge plant. While these reports came from relatively less developed countries, they are nevertheless pertinent because they reveal the natural inclinations of MNCs with respect to collective bargaining innovations, whether in developed or in developing countries.

In advanced Western European countries, managements of U.S.-based MNCs have transferred practices that are alien and repugnant not only to the workers directly affected, but also to the general public of those countries. Brutal layoff practices, for example, which are taken for granted in the United States, caused national scandals in France when applied there by certain major U.S.-owned MNCs.

Similarly, MNC transfers related to bargaining procedures appear to be determined solely by considerations of corporate advantage rather than designed to achieve healthy relationships with the workers involved. The Ford Motor Company's tactics in two countries illustrate the point. In Great Britain, Ford, like General Motors and Chrysler, bargains on an individual company basis with the unions representing its workers, whereas British automotive companies are represented in bargaining by the employer association comprising most firms in the shipbuilding and engineering industries. Separate company bargaining reflects a transfer to Britain of U.S. auto industry procedures. Ford also bargained separately from the employer association in West Germany for a long period during which the German metalworkers' union represented only a small fraction of its workers. Ford reversed its policy, however, after union membership at the giant Cologne plant increased so that it could have conducted an effective strike against the company. At that point, Ford hastily joined the employer association and hid behind the protection of the no-strike clause in the latter's agreement with the union.[10]

In the vast majority of cases, MNCs will tend to resist international transfers of collective bargaining practices sought by their workers in countries where those practices have not already been established. In addition, despite their oft-proclaimed desire for nondiscriminatory "national treatment" in host countries (that is, the same treatment as is given purely national companies), MNCs will try to escape from innovations applied to national firms in those countries. One example is the effort by the U.S.

---

10. The union refrained from striking because it felt compelled to take seriously Ford's threat of a lawsuit if a strike occurred. It is questionable whether such a unilaterally imposed contractual obligation would have binding force in other countries.

Chamber of Commerce in West Germany to obtain the intervention of the American government to gain for U.S.-owned MNC subsidiaries an exemption from the new codetermination law under consideration in the Bundestag.[11] In response, the chairman of the German Confederation of Trade Unions reminded the American MNCs that West Germany is no "banana republic" and that "Colonialism in Europe is dead."[12] Undoubtedly, one of the fears of the MNCs is that, if they are brought under the proposed new form of codetermination in Germany, their workers elsewhere might seek to transfer similar legislation to their own countries.

The German case is an illustration of the influence of the MNCs on national labor legislation. The efforts of the American MNCs, in this instance, did not prove successful. (My guess is that they were too blatant and direct affronts to German public opinion.) Another illustration is the transfer to Britain, in the form of the now-repealed Industrial Relations Act, of major features of the U.S. Taft-Hartley Act—a transfer in which U.S.-owned MNCs played a leading role. One example in developing countries is the restrictive labor legislation adopted by Singapore in 1968, which applied a particularly tight straitjacket to unions in "pioneer" industries, which consist mainly, if not entirely, of subsidiaries of MNCs. Malaysia adopted similar legislation. The influence of MNCs on legislation, of course, extends far beyond the field of labor and is successfully exerted in developed home as well as in developed host countries. Massey-Ferguson, the largest Canada-owned MNC, threatened to move its headquarters out of that country when legislation was adopted that taxed certain portions of foreign profits not previously taxed. The Canadian government responded to the threat by suspending the effectuation of the law for two years. Similarly, legislation recently proposed in Britain to stiffen taxes applicable to expatriate employees of foreign MNCs was either dropped or drastically modified as a result of the violent opposition and threats to relocate coming largely, if not mainly, from U.S.-owned MNCs.

The inescapable conclusion is that MNCs, in their roles as innovators and change agents, will seek to bring about retrogressive changes in collective bargaining and in labor legislation. They will push constantly, everywhere they operate, toward the lowest attainable level of social responsibility; the international transfers they seek will be those that are the least burdensome to them and the most disadvantageous to their workers. They will try to play off national groups of workers against each other in mutually destructive competition for employment opportunities that undermines existing labor standards and retards improvement of standards. As an example, certain U.S. MNCs have cited lower wages paid by the "competition" in other countries as an argument against the wage

---

11. *New York Times,* October 13, 1974, p. 17, and October 19, 1974, p. 40.

12. Ibid., October 19, 1974.

demands of their U.S. workers, while failing to note that the "competition" in many cases consisted of their own foreign subsidiaries.

Unions As Innovators and Change Agents

What of innovations, changes, and transfers initiated from the union side? Despite the severe handicaps that unions face in this regard, some transfers have occurred already and more are likely in the future. They will not always be accomplished through coordinated action of unions in different countries. Communication, though difficult and limited, often alerts national worker groups to gains won by their counterparts in other countries that they may achieve without outside support. This process is likely to be accelerated by improved communication among unions, which the rise of MNCs makes necessary despite cost and other obstacles.

Probably more has been transferred already through mere communication than is easily visible, but there are a number of fairly well-known examples. The extended vacations won by the United Steelworkers in the United States are an adaptation of the Australian "long service leaves." Vacation bonuses in the U.S. steel, can, aluminum, and agricultural implement industries, among others, reflect transfers from certain Western European countries. In 1955 Renault in France adopted a version of the cost-of-living-annual-improvement-factor wage formula in effect in the U.S. auto industry. The workweek has been reduced to forty hours in the metalworking industries in most of Western Europe substantially as a result of a campaign launched by the International Metalworkers' Federation (IMF) in the mid-1950s. There has been mounting pressure for increased relief time for auto industry assembly line workers, again in emulation of U.S. gains, in many of the countries in which the industry operates. In 1958 the French central employers' federation, Conseil National du Patronat Français (CNPF), adopted a nationwide unemployment benefit program, which has certain strong resemblances to the supplemental unemployment benefits (SUB) plans bargained with individual firms in the United States.

The transfers mentioned were not all directly related to the MNC phenomenon as such, but in many instances the ability of unions to cite practices already established in affiliates of the same corporation in other countries undoubtedly was helpful. Inevitably, as some companies within a country acquiesced in transfers of the types noted above, the practices involved tended to spread via the demonstration effect, backed up by worker pressure, to other firms in the same country, both national and multinational.

Changes in Bargaining Structures and Procedures

The future growth and spread of MNCs will be a major factor impelling unions to seek changes in bargaining structures and procedures in many countries. In order to facilitate coordinated action by unions representing workers of the same MNC in different countries, those unions that now bargain with MNCs through employer associations will feel a need to shift to individual bargaining with these firms. Similarly, where an MNC has two or more plants in the same country, and separate plant bargaining is conducted (whether by the same or different unions), there probably will be a tendency on the union side toward coordinated or joint bargaining on a nationwide basis as a step toward international coordination.

Within regional groupings of countries, such as the European Community, bargaining with MNCs may soon shift from a local or national basis to a regional basis.[13] Even though the United States and Canada are not members of a formal regional organization, there already are collective bargaining agreements covering workers in both countries (for example, the UAW-Chrysler agreement). It is possible that, in some cases, regional coalitions of national unions will confront similar coalitions of employer associations in bargaining. In that case, all the regional subsidiaries of the involved MNCs would be covered by the same collective bargaining agreement, thus achieving, or at least advancing toward, the unions' goal of "harmonization" without separate company bargaining. If association bargaining on wages is confined only to the setting of minima, however, additional action would be necessary to harmonize actual wage rates. Ultimately, and in some MNCs sooner than in others, bargaining will take place on a global rather than a regional basis—with perhaps some variations in agreement terms to allow for regional or national differences.[14]

Since, in the overwhelming majority of cases, the agents of international union coordination will be national rather than local unions, joint action with respect to in-plant problems will require that, where such matters are now dealt with by works councils or local bodies, the national unions become directly involved. Thus, present European practices would be brought closer to those in the United States and Canada. In these countries, national unions (or "international" unions with members in both countries) normally do not bargain all the details of working conditions in each plant with the central management of multiplant companies, but they do negotiate for uniformity in certain conditions and disputes procedures and they provide staff and other forms of assistance to their local unions in local bargaining on local issues.

---

13. The Commission of the European Communities' "Proposed Statute for the European Company" requires such bargaining where the unions request it.

14. There are such variations between the United States and Canada in the UAW-Chrysler agreement.

Harmonization of Wages and Working Conditions

A major demand of the international labor movement is for upward harmonization of wages and working conditions. Wage parity between the United States and Canada is already a fact in certain companies and is closely approximated in whole branches of industry in a few cases.[15] Wage parity may soon be a possibility in the European Community, perhaps together with certain nonmember countries in Western Europe. It seems reasonable to expect that wage parity will first be achieved on a regional basis, with harmonization among regions, at least in the industrially developed countries, reserved for a later period.[16]

As far as fringe benefits are concerned, those that are wage-related (such as paid holidays and vacations, overtime and night shift premiums, and layoff and severance pay) more readily lend themselves to upward harmonization than do wage rates as such because, proportionately, their uniformity would add no more to unit labor costs in low-productivity countries than in high-productivity countries. There are indications that "coercive comparisons" on an international basis already have contributed to improved fringe benefits (particularly holidays, vacations, and overtime premiums) in lagging countries.

The costs of certain working conditions (for example, rest and relief periods) are also wage related and therefore the same reasoning applies. Besides, such working conditions relate to elementary human physical needs, which are essentially the same throughout the world.[17] There is no logical or moral justification for denying to some workers, merely because of country, the fulfillment of such needs to the same degree as has been found reasonable elsewhere. Upward harmonization of occupational health and safety standards is clearly a moral imperative. No corporation has the right to make profits at the cost of avoidable maiming and killing of its workers. In pursuing upward harmonization of working conditions affecting the physical well-being of workers, the international labor movement should be able to count on the support of important sections of public opinion to accelerate the process.

---

15. It is noteworthy that parity or near parity has been achieved in these cases despite a substantial difference in levels of national productivity between the two countries.

16. Since this paper is focused on the developed countries, I will not discuss the more remote prospects for wage parity on a worldwide scale, including the poor nations, except to say that the levels at which parity is attained in the developed countries and the pace at which their wage rates advance thereafter will depend in large part on the course of wages in the economically underdeveloped countries.

17. The need for relief time, as one example, may in fact be greater in the less developed countries than elsewhere because of the workers' poor diets and, in many cases, debilitating climates.

Layoff Practices, Lifetime Employment, and Job Enrichment

With respect to layoff practices, I would expect to see unions press for two-way transfers between the United States and the rest of the noncommunist industrialized world. In countries where public unemployment insurance benefits are low relative to wages (as in the United States), it seems likely that unions, particularly in industries where employment fluctuates widely, will borrow from U.S. experience with SUB plans. In the United States I think that unions will seek, and eventually succeed in winning, the right to meaningful advance consultation in connection with short workweeks and layoffs, including reductions in force, resulting from market shrinkage or technological change, transfer of operations, or plant shutdowns or removals.

The sensitivity and militance with which European workers react to layoffs undoubtedly affect practices, laws, and the attitudes of employers. The responsibilities that European employers accept in this regard are reflected in Volkswagen's recent offer, when confronted by the need to reduce its work force, to pay $3,600 to each worker who would agree to quit. In the United States, in contrast, the UAW has had as little as thirty days' notice from the Ford Motor Company of the permanent shutdown of old plants manned largely by older workers who were faced with extreme difficulties, if not insuperable barriers, in obtaining comparable jobs. Provision of SUB and severance pay in some U.S. industries only moderately cushions the impact, especially since the United States persistently maintains far higher unemployment rates than other industrialized countries. High unemployment, obviously, increases the obstacles to reemployment of displaced workers.

A more remote possibility, although one that cannot be ruled out entirely, is that with the increasing number of Japanese subsidiaries operating in the United States, there may be a transference of some form of Japan's life-tenure employment system.[18] Considering the accomplishments of the Japanese economy, this system certainly cannot be dismissed as causing inefficiencies. Reports that it is disappearing in Japan seem to be somewhat exaggerated.[19]

---

18. Reliance on attrition to achieve work force reductions, fairly common in U.S. railroading and a feature of the Kaiser Steel agreement, represents an approximation to life tenure, although it was not borrowed from Japan.

19. The *New York Times*, October 24, 1974, pp. 1, 61, reported that under pressure of the current Japanese recession a small number of firms in Japan gave workers "temporary home rest," that is, a holiday at 90 percent of their regular pay, instead of laying them off. The payments bear a resemblance to SUB in the United States, but they apparently do not affect continuance of the rights of the recipients under the lifetime employment system. Another article in the same issue of the *Times*, p. 61, reported a suicide attempt by a union officer who, after having agreed that a company could shut down a plant and transfer the 900 workers affected to other plants of the same company (or give them incentive payments to quit), learned that the company had decided to dismiss the same number of workers from other plants.

As for experimentation in improvement of the quality of working life, including genuine involvement of workers and their union representatives, there are already some significant beginnings of transfers from Europe to the United States. Present UAW contracts with the Big Three, for example, provide for joint union-management design and evaluation of such experiments. A few of the experiments in the United States reflect some aspects of the new and rapidly mounting pressure of European unions for "democratization" of the workplace.

Among other recent European innovations that may be candidates for transference to the United States are "flex-time" (flexible workday and workweek arrangements) and salary status for workers presently employed on an hourly basis. Flex-time is already in effect in a number of American firms although the role, if any, that unions may have played in its introduction is not readly ascertainable. A demand for conversion of hourly workers to salary status was pressed, unsuccessfully, by the UAW in 1968 negotiations in the automobile and agricultural implement industries. Continued European progress in eliminating invidious distinctions in methods of payment as between blue- and white-collar workers could increase interest in that demand in both the United States and Canada.

Transfers of Industrial Relations and Social Legislation

As communications among unions of separate nations continue to improve, there may well be efforts to transfer certain legal provisions as well as collective bargaining provisions. After Britain's disastrous experience, it seems unlikely that many other industrialized countries will want to import the Taft-Hartley Act or any close copy of it. On the contrary, the MNC problem is likely to result in increasingly insistent demands for amendment of the Taft-Hartley Act to eliminate the prohibitions against sympathy strikes and secondary boycotts. These provisions prevent U.S. workers from coming to the aid of fellow workers in other countries, including those employed by the same corporations, no matter how outrageously exploited or oppressed. Brazilian GM or Ford workers can do little to help themselves under the brutal dictatorship that rules their country but UAW members, if freed to do so, could do much to relieve their plight.

The report of the UN Group of Eminent Persons recognized the problem and took note of the union "tradition of the stronger and more experienced helping the weaker." Accordingly, it recommended that "in the matter of sympathy strikes or other peaceful forms of concerted action, governments should follow liberal rather than restrictive policies.[20] If mounting realiza-

---

20. United Nations, *Impact of Multinational Corporations*, p. 78. In addition, the UN Group made the interesting suggestion that, where sympathy strikes "may be contrary to the terms of labor settlements or too costly for the workers," and an MNC tried to circumvent a

tion of the MNC problem leads Congress to act on this sound advice, U.S. collective bargaining agreements will have to be amended to enable the workers covered by them to take strike action, or conduct boycotts, in support of their counterparts in other countries. That, in itself, may lead to bitter strife because the MNCs are undoubtedly pleased with the divide-and-rule advantage that present U.S. law gives them.

Aside from freedom to engage in sympathy strikes, there is a great deal that the United States could usefully learn and borrow from legislation in effect or proposed in other democratic countries. American backwardness in social and labor legislation is probably largely a result of the absence from the United States of a powerful labor or social democratic political party of the kind that, in Western Europe, Australia, and New Zealand, often decisively influences such legislation.

The deficiencies in labor and social legislation, among other things, place a heavy burden on the collective bargaining process in the United States that, to my knowledge, is matched nowhere else in the industrialized world. The United States is the only economically developed country without some form of national health insurance. Its Social Security system provides pensions that, relative to wage levels, are far below those paid in other developed countries. The same is true of the relationship between public unemployment compensation benefits and average wages.[21] Except for a handful of states, the United States also lacks public disability insurance programs, common in other countries, to provide income for the families of workers who temporarily are unable to work. Despite the long-standing existence of examples elsewhere, the United States does not even provide by law minimum paid vacation periods for workers.

As a result, American unions are compelled to bargain for costly and inefficient private health insurance, complex private pension plans to supplement inadequate public pensions, supplementary unemployment benefits, sickness and accident benefits, and paid vacations. Leaving these matters to collective bargaining also leaves uncovered, or with grossly inadequate coverage, unorganized workers and those whose unions are weak, while fostering a proliferation of unsound private programs such as the

---

strike in a particular country, other governments might embargo exports or imports by the parent or affiliates of the struck plant "which could be a substitute for the interrupted production." (Ibid.)

21. In the United States, as of June 1974, average weekly unemployment compensation benefits amounted to 38 percent of *1973* average weekly wages in covered employment and a much smaller percentage of the total remuneration lost by unemployed workers when account is taken of the value of the fringe benefits they receive while working. In France, where privately financed fringe benefits are negligible, the government responded to the recent rise in unemployment by raising unemployment compensation benefits to approximately 100 percent of the workers' take-home pay. Other industrialized countries, while not matching the French level, replace a far higher percentage of jobless workers' lost wages than the United States.

chaotic private pension system that necessitated enactment of the incredibly complicated Employee Retirement Income Security Act of 1974.

Employee Participation in Management and Ownership

As the United States begins to catch up to countries that have more civilized social and labor legislation, American unions may seek to emulate other forms of worker-oriented legislation, now spreading in Western Europe, in which U.S. labor has shown little interest. One example is legislation that provides for union representation on the policy-making bodies of corporations (that is, codetermination or, going even further, workers' control) and for giving workers shares in the ownership, and thus the profits, of industry.

Hitherto, American unions, except for rare individual union officers, have shied away from such ideas because of legitimate fears that their involvement both in management decisions and in representing worker interests in conflict with management would make them schizophrenic. Besides, the experience of German codetermination and labor representation on the boards of Great Britain's nationalized industries, so far, has not produced particularly encouraging results. Nevertheless, there is persuasive general evidence of a strong democratic urge in human beings that impels them to seek an effective voice in the making of all decisions that affect them.

American workers are not immune from that urge. Indeed, they have shown no hesitation in invading areas that corporations consider sacred "managerial prerogatives." As UAW Vice-president Douglas Fraser once said (I paraphrase from memory), "A managerial prerogative is something we haven't so far gotten around to taking away from them." In some matters, American workers have limited the scope for management discretion more than their European counterparts. A German metalworker who had worked at Ford's Rouge plant told me that "You have more codetermination on the shop floor than all the codetermination we have in Germany." The intensity of the UAW drive for legislation to restrict managerial discretion in plant relocation is symptomatic of the refusal by American workers to recognize any managerial decision that affects them as out of bounds. In this connection, it is pertinent to recall that the UAW in 1945-46 struck General Motors for 113 days with one main goal being an agreement from GM that it would not increase its prices.

Sooner or later, U.S. workers will join their European colleagues in seeking a direct role in corporate decision making. I would, however, expect them to develop institutional mechanisms that would not detract from their unions' main function of defending and promoting workers' interests with regard to wages, hours, and working conditions.

As for workers gaining an ownership share in industry, a small step in that direction was taken in the United States under the UAW-American Motors agreement of 1961. Under a profit-sharing provision, workers received shares of the company's stock as well as certain other benefits. This stock feature was abandoned because American Motors fell on hard times soon after 1961. The UAW agreement with Chrysler provides that clerical and engineering employees participate in the "Thrift-Stock Ownership Program" under which the firm supplements savings set aside by workers to purchase corporation stock.

The demand for a share in ownership is likely to grow partly as a result of the heavy and probably increasing reliance of corporations on self-financing for expansion purposes. A persistent self-financing policy is a sign that prices and profits are higher than would be possible under genuine price competition and, as such, reflects the existence of monopoly or oligopoly. The excessive profits that permit self-financing are extracted either from workers, who receive lower wages than the firm's revenues could reasonably provide, or from consumers, who pay prices above those that would be set by competition, or from a combination of the two. Exclusive reliance by a corporation on self-financing also makes it evident that its stockholders are performing no useful role because, if they all sold their stock and thus sharply depressed its prices, the corporation could still expand because it would not need to go to the capital market to raise investment funds. Thus, the stockholders of a self-financed corporation become, in effect, parasites who give nothing in return for the income they receive. Their parasitic role is underlined by corporate propaganda, such as is frequently heard today from oil companies and public utilities, urging the need for increased prices (or rates) to finance expansion. If consumers are required to provide investment funds, why should the return on the investment go only to the existing stockholders? Why should not the consumers receive shares of stock and related dividends based upon their involuntary investments?

Thus, as the legitimacy of present stockholders' claims is brought into question by the corporations themselves, it is almost inevitable that American workers will demand an ownership interest in industry. The form of these demands, however, cannot be predicted.

Conceivably, legislation might require corporations that financed expansion out of profits to deposit a corresponding number of shares into a national mutual fund in whose income all citizens (workers and other consumers) would share. If the effect were to increase dividend payments, tax revenues derived from stockholders would rise and the tax load on others could be lightened, thus reducing irregularities in the distribution of after-tax income. If the effect were to reduce prices, thus forcing corporations to rely on the capital market rather than on self-financing, there would be a double social gain in the form of a lower price level and, probably, a sounder allocation of capital resources.

As a further step in gaining a voice in what are now managerial decisions, U.S. and Canadian workers also may seek legislation to bring layoff practices in North America nearer to those prevalent in much of Western Europe. Thus far, they do not have, as workers in some European countries do, the legal right to be consulted well in advance of layoffs or the ability to delay and sometimes to prevent them. The Commission of the European Communities has proposed adoption of uniform legislation to govern broadly defined "mass dismissals" throughout the Common Market under which "workers' representatives" (that is, unions or works councils, depending upon the country involved) would play a major role in determining whether or not a proposed layoff should occur and its extent if permitted to occur.[22] A more recent EC Commission proposal is concerned, in considerable detail, with the preservation of the rights of workers and their representatives in cases of merger.[23] As noted, the UAW already is pressing vigorously for U.S. legislation on plant relocation that, in some respects, resembles both existing practice in much of Western Europe and the EC Commission's proposal.

National Standards for MNC Industrial Relations

Undoubtedly, laws requiring improvements in financial disclosure will be encouraged by the rise of MNCs. Today MNCs have considerable freedom to withhold information, and when required to publish, they can make their profits, or the bulk of them, appear in whatever countries they choose. Through imaginative accounting and the manipulation of transfer prices (including charges to foreign subsidiaries for licenses, royalties, and equipment, and allocation of worldwide overhead costs as well as prices for materials, parts, and components), MNCs can not only evade national taxation and foreign exchange controls, but also deceive national unions concerning profits or losses attributable to operations in individual countries. In fact, MNCs may keep different sets of accounts for different self-serving purposes. In separate collective bargaining with individual plants of a multiplant corporation within the United States (particularly if the local unions involved are affiliated to different national organizations), management may tell the union bargaining with plant A

---

22. Commission of the European Communities, *Amended Proposal for a Council Directive on the Harmonization of Legislation of the Member States Relating to Mass Dismissals,* Brussels, November 26, 1973.

23. Commission of the European Communities, *Proposal for a Directive of the Council on Harmonization of the Legislation of Member States on the Retention of the Rights and Advantages of Employees in the Case of Mergers, Takeovers and Amalgamations,* Brussels, June 21, 1974.

that that plant is losing money and all the company's profits come from plant B, while telling the latter's workers exactly the reverse. This game is played even more easily by MNCs bargaining with unions in different countries.

The answer is the development of uniform accounting standards and principles to be applied by MNCs to each of their separate national branches (and, in the case of conglomerates, to each line of business within each nation) with the data to be published separately for each together with the global figures for the MNC as a whole. The EC Commission has made a proposal pointing in that general direction. The commission properly noted that effectuation of the proposal would contribute to making available information on MNCs "the economic and social importance of which can no longer justify the degree of secrecy with which they surround themselves."[24] The report of the UN Group of Eminent Persons also proposed moves toward international standardization, specifically "that the international standards of disclosure, accounting and reporting . . . should include the data which are of special relevance for the purpose of collective bargaining."[25] Home countries could and should require "their" MNCs to provide such data with respect to all countries in which they operate and ultimately it should be made a universal requirement by international action.[26]

In other fields, home country governments could do much to compel MNCs to act as innovators of sound industrial relations practices and decent labor standards in host countries. Such compulsion would be entirely proper. The MNCs claim to be the bearers of material progress and of advanced technology, managerial and marketing skills to their host countries. Why should not society also require them to be bearers of social progress in return for the privilege of operating on an international basis? The propriety of such a requirement was to a large extent accepted in the discussions of the UN Group of Eminent Persons where it was referred to variously as the beachhead, bridgehead, or spearhead principle.

The principle, which is reflected in a number of the group's recommendations, was probably first advanced by the UAW in 1968.[27] In a later adap-

24. Bulletin of the European Communities, Supplement 15/73, *Multinational Undertakings and the Community*, p. 13.

25. United Nations, *Impact of Multinational Corporations*, p. 79.

26. All national actions discussed in this section should be considered interim measures to be replaced as rapidly as possible with enforceable international regulations directed toward the same ends.

27. The principle is reflected in the resolution on "International Labor Solidarity" adopted by the UAW's convention held May 4-10, 1968. (See p. 179 of the convention's proceedings.) That same year, on the urging of the UAW, the same principle was incorporated in a resolution adopted by the Congress of International Metalworkers' Federation. In both cases, the principle was to be applied to MNCs operating under international corporate charters, such as George Ball and others have proposed.

tation of the idea (June 1971), the UAW International Executive Board adopted a resolution on "Licensing U.S. Corporations' Foreign Investments," which proposed legislation under which foreign investment by U.S.-owned corporations (including reinvestment of foreign profits) would be permitted only where the firm met certain conditions, including requirements that "(1) the foreign establishment pay fair wages, reasonably related to the productivity of the workers employed, and otherwise maintain fair labor standards, (2) the workers' right to free collective bargaining through representatives of their own choosing be recognized and (3) the establishment will not discriminate against any worker or applicant for work on the basis of race or creed."[28] Sweden tried to apply the beachhead principle by requiring its MNCs, in order to qualify for guarantees of their foreign investments, to comply with a long list of "social conditions," including recognition of trade union rights and nondiscriminatory racial policies. Unfortunately, the effort failed because Swedish guarantees were available for investments only in a limited list of developing countries and, even as to them, the MNCs could avoid obligating themselves to comply with the social conditions by not applying for the guarantees. The UAW's licensing proposal would avoid these problems because it would cover all foreign investments by U.S.-owned MNCs.

The UN group in adopting the beachhead approach recommended that "through appropriate means, home countries prevent multinational corporations from going into countries where workers' rights are not respected, unless the affiliate obtains permission to apply internationally agreed labor standards, such as free collective bargaining, equal treatment of workers and humane labor relations."[29] Even Giovanni Agnelli, president of Fiat, the giant auto industry MNC based in Italy, when questioned at the UN group's Geneva hearings, agreed that the recommendation "makes sense."[30] Unfortunately, few countries have ratified the ILO's Conventions and those that have, in many cases, do not enforce them. ILO recommendations, also, are widely ignored. Application of the beachhead principle, as suggested by the UN group, would put teeth into what are now little more than expressions (often hypocritical) of good intentions.

Similarly, the UN group recommended that "home countries should re-

28. Cited in International Union of United Automobile, Aerospace and Agricultural Implement Workers of America, *Proceedings of the Twenty-third Constitutional Convention* (1972), p. 345.

29. United Nations, *Impact of Multinational Corporations*, p. 80. "Internationally agreed labor standards" is intended to mean the "International Labor Code," i.e., the Conventions and Recommendations adopted by the Conferences of the International Labor Organization (ILO), a specialized agency of the United Nations.

30. Agnelli's remark appears in the "Informal Verbatim Transcript" of the group's public hearings for November 7, 1973. I believe, however, that the transcript is not available for public distribution.

quire multinational corporations to declare in all countries in which they operate, all measures of safeguards and special working conditions which they observe in their home countries to protect the health and safety of workers and to observe those measures in similar production processes in host countries with such changes and adaptations as the host government may specify."[31]

If the beachhead principle were applied by home country governments, South Africa, for example, would be confronted with the choice of either exempting MNC subsidiaries from apartheid legislation or foregoing the investments of such firms. Spain, for example, would be faced with a similar choice with respect to the granting of rights of association and free collective bargaining to workers in Spanish subsidiaries of MNCs. This would not be an infringement of sovereignty since the potential host government is entirely free to make either choice. At the least, powerful political pressures would be generated within potential host countries to exempt MNC subsidiaries from racially discriminatory or repressive labor legislation. If the pressures succeeded, islands of decency would emerge and the demonstration effect could be expected to spread a measure of civilization beyond the confines of the MNC operations. Thus, the MNCs could become vehicles for the international transfer of progressive and beneficent innovation instead of, as is often the case now, socially retrogressive and even malignant change.

International Standards for MNC Industrial Relations

Home country regulation of the foreign operations of MNCs, however, is not sufficient. Many governments will refrain from such regulation on grounds that they might put "their" MNCs at a disadvantage relative to those based in other countries. Besides, as the Massey-Ferguson example cited earlier demonstrates, MNCs will change their home countries if the advantages sufficiently outweigh the disadvantages.

This was foreseen long before the rise of MNCs by two respected and perceptive historical figures. Adam Smith wrote, "A merchant, it has been said very properly, is not necessarily the citizen of any particular country. It is in a great measure indifferent to him from what place he carries on his trade; and a very trifling disgust will make him remove his capital, and together with it all the industry which it supports, from one country to another."[32] Thomas Jefferson, possibly paraphrasing Smith, expressed the same thought: "Merchants have no country. The mere spot they stand on does not constitute so strong an attachment as that from which they draw

---

31. United Nations, *Impact of Multinational Corporations*, p. 80.
32. *Wealth of Nations*, p. 395.

their gains."[33] The views of Smith and Jefferson were strikingly confirmed by an MNC insider, Carl A. Gerstacker, president of the Dow Chemical Company, when he said, "I have long dreamed of buying an island owned by no nation, and of establishing World Headquarters of the Dow Company on the truly neutral ground of such an island, beholden to no nation or society."[34]

These two factors—fears, genuine or specious, of putting home country MNCs at a disadvantage and the absence of MNC loyalties to their home countries (or to any other for that matter)—make international, rather than purely national, regulation imperative if MNCs are to be used as vehicles for constructive rather than destructive innovation in industrial relations.

It is also clear that enforceable regulation backed up by effective sanctions is required rather than toothless codes of conduct. Conceivably, the latter might be a step toward regulation, since widespread violations would soon make it apparent that more than expressions of good intentions are necessary. On the other hand, codes without sanctions would have the serious drawback that responsible firms, which might follow them, would be placed at a serious disadvantage relative to the irresponsible ones that would blithely ignore them.

Moreover, there is a wide variety of matters on which only international action can achieve the desired purposes. This is obvious in cases of evasion of national taxes and foreign exchange controls through manipulation of transfer prices, disadvantages to the international monetary system resulting from or aggravated by currency speculation by MNCs, and the sabotage of efforts to protect the environment through MNC relocation, actual or threatened, to countries with the least stringent standards.

The need for international action on labor matters is equally urgent if the best rather than the worst practices are to be transferred across national boundaries and if competitive degradation of labor standards is to be avoided. For example, only by intergovernmental action—by international agreement—can governments be inhibited from competing for investments by MNCs by outbidding each other in offering concessions at the expense of workers' welfare.[35] How, in the absence of health and safety standards, agreed on and enforceable at the international level, can any country hope to both protect its workers against corporate slaughter and still keep them employed? How, in the absence of enforceable international

---

33. John Bartlett, *Familiar Quotations*, 13th ed. (Boston: Little, Brown, 1955), p. 375b.

34. "The Structure of the Corporation," speech delivered at the White House Conference on the Industrial World Ahead, held in Washington, D.C., February 7-9, 1972, p. 9 (multilith). I have been told, but have not yet been able to confirm, that the quoted sentence was omitted in later versions of the text.

35. Inhibition rather than outright prevention is probably the most that can be hoped for in a world of national sovereignties.

rules, can workers throughout the world be assured of fair shares in the fruits of their productivity?

Specifically on this last point, the UN group's report noted the problems that arise when an MNC introduces an advanced technology, designed for a high-wage, economically advanced country, into a low-wage developing country. One consequence, of course, is excessive profits. Another is likely to be a drain on the host country's foreign exchange resources as those profits are repatriated. Still another is the loss of domestic demand for wage goods and accompanying increases in employment that would be created if the MNC's workers received pay commensurate with their productivity.

But the consequences are not confined to the developing host countries. The low unit labor costs resulting from the combination of high technology and low wages create serious disturbances in international competition and tend to undermine reasonable wage standards established elsewhere. A clear-cut case of unfair competition based on exploitation arises, exploitation being denial to workers of their fair share of the values they produce. There is no way, barring protectionism, that this problem can be dealt with by purely national action.

International action was proposed as long ago as the 1940s by the drafters of the Havana Charter for a UN international trade organization. The charter, which was signed in 1948 by representatives of fifty-odd nations, but, unfortunately, never ratified, included an Article 7, headed "Fair Labor Standards," which recognized that "all countries have a common interest in the achievement and maintenance of fair labor standards related to productivity" and provided (by reference to other articles) for means to enforce such fair labor standards in international trade. The UN group urged that consideration be given to amendment of the General Agreement on Tariffs and Trade (GATT) to include Article 7 of the Havana Charter.

"Fair labor standards related to productivity," of course, means an approximation to uniformity of unit labor costs. That, in turn, means that human beings would no longer be treated as just another economic resource to be bought at the lowest obtainable price. International competition would have to take place on a basis other than the degree of exploitation to which governments are willing to subject their workers.

This thought may horrify some economists who have forgotten that economics is a human science. But it would be harmonious with the principle laid down in both the Clayton Act and the Declaration of Philadelphia (an annex to the constitution of the ILO) that the labor of human beings is not a commodity.

The international labor movement was the first institution of any significance to call attention to the problems presented, not only to workers but to society as a whole, by the rise of the MNCs and their growing power. The labor movement recognized early that collective bargaining alone could not contain the beast nor tame it so that its behavior would be compatible with the general social interest. Effective intergovernmental regulation was perceived from the outset as imperative.

Fortunately, the labor movement is not helpless in pursuing such regulation. In many of the small group of countries that plays the decisive role in world economic affairs, unions are closely allied with Labor and Social-Democratic parties that have been and likely will again be the (or in the) governments of their respective countries. Those governments are in a position to raise the MNC problem in intergovernmental bodies and to press for internationally agreed solutions.

Accordingly, as a result of a proposal made in a resolution adopted by the 1971 Congress of the International Metalworkers' Federation (IMF), there already exists a working party organized by the International Confederation of Free Trade Unions, which includes the major international trade secretariats concerned with MNCs and is beginning to involve representatives of the labor-based political parties. Its task is to draft proposals for a comprehensive and enforceable international regulatory code for MNCs covering not only matters of direct interest to the labor movement, but also, in the words of the IMF resolution, "all other matters with respect to which the activities of the international corporations endanger the social interest, nationally and internationally."

The EC Commission has taken note of "much anxiety among workers" arising out of the growth and spread of MNCs. It has declared that it "considers the setting up of a trade union counterweight as essential" and has undertaken to "encourage it."[36] Such a counterweight can do much to curb the inclinations of the MNCs to take the world back to the dark ages of industrial relations and, instead, to spread civilized labor practices to those parts of the world where oppression and exploitation prevail. But what the labor movement alone can do is limited. It needs the support of relatively enlightened governments and, through them, of the many intergovernmental organizations that have important roles to play in improving the conditions not only of the world's workers but of all the underprivileged.

---

36. *Multinational Undertakings*, p. 10.

MULTINATIONALS' IMPACT ON HOST COUNTRY INDUSTRIAL RELATIONS

Roger Blanpain

One of the most debated issues raised about multinational corporations concerns their impact on the industrial relations systems of the host countries. Do multinationals try to improve and transplant homemade solutions, systems, rules, and techniques? Do they succeed in doing so or do they conform, eventually out of necessity, to local practices and values? How much do they change and innovate in labor relations?

There is a widespread belief, shared by others than trade unionists, that multinationals are "cultural invaders" that do not respect local traditions. This outcry received international publicity in 1965, when more than five thousand workers at Genk, Belgium, struck the Ford Motor Company for several weeks and a "black book" was published, which started with an introduction that can be fairly translated as follows: "In this report we want to denounce the introduction into Belgium of a kind of American capitalism that completely disregards our social legislation, our labor relations practices, and our revered traditions."

The Roberts-Arundel recognition dispute in the United Kingdom is widely known. In 1965 the Roberts Company, an American manufacturer of textile machinery, bought out Arundel-Coulthard, a British firm in the same business. The new firm concentrated its activities in one plant after closing down four of the five facilities. Subsequently a dispute resulted from the engagement of women as machine operators, work that previously had been done only by men, without any consultation with the unions.

Roger Blanpain is professor of law and director of the Institute for Labor Relations at the University of Leuven, Belgium.

As a result of this dispute, all the union members were dismissed and replaced by nonunion labor. This led to tremendous difficulties and picketing, demonstration strikes, and so on. A twelve-month strike, beginning in November 1967, for the reinstatement of union members and for recognition of the trade union followed. There were token strikes by several thousand workers in other firms as well. Eventually the company agreed, but in January 1969 it closed down.[1]

The situation at Roberts-Arundel led to the following remarks:

> It is bad enough when you have major industrial warfare arising out of really important matters of principle. But when they arise out of relatively minor, unimportant issues, such as were involved in the Roberts-Arundel dispute, then something is seriously wrong. I think what really probably was wrong was simply a matter of ignorance by the company concerned of the practices, the traditions, the matters regarded as of importance in the United Kingdom, and an assumption that methods hallowed by tradition and supplemented by law in the United States must be right wherever they are exported.[2]

One could give many more examples of conflict between the aspirations and insights of the foreign firm and the host community. These conflicts may be due to management's failure to recognize fundamental differences between foreign and domestic policies, or to the fact that the multinationals deliberately want to impose their own systems, or to both. Clyde Summers has illustrated the failure of an American management to understand European policies, practices, and attitudes in the following example:

> In 1962 an American pump manufacturing company bought out a Belgian firm. . . . At the time the acquisition took place, the Belgian plant was covered by an industrywide collective agreement, and labor relations had been stable for a number of years. No sooner had the American company taken control than the Belgian labor union demanded a 10% wage increase. The company pointed out that the wages being paid were already 20% above those provided for in the collective agreement, but this was dismissed by the union as irrelevant. The company then offered to match the wages paid by its chief European competitors, but this, too, was rejected.
>
> In justification of its demands, the union declared that until two years earlier, when the owners faced financial difficulties, the plant had always paid more than any other continental pump producer and insisted that this premium should now be reinstated. The deadlock resulted in a six-week strike. Later, when the company learned that among other Belgian employers the union's demands were considered normal and quite appropriate and that the company's position was viewed as unduly rigid, its resistance to the wage insistence of the union collapsed.
>
> This very costly and unnecessary strike had its primary source in the failure of

1. Samuel C. Silkin, "American Investment and European Cultures: Conflict and Cooperation," in *Western European Labor and the American Corporation*, ed. Alfred Kamin (Washington, D.C.: Bureau of National Affairs, 1970), p. 442-44.

2. Ibid., p. 444.

American management to understand European collective bargaining processes.[3]

In light of the above, it is interesting to note that all collective bargaining agreements in the European Economic Community (EEC) provide only for minima. There is always room for improvement and, consequently, for more bargaining. The conclusion of a central national agreement is not the final settlement; it is the first round of negotiations and a prelude to bargaining at the local level. The second round is far more important in fixing actual terms. At the local level the union's policy is to adjust its demands according to the employer's ability to pay. Once negotiated, these differentials become a matter of vested rights. This is what the American pump company failed to understand.

There are many examples of multinationals attempting to impose foreign solutions that conflict with local traditions and values. In Japan unsuccessful attempts were made to introduce wage systems based on job evaluation and merit rating, as opposed to the traditional criteria of educational qualifications and seniority.[4] Other firms, too, discovered that the application of some techniques violates social values. In Italy, for example, it is unacceptable to pass over an individual for an annual increase merely because of unsatisfactory performance.[5] In Germany a strike resulted when John Deere-Lane, A.G., reduced the length of the breakfast break, and in Canada General Motors had to abandon the attempt to replace the traditional fixed rest period by a rotating rest period.[6]

Other changes introduced after negotiations were not necessarily felt to be incompatible with local values. In the United Kingdom, for example, Ford, General Motors, and Chrysler applied a measured-day work system, and only Chrysler had great difficulty in gaining acceptance of the system.[7] Another example is from the Ford Motor Company in Genk where an attempt to change the rotating shift assignment pattern was partly accepted by the unions without specific strife.[8]

From this list of examples, which is by no means exhaustive, it is clear that some industrial relations decisions of multinationals imposed changes that were looked upon as unacceptable by local standards whereas

3. Clyde W. Summers, "Labor Relations in the Common Market," *Harvard Business Review* 43 (1965): 148.

4. ILO, *Multinational Enterprises and Social Policy* (Geneva, 1973), p. 79.

5. John C. Shearer, "Manpower Environments Confronting American Firms in Western Europe," in *Western European Labor*, p. 389.

6. ILO, *Multinational Enterprises*, p. 79.

7. Ibid.

8. Duane Kujawa, *International Labor Relations Management in the Automotive Industry: A Comparative Study of Chrysler, Ford, and General Motors* (New York: Praeger, 1971), p. 234.

other decisions were regarded as "innovations" that were eventually acceptable. The question is whether these cases of change and innovation, accepted or not, are exceptional or typical? Do multinationals conform to local patterns or not?

Unfortunately, there is not a lot of comprehensive empirical research available on Africa and South America.[9] For Europe, there are mainly the contribution of Max Steuer and John Gennard for the United Kingdom,[10] the study of Mark Beckers and his colleagues for Belgium,[11] and the research by Duane Kujawa concerning the automotive industry. The first two studies cover the industrial relations behavior of foreign firms within one country; the Kujawa study compares the labor relations policies and practices of three automobile companies (Chrysler, Ford, General Motors) in several countries (Canada, the United Kingdom, the Netherlands, Belgium, West Germany, France, and Spain). Another study, confined to the electronics industry in the United Kingdom, was undertaken by Malcolm Warner and others, and research concerning corporate headquarters' involvement in the industrial relations policy and practice of subsidiaries was done by David Blake.[12]

These studies, which are certainly neither final nor exhaustive, differ in scope, method, and depth, and provide no general conclusions of any kind. They do, however, allow a concentration on the industrial relations behavior of the foreign firms in the United Kingdom and Belgium, which is especially useful because the two countries are comparable as far as the importance of foreign investment is concerned.[13] In addition, they both

9. M. Jadi, "Multinational Corporations and Labor in Africa: A Review of Research" and R. Bolivar-Velez, "Report on Research Findings for Latin America," (papers presented at Research Meeting on Multinational Corporations, International Institute for Labor Studies, Geneva, December 1973).

10. Max Steuer and John Gennard, "Industrial Relations, Labour Disputes and Labour Utilization in Foreign-owned Firms in the United Kingdom," in *The Multinational Enterprise*, ed. John Dunning (London: Praeger, 1971), pp. 89-146. See also David J. C. Forsyth, "Foreign-owned Firms and Labour Relations: A Regional Perspective," *British Journal of Industrial Relations* 11, no. 1 (1973): 20-28, which contests the findings of Steuer and Gennard "that foreign-owned firms in the U.K. had a labour relations 'performance' (measured in terms of strike activity) superior to that of indigenous firms in the years 1963 and 1968." Forsyth argues that data on strike activity in Scotland between 1960 and 1969 give a different picture. There is a particularly heavy concentration of foreign-owned firms there, and "the U.S.-owned sector . . . is shown to be characterized by a much heavier incidence of strike activity than is the indigenous sector."

11. Mark Beckers et al., *La Belgique face aux investissements étrangers: Une approache sociologique*, étude réalisée sous la direction de Pierre DeBic, (Leuven: Acco-Leuven, 1973).

12. Malcolm Warner et al., "The Comparative Measurement of Industrial Relations in Multinational Firms," in *Multinational Corporations and Labour Unions*, Nijmegen Conference, May 17-19, 1973, pp. 143-51, and David Blake, "Cross-national Cooperative Strategies: Union Response to the MNCs," ibid., pp. 223-47.

13. In 1968, 192,000 workers were employed by foreign multinationals in Belgium. This constituted 18 percent of total Belgian employment in industry: U.S. firms and EEC firms each employed 8 percent. Of the workers in the rubber and petroleum industry, 46 percent

have well-developed systems of "voluntary" industrial relations, with a
rather strong degree of unionization (70 percent in Belgium and 40 percent
in the United Kingdom); no legally binding collective agreements; collective bargaining at different levels (national, regional, and plant); and
employer associations that play an important role in collective bargaining
as well as in representing employers' interests with governmental
authorities.

   The strength of these characteristics means that in both the British and
the Belgian systems multinational corporations must take local realities
into account in developing their own labor relations policies. Thus, a basis
may be provided to test the propositions of Shearer and Warner concerning the labor relations conduct of foreign multinationals. Shearer
suggested that "American firms which operate in foreign countries usually
premise their industrial-relations policies on the base of the values,
assumptions, and habits they have developed in the United States. They
then may or may not modify them in response to the different circumstances abroad." [14] Similarly, Warner, discussing the approaches of

---

worked in foreign firms, and in the paper industry, 36 percent. See J. DeSloovere and O.
VanDen Bulcke, "Buitenlandse industriele bedrijven in Vlaanderen, Wallonie en Brussel,"
Economie in Vlaanderen, December 1972, p. 45. In 1973, 56 percent of Belgian metalworkers
were employed by foreign-owned companies. See Dienst voor Collectieve
Arbeidsverhoudingen, *Driejaarlijks verslag, 1970-1972* [Service for Collective Labor
Relations, *Triannual Report, 1970-1972*] (Brussels, 1973), p. 19. In 1970, the number of people
employed in 270 U.S. industrial subsidiaries in the United Kingdom was said to be 481,268.
ILO, *Multinational Enterprises,* p. 47.

   14. John C. Shearer, "Industrial Relations of American Corporations Abroad," in *International Labor,* ed. Solomon Barkin et al. (New York: Harper and Row, 1967), p. 117. "In
many developing countries governments and trade unions were in such a weak position that
multinational corporations could often impose their own pattern, while in developed countries they had to respect the local patterns." J. Harrod, "Multi-national Corporations, Trade
Unions and Industrial Relations: A Case Study of Jamaica," in *Transnational Industrial
Relations,* ed. Hans Günter (London: MacMillan, 1972), p. 371. Roberts suggests that
Shearer's point "might well be made about British and European firms, when operating in
underdeveloped countries, but not when operating in advanced industrial countries, such as
Australia, the United States or European countries." Ibid., p. 127. "In Japan, where foreign
investment accounts for only 0.6 percent of all Japanese employers, the three main
characteristics of the Japanese employment system—lifetime employment, the security wage
system and the enterprise union—are being adopted with slight revisions by most foreign
enterprises in Japan." T. Hanami, "The Multinational Corporation and Japanese Industrial
Relations," *IRRA International Conference,* 1973, p. 10. In Korea, on January 1, 1970, "a
special law on Trade Unions and Mediation of Labor Disputes in Enterprises invested by
Foreigners" was promulgated, with supposedly obligatory procedures for mediation and conciliation. IMF, *The Subsidiaries of Automotive Multinational Companies in Developing
Countries, Their Production Facilities in Asian Developing Countries: Social Conditions and
Trade Union Problems* (Geneva, 1973), pp. 18-19. In Malaysia, the IMF reported that the
government, anxious to attract foreign investment, introduced new legislation which supposedly states that in an entirely new industry, trade unions may not be established for three
years. It further stipulates that during five years after a multinational has moved in, fringe
benefits of its subsidiaries cannot be improved above the level set by law. Ibid., p. 25.

multinational firms, developed the following proposition:

> Multinational firms, largely American, although not necessarily, originally tried to transfer their industrial relation style to other sites abroad in a wholesale fashion. . . . They found . . . later that they ran into trouble as the unions opposed certain 'alien' labor relations practices, and eventually . . . moved to an accommodation *grosso modo* with the socio-industrial norms dominant in the national culture.[15]

Blake has concluded that corporate headquarters rarely, if ever, become involved in industrial relations matters concerning local contract administration and subsidiary grievance procedures. But in subsidiary collective bargaining and strike settlements, the "pattern shifts dramatically."

> While a large number of respondents indicate that headquarters rarely or never become involved in these issues, an equal or larger percentage say that their regional or parent company headquarters participate sometimes or with even greater frequency in subsidiary collective bargaining and strike settlement efforts. . . . [In that case] the nature of that involvement is likely to be more active than just the giving of advice and the setting of standards.[16]

Moreover Blake continues, "labor union officials do feel that corporate headquarters does play an active and more important role in labor-management relations."

To a certain extent, these research findings concerning Belgium and the United Kingdom supply evidence supporting Shearer's and Warner's propositions. The local labor relations system may compel the multinational corporation first to decentralize the handling of industrial relations and, second, to adjust to local conditions. According to Kujawa, the features of national labor relations systems that have a major influence on this decentralization process are employer association membership, the employee representation unit, local law and administration, direct government participation in the collective bargaining process, and cultural and social values that directly affect the content of collective agreements.[17] These features also may compel the multinational eventually to adjust and integrate within the system and to try to change it from within.[18] Such an evolution, which seems logical, is illustrated by some convincing evidence in the research findings regarding trade union recognition, employer association membership, duration and nature of collective agreements, job security, and productivity bargaining and relative wages.

---

15. Warner et al., "Comparative Measurement of Industrial Relations," p. 148.

16. Blake, "Cross-national Cooperative Strategies," pp. 226-28.

17. Kujawa, *International Labor Relations in the Automotive Industry*, p. 181; see also Steuer and Gennard, "Industrial Relations in the United Kingdom," p. 112.

18. Hans Günter, *Multinational Corporations and Labor: A Prospective View*, IRRA, London Congress, 1973; Beckers et al., *La Belgique*, pp. 84-85.

Trade Union Recognition

In the United Kingdom, the failure to recognize and negotiate with trade unions (manual workers) does not appear to be a significant problem with foreign firms from Western Europe. But some American firms, for example, IBM and Kodak, have refused to recognize British trade unions.[19] Ford Motor Company in Britain did not recognize trade unions until 1944, when it began to operate an aircraft engine plant subject to government policy that management deal with trade unions.[20]

In 1966 the Amalgamated Union of Engineering Workers, the same union that was involved in the Roberts-Arundel recognition dispute, was refused recognition by Caterpillar Tractor Company at its West of Scotland establishment. Twelve hundred employees went out on strike for thirteen weeks. When the union withdrew 600 of its members from another factory of the same company where recognition had been granted, the company agreed to recognize and to negotiate with the union.[21]

Steuer and Gennard have concluded that nonrecognition of manual worker trade unions among foreign-owned firms is not worse than among domestic firms in the United Kingdom. Both types of firms, however, appear to have a fear of white-collar unionism.[22] In 1973 Britain's Commission on Industrial Relations had twenty-two new court references concerning applications by unions for recognition as a sole bargaining agent, mainly, though not exclusively, in banking, insurance, and betting.[23] Warner concluded that the multinational firms surveyed seemed neither stronger nor weaker in their degree of recognition of unions. The extent of union membership in these firms was lower than in domestic companies and could suggest that company policy tended to discourage unionization, but the accuracy of this statement is unclear.[24]

The foreign "nonrecognizers" tend to be large and conspicuous and to have many resources at their disposal to resist demands and industrial action designed to force recognition. Nigel McCrea concluded that "the issue of union recognition is frequently a polemical one. In a class society, why should employers be expected to grant automatic recognition? One could argue that the minority of foreign-owned firms which withhold recognition are being more logical and true to their fundamental aims than com-

---

19. Steuer and Gennard, "Industrial Relations in the United Kingdom," p. 97.

20. Robert Copp, "Negotiating a New Wage Structure at Ford of Britain," in *Western European Labor*, p. 109.

21. Steuer and Gennard, "Industrial Relations in the United Kingdom," p. 98.

22. Ibid., p. 99.

23. CIR Report No. 65, *Annual Report for 1973* (London: HMSO, 1974), p. 5.

24. Warner et al., "Comparative Measurement of Industrial Relations," p. 147.

panies which automatically concede it.''[25]

In Belgium, the degree of unionization is higher in foreign firms than in the labor force as a whole. A 1971 survey of sixty-three foreign enterprises, employing 59,195 workers, showed unionization to be 82.4 percent, while the general degree of unionization in Belgium, in 1970, was slightly above 70 percent. In implantations since 1955, 83 percent were organized, and in the case of takeovers the proportion was 90 percent, which is extremely high. The reason for this high degree of unionization apparently is the demanding work conditions: high speeds and the "Taylorisation" of the jobs to be performed. Thus, the workers, regardless of age, sex, nationality, or trade union past, have only one recourse: the union.[26] In nonintegrated regions, unionization tended to be less than 40 percent in four large enterprises.[27] In three cases, the foreign firms had to reckon with firm trade union action at the moment of the implantation. In six other cases, the employers had agreed to negotiate an agreement even before recruiting workers. One of the clauses of these agreements involved the union in recruitment by allowing a delegate to talk with each newcomer and to participate at his or her reception in the firm.

At the beginning, most managers of foreign firms in Belgium were not willing to accept the Belgian industrial system. In integrated regions the unions forced the firms to recognize them and to accept them as the spokesmen of the workers; but in nonintegrated regions this was not always the case, and in some instances foreign managers even refused to meet with the representatives of the workers.[28] The Belgian Ministry of Labor reported that some foreign companies refused to recognize union delegations and set up consultative organs composed of their nonunionized employees. As such, "they tried," the report concluded, "to introduce a duality in our collective relations, which is contrary to the spirit and the system which we developed in the course of the recent decennia and which was gradually extended." [29]

Membership in an Employer Association

In the EEC countries, employer associations play a very important role. They not only give legal, fiscal, economic, and other advice, but they also

25. Nigel McCrea, "Report on Research Findings relating to Great Britain," Research Meeting on Multinational Corporations and Labor, International Institute of Labor Studies, Geneva, December 1973, p. 17 (mimeographed).

26. Beckers et al., *La Belgique*, pp. 58-59 and 79.

27. Integrated regions are those where the firms are concentrated with regard to the labor force, are complementary as far as products are concerned, and where the socioeconomic groups are formally organized. Nonintegrated regions lack one of those features.

28. Beckers et al., *La Belgique*, pp. 62, 84-85.

29. Dienst van de Collectieve Arbeidsbetrekkingen, *Driejaarlijks verslag, 1970-1972*, p. 20.

engage in collective bargaining. Consequently, joining an employer association reduces the members' freedom to negotiate separately with their employees. In the United Kingdom, Chrysler, Ford, Vauxhall, Esso, Shell, Mobil Oil, Brown and Polsons, Heinz, Kellogg, Alcan, Massey-Ferguson, Kodak, International Nickel, and Woolworths are not members of national employer associations; thus they negotiate independently. The foreign firms that deliberately have opted in Britain for company and plant bargaining are predominantly American-owned, contrary to the case for foreign firms of Western European origin.[30]

In some countries, like Belgium and the Netherlands, national or regional agreements negotiated by employer associations can have a binding effect on all employers, regardless of whether the employer is a member of the association or not. This may have influenced foreign-owned firms such as Ford-Genk, Caterpillar, Esso, and Shell to join Belgian employer associations.

At one time, the subsidiary of Ford Motor Company in Cologne, Germany, was not a member of the Gesamtmetal employer association. But when the auto union, Industriegewerkschaft Metall, demanded that all premiums paid by Ford that were above association-established rates be included in a plant collective agreement and threatened to strike if this was not done, Ford hastened to join the employer association. It thus got the protection afforded by the union's duty to keep peace during the duration of the agreement between the union and the association. The union felt cheated by such tactics.[31] In the United Kingdom, however, Chrysler left the Engineering Employers' Federation to exercise "more direct control over bargaining issues and to be able to exercise a greater degree of local control over its labor relations."[32]

The Beckers survey involving eighty-one foreign firms in Belgium revealed that seventy-five were affiliated to the respective employer association.[33] In 1968, 71 percent of the American firms engaged in the metalworking industry belonged to the Fabrimetal employer association. Nonmembers offered the following reasons for not joining: high membership dues; insufficient services; the need for members to be bound by the collective agreements concluded by the association; the obligation

---

30. Steuer and Gennard, "Industrial Relations in the United Kingdom," p. 95.

31. Franz Gamillscheg, "Outlines of Collective Labor Law in the Federal Republic of Germany," in *Western European Labor*, ed. Kamin, pp. 262-63. It should be noted, however, that Volkswagen is not a member of an association and has its own relationships with the Industriegewerkschaft Metall.

32. Kujawa, *International Labor Relations in the Automotive Industry*, p. 183. See also the case of Massey Harris, in Steuer and Gennard, "Industrial Relations in the United Kingdom," p. 95.

33. Beckers et al., *La Belgique*, p. 148. Of the six nonmembers, two were recent implantations; four were implanted in nonintegrated regions.

for the employer to pay a premium for "trade union guarantees."[34] It is mainly the American firms that are hesitant to join, but most of them do within five years after implantation.[35]

In the metalworking industry foreign firms do play an active role in the employer association, particularly with regard to the collective agreements concluded by the association. Their participation in Fabrimetal's social committee, which develops industrywide collective bargaining policy, is expanding. The Beckers survey revealed that 42 percent of the members of the social committee were made up of representatives of foreign enterprises, including Ford, GM, and Caterpillar.[36] One could say that the same reason for which Rootes (Chrysler in the United Kingdom) left the employer association has encouraged foreign companies in Belgium to join: they want to control negotiations and industrial relations policy at the decision-making level. Indeed, Beckers has suggested that in some sectors the associations have adapted to the multinationals and not vice versa.

Duration and Nature of the Collective Agreements

In the United Kingdom where the collective agreements are usually open-ended and not legally binding on the contracting parties, attempts were made by certain foreign multinationals to negotiate binding agreements of a definite duration. In 1968 H. Wiggins, a subsidiary of International Nickel, succeeded in negotiating a legally binding collective agreement. The agreement clearly stated the length of the agreement, the circumstances under which negotiations could be resumed during its term, and when during its life industrial action was acceptable. In addition, an arbitration board was established to resolve claims that the company had breached the agreement, and a penalty was introduced consisting in the loss of a premium rate if employees assisted or took part in any industrial action that was in breach of the agreement.[37]

In 1969, after an unofficial strike against a bargain struck with its joint union negotiating committee, Ford of Great Britain decided to test the no-

---

34. In the metalworking industry trade unions guarantee social peace during the life of the collective agreement. In return for safeguarding social peace, trade unions receive a financial "subvention" from the employer association. See Roger Blanpain, "Labor Relations in Belgium" in *Western European Labor*, p. 245.

35. Beckers et al., *La Belgique*, p. 150.

36. Contrary to what Kujawa (*International Labor Relations in the Automotive Industry*, p. 182) has stated, Ford plays an extremely active role in Fabrimetal of Belgium. An active member since 1956, Ford is represented in the social committee and in the executive committee of the social committee, in the board of governors and its executive committee. Ford is also a member of the regional employer association of Fabrimetal (where the national agreements are ratified) and in the regional joint committee, which plays a special role in the conciliation of industrial disputes at plant level.

37. Steuer and Gennard, "Industrial Relations in the United Kingdom," p. 107.

tion that collective agreements were not legally enforceable in the United Kingdom.[38] Controversial aspects of the agreement were the size of the pay increase and the introduction of sanctions against individual participants in wildcat strikes and similar forms of concerted "unconstitutional action." Specifically, a participant in such unconstitutional action forfeited eligibility for layoff benefits for six months after the incident and the additional twenty pounds of the annual vacation bonus.[39] Subsequently a high court ruling that the operative disputes procedure was not a contract decided the case in favor of the union for Ford had no legal rights that might be infringed.[40] Although the Heath government followed the American example and encouraged legally binding collective agreements, according to McCrea, there has been no growth in such contracts.[41]

Foreign-owned firms in the United Kingdom seem to favor fixed-term agreements more than the domestic producers: Esso (1960, two years); Massey-Ferguson (1962, four years); Wiggins (1968, two years); and Ford (1969, two years). In 1969 a number of foreign multinationals also concluded company agreements with a termination date—Chrysler (two years), Otis Elevator, International Harvester, and Vauxhall.

Until the 1960s collective agreements in Belgium were open-ended. This has changed and now many agreements are for a definite duration, varying mainly between sixteen months and three years.

In 1962 Ford in Genk negotiated a contract for a five-year period. The ensuing conflicts mainly concerned the extent of the agreed peace obligation. The unions' position was that they could discuss, bargain, and strike on all items that were not expressly covered by specific contract language. This was not the view of the employer. Eventually, however, Ford got satisfaction through a social programming agreement containing a no-strike clause with a trade union guarantee of social peace during the life of the agreement. The peace obligation was accompanied by a clause providing benefits for union members only and gearing the payment of benefits to the faithful observance of the collective agreement and the maintenance of social peace during the life of the agreement. Such benefits typically take form as a productivity bonus, supplementary unemployment and pension benefits, or a flat rate payment.[42]

In generalizing about the overall effect of multinational enterprises on

---

38. Copp, "Negotiating a New Wage Structure," p. 117.

39. Ibid., p. 116.

40. Roy Lewis, "The Legal Enforceability of Collective Agreements," *British Journal of Industrial Relations* 8 (November 1970): 324-36.

41. McCrea, "Research relating to Great Britain," p. 16.

42. For more details see Roger Blanpain, "Recent Trends in Collective Bargaining in Belgium," in ILO, *Collective Bargaining in Industrialised Market Economies* (Geneva, 1974), pp. 214-15.

bargaining structures the ILO concluded:

> They have been negligible where the multinational enterprises have made no attempt to operate their branches outside the framework of established collective bargaining systems but instead have sought to fit themselves into existing practices and procedures. On the other hand, they have had a decentralising effect where the policies followed by multinational enterprises with respect to collective bargaining have been independent of those of the employers' associations in the industry in the host countries of their subsidiaries: in a substantial number of firms, especially those with headquarters in the United States, the European subsidiaries have followed their own course, including the conclusion of their own collective agreements with trade unions, instead of subscribing to the obligations inherent in membership in an employers' association. To this extent, multinational enterprises have in certain countries contributed to general movement towards a more decentralised bargaining structure.[43]

Job Security

A general assumption made concerning multinationals is that they provide less job security for their employees than do domestic firms. This is one of the fears expressed by the British trade unions.[44] A case deserving mention in this context involved a Belgian shoe manufacturing and leather firm that was taken over by an American company. The American purchaser decided immediately to automate the plant and an American industrial engineering consultant flatly stated that more than 50 percent of the work force would be dismissed. The issue was immediately taken up in the joint committee—at industry level with representatives of the employer association and the unions—under heavy union pressure. No strike occurred because a job security system was worked out providing better employment guarantees than in almost any other sector of Belgian industry.[45] The unique American casualness with respect to laying off workers, even when the company follows the rules, causes great difficulties. When a pharmaceutical firm in Rome laid off 350 employees it precipitated a worker takeover of the plant. "The firm was obliged to rescind the mass layoff and deal with each case individually. For those who could be induced to resign voluntarily the company had to provide, in addition to the mandatory severance pay, an indemnification of 900 hours' wages or three months' salary."[46]

Beckers and his colleagues stated, without too much evidence to sustain their assertion, that job security is less guaranteed in new foreign firms

43. ILO, *Collective Bargaining in Industrialised Market Economies*, p. 129.

44. See Everett Kassalow, "The International Metalworkers' Federation and Multinational Automobile Companies: A Study in Transnational Unionism," 1974, p. 292 (mimeographed).

45. Blanpain, "American Involvement in Belgium," p. 461.

46. Shearer, "Industrial Relations of American Corporations Abroad," p. 120.

than in former Belgian firms that have been taken over. They also stated that foreign firms tend to have a higher turnover rate and that a good number of foreign firms threaten a loss of jobs if productivity diminishes.[47] In the United Kingdom, however, Warner found no differences in job security between multinational and national firms.[48]

Productivity Bargaining and Relative Wages

The development of productivity bargaining has been hailed as a major innovation in United Kingdom industrial relations, mainly due to the effects of foreign multinationals. The first agreements were concluded in July 1960 between the management of the Esso Refinery at Fawley, near Southampton, and the local representatives of the Transport and General Workers' Union and seven other unions representing the craftsmen. According to Allan Flanders "these agreements were without precedent or even proximate parallel in the history of collective bargaining in Great Britain." The Fawley agreements had two prominent features: (1) the productivity package deal in which the company agreed to provide large increases in pay—about 40 percent—in return for the unions' consent to certain changes in working practices that were hampering the efficient utilization of labor and (2) the reduction of overtime. The first feature included "some relaxation of job demarcations; the withdrawal of craftsmen's mates and their redeployment in other work; additional temporary and permanent shift working; and greater freedom for management in its use of supervision." The second feature reduced systematic overtime, which had become built into the firm's wage structure, labor policy and work habits.[49] The idea of the agreement was that the workers agreed to work changes in return for higher wages. Other foreign firms such as Alcan, Mobil Oil, and Shell have since negotiated similar agreements.

As Yves Delamotte has pointed out, British productivity agreements have not had much application in Continental Europe since there is no equivalent to the specific rules or practices that tend to impede the rational utilization of labor in the United Kingdom.[50]

Although Belgium does not seem to suffer from so-called restrictive work practices, production speeds seem to be much higher in foreign firms than in Belgian firms. Moreover, the foreign multinationals seem to be more

---

47. Beckers et al., *La Belgique,* p. 167.

48. Warner et al., "Comparative Measurement of Industrial Relations," p. 147.

49. Allan Flanders, *The Fawley Productivity Agreements: A Case Study of Management and Collective Bargaining* (London: Faber and Faber, 1964), pp. 13-14.

50. Yves Delamotte, "British Productivity Agreements, German Rationalisation Agreements and French Employment Agreements," *International Institute for Labor Studies,* Bulletin 9 (1972), p. 34.

strict on working time and absenteeism than Belgian enterprises.[51] This would explain why workers in foreign firms concentrate, especially in their trade union action, on "work organization issues" much more than Belgian firms do.

Finally, there seems to be no conclusive evidence in the United Kingdom about whether multinationals pay higher wages or not. Gennard found that contrary to a popular impression "the crude data suggest that in motor vehicles, the North American subsidiary does not pay better wages than the domestic company." McCrea argues that such comparisons are faulty.[52] In Belgium foreign firms tend to pay higher wages, with some minor exceptions.[53] Changing from a Belgian to a foreign enterprise, in general, the Belgian worker would gain a 5 percent wage advantage.

Some Conclusions

It is undoubtedly very difficult, in the absence of more reliable and comprehensive information, to evaluate the impact of foreign multinational corporations on national labor relations systems. Findings on the United Kingdom and Belgium by and large do not support the conclusion that the multinationals, up to now, have really had a great impact. In their approaches there has been less change and innovation than adaptation to local patterns and attitudes. Roberts concluded that

> considering that there are some two thousand foreign-owned firms in the United Kingdom of which 80 percent are American-owned, the degree of conflict arising out of national antagonism has been extremely small. It would have been much larger had the management of these companies insisted on foreign standards and practices. Even though not compelled to follow British patterns by law, most foreign companies have accepted them.[54]

The question is why these companies did accept local practices. There is evidence to sustain the proposition that although the larger corporations first tend to export their own industrial relations policies, eventually they have been compelled to accommodate to local patterns and to adjust to and integrate within the system. Some of these adjustments were, due to misunderstandings, the result of engaged strife. Nevertheless some important changes and innovations were introduced into the United Kingdom, such as the fixed term and the binding character of collective agreements, and

---

51. Beckers et al., *La Belgique,* p. 69; see also Blanpain, "American Involvement in Belgium," p. 458.

52. McCrea, "Research relating to Great Britain," pp. 10-11.

53. Beckers et al., *La Belgique,* p. 72. The exceptions are in two subsectors of the chemical industry and in pharmaceuticals.

54. "Factors Influencing the Organisation and Style of Management and Their Effect on the Patterns of Industrial Relations in Multinational Corporations," in *Transnational Industrial Relations,* p. 127.

productivity bargaining.

It is too early to make any definite statements on this subject. The influence of the multinational corporation within various national contexts is still growing because many multinationals are new and still adjusting. Once adjusted and integrated they may well achieve a dominating position in some employer associations—where this serves a purpose and is functional. Thus, they may bring about change through the existing system and become one of the dynamic factors in domestic industrial relations systems. In the intermediate term, however, fundamental characteristics of industrial relations systems are likely to remain basically unchanged.

> The major characteristics of a national industrial-relations system appear to be established at a relatively early stage in the industrial development of a country, and in the absence of a violent revolution in the larger community, a national industrial-relations system appears to retain these characteristics despite subsequent evolution.[55]

Of course it must not be forgotten that the rules in a given system are often flexible and thus provide a lot of possibilities for multinational companies, which command great resources and technical and managerial competence. Yet, the basic question for the multinational remains: how to adapt to local practice and at the same time manage the labor aspect of their business effectively?

The present gap about the labor relations operations and the impact of multinational corporations must be filled by comprehensive objective information. This would allow a debate based more on fact than on impressions, speculation, and random, spectacular examples.

---

55. John T. Dunlop, *Industrial Relations Systems* (New York: Holt, 1958), p. 307.

Comment
John A. Belford

Roger Blanpain's paper provides an overview of relevant research in this field that is extremely useful to the practitioner who does not always have the time to keep fully informed and up to date. It is particularly refreshing in its agnosticism. Blanpain holds to no absolutes; he presumes no final answers. His concluding suggestion is especially valuable: it is important that research in this field is not perceived as lacking in objectivity.

Blanpain approaches his subject with humility. He points out that some industrial relations decisions of multinationals have been unacceptable locally, whereas others have been regarded as constructive innovations. The problem has been stated by others like this: the multinational is damned if it does and damned if it doesn't. If it conforms to local practices it is criticized for exploiting lower labor standards, and if it innovates it is accused of being the agent of cultural invasion. There is, however, a simple answer to this: where the multinational innovates by convincing its employees and employee representatives—where it brings them along with it—it can successfully innovate, but there must be some form of employee participation or involvement.

On the locus of decision making, Blanpain quotes David Blake: "Corporate headquarters rarely become involved in local contract administration and subsidiary grievance procedures. . . . However, the whole pattern shifts dramatically when the industrial relations issues are concerned with collective bargaining and the settlement of strikes."

I tend to agree with Blake's statement. There are issues on which the corporate headquarters cannot responsibly divorce itself or avoid involvement; but it would be a brash corporate management that would substitute its judgment of an industrial relations situation for the judgment of the local management. If they do, they are asking for trouble. There is no substitute for local judgment. In this regard I feel strongly about the importance of senior industrial relations managers in every location being national and indigenous. You cannot in five years or ten years indoctrinate a foreigner with the cultural sensitivity that is brought to the problem by a national who has lived his life in the environment, who has been educated there. There is just no substitute for the national industrial relations director.

Blanpain gives examples of two industrial relations changes introduced by multinational corporations on which I should like to comment: non-

John A. Belford is vice-president of personnel and industrial relations of Massey-Ferguson, Ltd.

memberships in employer associations and productivity bargaining.

There is no evidence whatsoever that multinationals have firm policies with respect to being members of employer associations or not. I know of none that has such a policy. I know of no case in which the choice of becoming a member of the employer association or not has been a decision of corporate management; it has always, in my experience, been the decision of local management. Nor do I know of any multinational that follows the same pattern in all countries. Massey-Ferguson happens not to be federated in the United Kingdom, but to be federated in Germany and South Africa. It is a question of what is appropriate for a particular subsidiary in a given environment. This is pure speculation, but it may be that the management of multinationals may be more open to suggestions from local managements about approaches that do not strictly conform with local practice than their domestic counterparts in the same foreign location would be.

Productivity bargaining was also cited as a multinational's constructive innovation. I wish only to point out that this model innovation, which was introduced by Esso in the United Kingdom with the support and participation of the union representatives, has fallen into disrepute there.

So far as productivity bargaining centers on work rules and practices (and this is the basic approach), it introduces an interesting criterion for setting wages: the more inefficiencies in a plant and the more easily they are corrected, the greater the wage increases and the faster they come. There is hardly any room for such increases in the efficient work force. The *Economist,* March 31, 1973, stated it this way: "Productivity agreements . . . usually mean the theoretical easing of restrictive practices for whose enforcement the workers concerned should have been sacked long ago anyway."

I was fascinated by Nat Weinberg's paper, but I find it difficult to comment on constructively. The paper seems to me to contain three characteristics basic to all mythology. The first is that it is characterized by absolutes. There are no qualifications, no uncertainty. Second, it is characterized by internal inconsistencies. Third, it has no relation to the real world. Let me give some examples of each of these characteristics of mythology in the Weinberg paper.

The absolutes. Weinberg says the consequence of the practices of MNCs (and there are no qualifications in the text) is that "it is difficult for any country to establish or maintain decent standards." I simply raise the question whether the MNCs in Belgium, the United Kingdom, Germany, and Australia have made it difficult for those countries to maintain decent standards? Second absolute: "Thus, the MNCs [presumably all MNCs] are able, and not at all hesitant to threaten the job security of each national worker group in order to extract concessions and to impose management's version of collective bargaining." Where, I would like to know, in advanced industrial societies have the MNCs successfully imposed their version of collective bargaining on an unwilling union? I do not know of any such case. Third absolute: "These opportunities for MNC initiatives often enable MNCs to force host country unions into defensive battles, which dissipate their energies in resisting resented innovations rather than in fighting for the international transfer of practices they consider desirable." In our multinational we face unions fighting for what they want every day and I cannot recall a single dispute in which the union demanded the international transfer of an industrial relations practice. Next absolute: "MNC managements, to the extent they can get away with it, will tend to treat their workers not as human beings with human needs but as tools to be bought as cheaply as possible. . . ." Does Weinberg really believe that all multinational corporations work on this principle? That modern corporate management really believes that this will pay off in the 1970s and the 1980s? Next: "They will push constantly, everywhere they operate, toward the lowest attainable level of social responsibility. . . ." This would just not work in today's world, even if multinationals wanted it.

Internal inconsistencies. Weinberg contends that membership in an employer association "makes practically impossible international joint action by unions in relation to a single MNC belonging to an employer association." I infer from this that he thinks that international joint action is desirable. Yet, he criticizes the Big Three in the U.S. auto industry for bargaining separately in the United Kingdom. He cites this as an example of the international transfer of bargaining procedures, "determined solely by considerations of corporate advantage rather than designed to achieve healthy relationships with the workers involved." He makes it clear that he regards international joint action by unions as desirable and criticizes the Big Three for going for separate bargaining in the United Kingdom, which would foster, in his opinion, the evolution toward international joint action. Next inconsistency: at various points Weinberg contends that multinational corporations play the "divide-and-rule game" and "impose management's version of collective bargaining" and "force unions . . . into defensive battles." Yet he quotes a United Automobile Workers vice-president as saying, "A managerial prerogative is something we haven't so far gotten around to taking away from them." Another inconsistency: Weinberg is strongly of the opinion that U.S. workers will join their European colleagues in seeking a direct role in corporation decision making (implying they now have none). Yet he quotes a German metalworker who was employed at a U.S. Ford plant who said, "You have more codetermination on the shop floor than all the codetermination we have in Germany."

Unrealities. Weinberg expects unions to press for two-way transfers of layoff practices between the United States and the rest of the noncommunist industrialized world—presumably within the planning cycle of most unions and companies. He foresees increasing insistence to amend the Taft-Hartley Act to eliminate prohibitions against sympathy strikes and secondary boycotts, because the prohibitions handcuff workers from coming to the aid of fellow workers in other countries. Does Weinberg really believe that there is such a grass-roots drive in the United States, where the AFL-CIO supported the Burke-Hartke Bill and where, in an international dispute under coordinated bargaining between General Motors and UAW in both Canada and the United States, the union's master bargaining committee in the United States made a deal and left their union brothers in Canada on the picket line for weeks?

I do, however, express my appreciation to Mr. Weinberg. He has brought a unique point of view to the subject and enlivened the proceedings.

Comment
Kazutoshi Koshiro

From a Japanese point of view, Roger Blanpain's conclusion that the multinationals have not really had a great impact on industrial relations in host countries seems appropriate. As a host country, Japan's experience has been similar. It seems natural that, rather than causing problems by forcing unwanted changes on the host society, the multinational firm will find it more profitable to adjust itself to local expectations. If multinationals adapt themselves to the local value systems and cultural patterns, there probably will not be any big change in the industrial relations system of the host country. But this requires considerable adaptability on the part of foreign multinationals.

While foreign firms have managed to adjust themselves to Japanese ways of doing things, Japanese firms have not done so well in Southeast Asia. The anti-Japanese demonstrations in Thailand and Indonesia in early 1974 can best be understood as examples of unsuccessful accommodation by the Japanese multinationals in these countries. Because this conference is limited to multinationals in "advanced" societies, I will refrain from going further into the problems of MNCs in the underdeveloped countries.

Kazutoshi Koshiro is professor of economics at the Yokohama National University and research associate at the Japan Institute of Labour.

But let me make one point: if you concentrate your research on comparisons among advanced Western countries, multinationals will have relatively little difficulty in adapting to local practices because the differences between these countries are like the differences between whiskey and bourbon or between Moselle and Rhine wine. The problems of adaptability may be much greater between countries with very different cultures and traditions.

In the remainder of my comments I would like to discuss some recent developments involving Japanese multinationals and trace the reaction of trade unions to these developments. Then I would like to cite a few industrial relations problems experienced by foreign multinationals in Japan in recent years.

Japan's Multinationals Overseas

Foreign investment by Japanese firms totaled $10,270 million by March 1974, a 50 percent increase compared with March 1973, and a level comparable with that of West Germany and France. The geographical location of these investments is as follows:[1]

(in millions of dollars)

North America	$2,462	(24.0%)
Asia	2,391	(23.3%)
Europe	1,997	(19.4%)
Central and South America	1,811	(17.6%)
Near and Middle East	716	(7.0%)
Oceania	640	(6.2%)
Africa	254	(2.5%)
Total balance	$10,271	(100.0%)

Three responses in the field of industrial relations to the increasing amount of foreign investment by Japanese MNCs are of particular importance.

1. *The founding of the Nissan and Toyota World Auto Councils.* Japan's auto production exceeded 7 million units by 1973, of which 2 million were exported. In addition, Nissan has twenty-six foreign assembly plants, which produce a total of 200,000 cars per year, and four sales branches in-

---

1. The Ministry of International Trade Industry, *Wagakuni Kigyo no Kaigai Jigyo Katsudo* [The Overseas Business Activities of Japanese Firms] (Tokyo: Okurasho Insatsu Kyoku, 1974), pp. 75 and 80. Part of the figures for Europe include $780 million worth of stocks held in the Abu Dhabi Marine Areas. In addition, it should be noted that automobiles, electrical appliances, textiles, shipbuilding, and steel are the major industries in Japan that are multinational.

cluding those in the United States and West Germany. Toyota has eight foreign plants (in Australia, Canada, Costa Rica, Peru, Portugal, Brazil, Thailand, and Indonesia) with a total production capacity of about 60,000 units. It also has fifteen sales branches abroad.

Responding to this expansion of overseas production and sales activity, the Confederation of Japan Automobile Workers' Unions (JAW) established the Nissan World Auto Council (NWAC) and the Toyota World Auto Council (TWAC) in September 1973. Representatives from eighteen foreign unions in addition to a few international organizations joined the councils, three in the Toyota council and fifteen in the Nissan council.

As has been noted by Everett Kassalow, these councils have several unique features.[2] First, their organizational structure embraces (1) unions of salesmen which usually belong to the International Federation of Commercial, Clerical, and Technical Employees (FIET) instead of the International Metalworkers' Federation (IMF), and (2) employee representatives of foreign plants or offices where no bona fide trade unions exist. Kassalow raises some doubts about this latter point because it "seems to be a departure" from the usual approach to trade unionism.

Another problem to be mentioned concerning the organizational features of the councils is the fact that they have not yet obtained the participation of unions either in the three major Toyota subsidiaries—Australian Motor Industries, Canadian Motor Industries, Toyota Motors in Thailand—or in the three major firms associated with Nissan—Entreposts Comercial de Automoveis in Portugal, Datsun Motor Vehicle Distributors in South Africa, and P. T. Indocaya Nissan Motors in Indonesia.

2. *The growing importance of the Nissan-Toyota World Auto Councils in the international labor movement.* One objective of the councils is to encourage the unionization of Nissan and Toyota workers throughout the world. Along these lines, the NWAC helped to organize the Malaysian Tan Chong & Sons Motor Company in the spring of 1973 by threatening management that it would persuade Nissan in Japan to stop exporting Nissan-made cars and parts to the Tan Chong Motor Company, which engaged in the assembling and sales of Nissan cars. Thus, the Tan Chong Motor Company was forced to accept unionization.

In the field of international collective bargaining, in 1974 NWAC succeeded in promoting a wage settlent with Nissan Mexicana, a subsidiary of Nissan and Marubeni Trading Company. The union of Nissan Mexicana used to be affiliated to the IMF, but the left-wing faction within the

2. Everett M. Kassalow, "The International Metalworkers' Federation and the Multinational Automobile Companies: A Study in Transnational Unionism," 1973, p. 335 (mimeographed).

union manipulated its secession from both IMF and the Mexican TUC, demanding a tremendous wage increase of 80 percent. Since the union still remained a member of the NWAC, however, Ichiro Shioji, president of the JAW and the NWAC, took advantage of this situation to mediate in the dispute. As a result, a 22 percent increase was accepted (Mexican Ford and Volkswagen had already reached an agreement for a 20 percent increase).

The most impressive achievement of the NWAC and TWAC was the successful coordination of a policy concerning U.S. and Japanese auto production and foreign exports in the spring of 1974. On January 30, 1974, Leonard Woodcock, president of the United Automobile Workers (UAW), proposed an import restriction bill to protect the employment opportunities of American auto workers by controlling the increasing inflow of compact cars from West Germany and Japan. In January 1974 the market share of small cars, including American compacts, as a proportion of the total number of passenger cars sold, was 48.9 percent, and the market share of imports was 18.7 percent. A number of auto workers in American plants manufacturing large passenger cars were laid off. In order to protect the employment opportunities of its members, the UAW proposed that Japan exercise self-restraint in exporting to the United States, maintaining in the future a level not to exceed exports to the United States in 1973. Otherwise, the UAW would propose a law setting an import quota based on the average market share during the past three years. This meant for Japan that her share would be fixed at 5.8 percent of the estimated total sales of 10 million passenger cars. Some Japanese auto companies felt that the self-control formula based on the market share of individual firms in 1973 was not practical because some companies (Toyokogyo and Honda) would be able to maintain their temporarily bloated market share recorded in 1973, whereas others (particularly the Big Two—Toyota and Nissan) would receive a decreased share reflecting recent export behavior following the floating of the yen in February 1973. Toyota and Nissan had decreased their exports, whereas others had increased exports to a considerable extent since then. The proposed legislative formula, on the other hand, was considered less harmful for the Big Two, but more harmful for the others.[3]

---

3. According to the proposed legislative formula, the total import quota for Japanese auto producers was estimated at 580,000 passenger cars, of which Toyota's share was 265,000 units, Nissan's 192,000, Toyokogyo's 55,000, and Honda's 20,000. On the other hand, under the self-control formula, the total exportable number of passenger cars from Japan was figured as 584,000 units, which was less than the record of 654,000 in 1971 and 590,000 in 1972. The total of 584,000 units was to be divided among the Japanese producers on the basis of number of units exported by individual companies in 1973; Toyota and Nissan were to have 211,000 and 173,000 respectively, both of which were less than the quotas for each company mentioned above. On the other hand, Toyokogyo's quota would have increased to 118,000 and Honda's to 41,000. Confederation of Japan Automobile Workers' Unions, "On the Import Quota Proposal for Foreign Cars by the UAW," March 29, 1974, pp. 5-7 (mimeographed, in Japanese).

Therefore, the best solution for the Japanese auto workers was one which made the UAW feel that there was no urgent necessity for the United States to impose any form of restriction on the Japanese auto companies. In order to successfully carry out such a sophisticated strategy, Shioji managed to get government officials and the top management of Japan's automobile industry to meet on friendly terms with Herman Rebhan, then the director of international affairs for the UAW. In this way they could hear directly both about the serious difficulties of the American auto worker and the problems of an industry which was trying to transform its production facilities to produce more small cars within a year. At the same time, Shioji explained to Rebhan that the export of Japanese cars to the United States had been decreasing since the oil crisis because of increased prices. In fact, according to Ward's Automotive Report, the total number of Japanese cars sold in the United States during the first nine months of 1974 had decreased 19.8 percent, almost comparable with the 21.1 percent decrease in the sales of American cars. Rebhan and the UAW appreciated the thought given to this problem by the Japanese auto industry, and in June 1974 at the UAW Convention it was decided not to propose the import restriction bill in order to maintain friendly relations between the unions and the two countries.

3. Applause and criticism for the Japanese style of personnel management.
Some authors have suggested that the influx of Japanese multinationals may lead to "the transplantation of Japanese style industrial relations" to the host communities, with these practices acquiring "widespread acceptance in some countries."[4] But it is an exaggeration to say that it will be transferred on "a large scale to the developing countries."[5]

Paternalistic personnel management, based on lifetime commitment and seniority-oriented wage systems, seems to have taken root rather easily in Taiwan, but is completely unacceptable in Singapore. The basic differences between Confucian and British value systems may partially explain why these two Chinese societies react in different ways. Taiwan and Japan belong to the same Confucian culture, whereas Singapore has been infused more with British culture than with traditional Chinese culture.[6]

What makes the problem more confusing, however, is the applause given to the Japanese system of personnel management by two Stanford Business School professors who studied the causes of productivity differen-

4. Tadashi A. Hanami, "The Multinational Corporation and Japanese Industrial Relations," *International Industrial Relations Association, International Congress*, 1973, p. 17.

5. Ibid., p. 10.

6. For more detailed discussion, see the reports of the Japan Institute of Labour's Industrial Relations Study Teams in both countries. Summaries of these reports were published in *Nihon Rodo Kyokai Zasshi* 16, no. 12 (December 1974) and 17, no. 1 (January 1975).

tials between plants run by American managers and those run by Japanese managers in the United States. The Stanford professors declare that the Japanese companies operating in the United States are "outperforming American companies in the same industries."[7] Their argument can be summarized as follows:

What the Japanese have that Americans by and large do not is a finely cultivated sense of the importance of looking at the corporation as a social organization, not simply as a profit-oriented enterprise. This perspective has led to a system of management techniques that Westerners may find strange, but one that has made Japanese productivity the envy of the world. Japanese firms have been able to transplant this key cultural outlook by filling top managerial positions of their U.S.A. subsidiaries with Japanese nationals.

While Japanese management techniques foster high productivity, they also can make life difficult for American-born managers who must contend with what seems a topsy-turvy world. For one thing, the Japanese conceive of management as a process in which the most important information flows from the bottom up, rather than from the top down. Japanese managers expect change and initiative to come from those closest to the problem, from sales people and assembly line workers rather than from top executives.

More baffling to Westerners is the Japanese style of decision making. It involves a lengthy process of achieving consensus, and it often takes days or weeks to arrive at a decision that an American manager might make by himself in minutes. But, in the process, practically everyone who will be affected by the decision is consulted. Thus, when Japanese businessmen finally do reach a decision, they are ready to act with great speed. No time need be wasted trying to convince colleagues that the decision is correct, since they helped make it. In fact, the word "decision" doesn't have the same meaning in Japanese. We call "decision" the "action stage."

The most telling aspect of Japanese management is its concern for workers as individuals. Our philosophy is that you must care about the individual. Everyone, including top management, gathers in the warehouse to celebrate successful operations with beer and sandwiches. Some Japanese-run firms hold monthly birthday parties for employees at which the chairman personally presents gifts. Almost all Japanese managers make a practice of knowing the names of as many subordinates as possible.

Predictably, workers thrive under such treatment. American workers employed by Japanese companies report that they like the feeling of having many ties rather than just a work contract with their employer. The notion that the company is interested in their overall affairs and even in the well-being of their family is flattering and comforting. Indeed, it works so well that several American corporations have already adopted similar managerial styles—among them Eastman Kodak, IBM, and National Cash Register. All this seems to indicate that America's traditional antagonism between management and labor may well be anachronistic.[8]

7. Richard T. Johnson and William G. Ouchi, "Made in America (under Japanese Management)," *Harvard Business Review* 52, no. 5 (September-October 1974), p. 61.

8. This summary is quoted from a monthly journal of the National Trade Union Congress of Singapore, "Management: The Japanese Touch," *Perjuangan NTUC* (August 1974): 5. The summary of the Johnson and Ouchi study was publicized through *Newsweek* before its formal publication.

The report by the Stanford professors suggests that the attractions for American workers are (a) the participation of rank-and-file workers in the process of decision making and (b) the humanistic treatment of workers by management. (Personally, I imagine that these Japanese subsidiaries do not apply a wage system based on the years of age and service or a lifetime commitment system, accompanied by very slow pace of promotion even for workers with unusual capabilities.) Yet the Japanese companies operating in Singapore are criticized for forcing local workers to accept these negative aspects of Japanese-style personnel management.

Industrial Relations in MNCs Operating in Japan

According to a survey by the Ministry of International Trade and Industry in June 1973, there were 1,464 Japanese firms in which 20 percent or more of the capital was owned by foreign interests. Sixty percent of them were American firms. These foreign-owned firms, however, accounted for only 1.9 percent of the total sales by all corporations in Japan. Also, they accounted for only 3 percent of after-tax profits and hired only 1.1 percent of the employees in all Japanese corporations.[9] This rather limited role of foreign MNCs in Japan can be explained by the fact that a liberalization of policies concerning direct capital investment by foreign companies into Japan did not occur until the late 1960s.

Generally speaking, large-scale Japanese companies have been very interested in Western styles of personnel management, including job evaluation, merit rating, payment by results, quality control programs, and zero defect campaigns. These Western management techniques have been modified in Japan so as not to destroy the basic features of the lifetime employment system. Therefore, Japanese management is already aware of the differences between Western and Japanese approaches to personnel administration, and there is nothing new that the Japanese companies feel is worthwhile to be absorbed from the foreign MNCs. On the contrary, it is the foreign firm that must adjust to Japanese society and make innovations in industrial relations.

We have observed several labor disputes in the foreign companies operating in Japan. There have been at least nine significant cases regarding the subjects being discussed at this conference:[10] six cases were concerned with job security.

---

9. Ministry of International Trade and Industry, "Gaishikei Kigyo no Doko" [Trends of Foreign Firms Operating in Japan], No. 7, June 1974, pp. 15, 19, 28, and 35 (mimeographed).

10. There is no official published report on these labor disputes. A report by the Ministry of Labor, Bureau of Labor Policy, *Report on the Industrial Relations of the Foreign Firms Operating in Japan* (March 1974) contains only statistical information. Therefore, the disputes mentioned in this paper, which cover most of the major cases in this field, were compiled by the author from various sources.

1. Noble Oak Company laid off 200 employees in August 1966.

2. Japan Remington Rand Corporation closed down a plant and discharged 400 employees in April 1967.

3. BOAC discharged 16 employees when it closed down one of its offices in Japan in 1967.

4. Mercantile Bank's Osaka Branch discharged 70 employees when it was absorbed by the Hong Kong-Shanghai Bank in 1967.

5. Chase Manhattan Bank discharged 25 employees in cutting down its services for the U.S. Army. All the 25 discharged employees were reinstated by June 1973, due to an order of the labor commission.

6. Japan Allied Artists (Cinema) discharged 39 employees in 1967.

Three cases involved unfair labor practices.

1. American Express ignored union demands for wage negotiations. Such behavior was judged as an unfair labor practice in violation of the obligation to bargain in good faith with the union.

2. Japan Coca Cola is notorious for its repression of union organizing activities without having been officially caught for unfair labor practices. Any employee who has tried to organize at the company has been skillfully discharged on the other grounds.

3. In general, the foreign banks in Japan have refused to bargain collectively with the Federation of Foreign Banks Employees' Unions. The banks cite their lack of independent authority to bargain collectively. In the AP Tokyo Branch case in March 1955 and the Chase Manhattan Bank case in November 1966, the unions brought action to the Tokyo Metropolitan Labor Commission and the employers lost.

One case of accommodation to the Japanese wage system involves Japan IBM, which introduced a seniority-oriented wage system and paid a "housing allowance" for the first time in its history.

A most interesting case of foreign investment in Japan is the capital participation of Chrysler in Mitsubishi (acquiring 35 percent of Mitsubishi Automobile's authorized capital—15 percent of the paid-up capital) and of GM in Isuzu (acquiring 34.2 percent of Isuzu's capital). As a result of the Mitsubishi-Chrysler agreement, Chrysler began to import Mitsubishi-made cars as "the Dodge-Colt." Thus, a Chrysler plant in Los Angeles was closed down and 2,000 American workers, who were members of the UAW Local No. 6, were dismissed. The UAW denounced this policy with the slogan, "Chrysler, come home!"

Comment
Russell Bell

In 1974 I participated in a panel session on multinational corporations sponsored by the Canadian Export Association. I came away from that meeting feeling distressed about its consensus that effective controls over these corporations, particularly of the kind long advocated by the Canadian Labour Congress, would not likely become a reality for twenty-five years.

The position of the Canadian Labour Congress is that because Canada remains the most vulnerable of any major industrialized nation to the largely unbridled activities of the huge multinational corporations, guidelines must be established to determine what kinds of investments are required in Canada's economic interest and all such investments must be subject to Canadian laws and policies. We also have repeatedly urged our government to do everything possible to establish international ground rules to govern the activities of these companies and to seek to establish an international agency, perhaps under the jurisdiction of the United Nations, to implement these ground rules.

Multinational corporations conduct their business around the world with utter indifference to the national interests of the countries in which they operate, and we are very much concerned that they display the same indifference to the interests of the workers they employ. Capital is highly mobile; workers are not. Capital can be here today and gone elsewhere tomorrow, while workers are left to fend for themselves, often under circumstances of hardship.

Yet I want to make it plain that whatever criticisms we may have of these corporations, we recognize that they are an important economic fact of life in the 1970s and will be in the decades ahead. We also recognize that they are effective in mobilizing managerial, marketing, technical, and research skills on a worldwide scale and that, consequently, they have an enormous potentiality for uplifting the world's economic standards. But that can be realized only if they are properly regulated and made to comply with the interests of the host countries.

The developing countries are particularly fearful that these powerful companies may affect their national cultures and erode their political sovereignty. It does not require much imagination to understand these fears, especially by small developing countries, which could easily be dominated economically and politically by corporate giants.

Russell Bell is director of research of the Canadian Labour Congress.

To cite a specific example of the lack of governmental control exercised over multinational corporations, I would refer to a 1969 report to the Canadian Royal Commission on Farm Machinery, which was highly revealing in its account of how international corporations operated in the marketing of farm machinery.

A decision may be made in Chicago, Detroit, or London to supply Canada with tractors or combines from Britain, France, or West Germany and to charge the Canadian selling organization a given price for them. The same executives may decide to supply the U.S. market from the same or a different source. The motives for these decisions may be varied. The company concerned may wish to protect the higher price and profit level that exists in one market. The company may have excess capacity in one factory which it wishes to utilize. There may be a tax advantage in realizing a larger share of their profits in one country rather than another. Yet the country whose interests are adversely affected may be quite different from the country in which the decisions are being made. The country adversely affected may find there is little it can do, acting by itself, to change the policy in question. To an important degree, these multinational corporations are independent of the national authority of individual countries.[1]

How we can best develop institutions to enable organized workers to match the prowess of these international corporate giants is a major trade union concern. From my perspective, this is a formidable problem. The Canadian Labour Congress's policy is to develop multinational union councils to represent those unions that have to deal with international corporations. This should enable these unions to develop global strategies for effective bargaining purposes. It seems to me that it is also in the interest of corporations themselves, as well as in the interests of employees who work for them, to have unions representing those employees. International corporations that do not accept the rights of workers to organize for the purpose of collective bargaining, whether in the Western industrialized world or in the developing countries, I predict, will soon find themselves in trouble. These are "real world facts"; to ignore them is to run the risk of industrial, social, and political turmoil, and obviously no rational person wants to risk that.

Often, trade unionists are accused of being irresponsible in their demands. The test of responsibility or irresponsibility, however, surely has to be determined through the disclosure of adequate financial and other economic information with regard to these corporations. One of our great difficulties as trade unionists is to get adequate financial information about the operations of multinational subsidiaries. How can we bargain rationally without access to that information?

Finally, we have made some progress toward control of multinational corporations in Canada. Previously, we had a very weak bill before the

1. Royal Commission on Farm Machinery, *Special Report on Prices of Tractors and Combines in Canada and Other Countries* (Ottawa: The Queen's Printer, 1969), p. 93.

House of Commons dealing with this subject, but it fell by the wayside when an election was called. Then a minority government came in—it is surprising what progress you can make under a minority government—and we got a stronger bill, the Foreign Investment Review Act, which is now in effect. While we are not entirely satisfied with this new act, time will tell if it is a significant step toward controlling multinational corporations in Canada.

Comment
George B. McCullough

Nat Weinberg describes MNCs as crass, money-grubbing organizations, callous to human needs, with primary objectives of keeping unions out and underpaying and overworking their employees. There are probably a few irresponsible companies that fit this description, just as there are a few irresponsible unions that sacrifice their membership for personal gain of the leadership. It has been my experience, however, that large North American- and European-owned MNCs are socially responsible, deal fairly with unions, have good relations with their workers, and are responsive to the human needs of workers at all locations.

Weinberg argues that MNCs are hierarchical and authoritarian. I agree, but I feel that he overstates the case. He further suggests that multinationally, unions are loose conglomerates, weak financially, with little capacity for cooperation. I do not disagree with this point, but I fear that it could be misleading. In most countries in which MNCs operate, strong *national* unions are a major countervailing force, and national labor legislation often makes them more difficult to deal with in host countries.

The Weinberg paper supplies several specific examples of trends in collective bargaining crossing national boundaries. These included the forty-hour workweek in Europe; "long vacations" from Australia to the United States; cost-of-living agreements from the United States to Renault; and the concept of supplementary unemployment benefits to France. It is my opinion that this trend will accelerate. As managements move from country to country, as unions become more cooperative and exchange contract terms more effectively, and as the media continues to publish "breakthrough" settlements, the trend will be to spread industrial relations

George B. McCullough is manager of the employee relations department of the Exxon Corporation.

topics across national boundaries.

Weinberg also predicts "coordinated bargaining," which I translate as transnational bargaining. If transnational bargaining does take place, it will occur between individual MNCs and a federation of national unions or possibly a transnational union. Obviously, a major union objective will be standardized wages, benefits, and working conditions, probably involving "upward harmonization." In some cases, these agreements may not be in the best interests of some of the host nations. As a result, unless and until these sovereign states establish common goals, especially some common political goals, I predict that transnational bargaining, even if desired by both managements and unions, will fail to develop.

I would like to conclude my comments on the Weinberg contribution with the following quotation from his paper:

> Fortunately, the labor movement is not helpless in pursuing such regulation. In many of the small group of countries that plays the decisive role in world economic affairs, unions are closely allied with Labor and Social-Democratic parties that have been and likely will again be the (or in the) governments of their respective countries. Those governments are in a position to raise the MNC problem in intergovernmental bodies and to press for internationally agreed solutions.

I agree wholeheartedly, but uncomfortably, with his first statement. The labor movement has been highly successful in politics. Labor parties control many governments of the world today and unions have been far more successful than corporate managements in the political arena. I am not sure that in the long term this is necessarily good for society. I disagree, however, with his last statement. Obviously, the question of MNCs has been raised by various intergovernmental bodies—ILO, OECD, and ECOSOC of the UN to name a few. I submit, however, that even if they identify a problem—which has not yet been done on a factual basis—and they develop viable solutions to the identified problem, it will not necessarily change anything. Except for the European Economic Community (EEC), which is pursuing a course of political union, no sovereign nation is going to accept imposed solutions unless it is clearly in its national interest to do so. I must conclude then that to expect translatable actions in this area by international bodies is self-deluding.

Let me now turn to Roger Blanpain's paper, which raises three basic questions: Do foreign multinationals try to transplant industrial relations, home country solutions, systems, rules, and techniques? Do they succeed, or do they conform to host country practices and values? How much do they bring about change and innovation in host country industrial relations?

First, I believe that Blanpain's use of the term MNC is too general. To me, MNCs are those companies that derive a substantial part of their sales volume from overseas operations and that have as many or more host country employees than home country employees. Therefore, Unilever, Bayer, Philips, Nestlé, Royal Dutch/Shell, Ford Motor Company, and Exxon would all qualify as MNCs. The Joe Zilch Pump Company with five U.S. plants employing 6,000 workers and one Canadian plant with 250 workers, under my definition, would not qualify as an MNC.

Blanpain suggests a number of examples of U.S.-owned companies making mistakes in contravening local practices, many of these instances resulting in unnecessary strikes. His data are irrefutable; however, I would point out that during the late 1950s and early 1960s, U.S. national companies made the same mistakes with the same consequences when a number of northern and eastern U.S. companies first located plants in the South. Again, this demonstrates a common failing—managements from one area of the country making decisions that fail to recognize cultural differences in the local area.

The paper quotes John C. Shearer as follows: "American firms which operate in foreign countries usually premise their industrial-relations policies on the base of the values, assumptions, and habits they have developed in the United States. They then may or may not modify them in response to the different circumstances abroad." I would agree with the first statement and would apply it to all multinationals—American based and otherwise—but not with the second. I think the vast majority have modified their policies over time. Duane Kujawa also is quoted: "The following features of national labor relations systems have a major influence on this decentralization process: employer association membership, employee representation unit, local law and administration, direct government participation in the collective bargaining process, and cultural and social values directly affecting collective agreements." This confirms my experience. My company operates in 137 countries. The variations in our labor relations processes, the manner in which we go about collective bargaining, and the differences in items included in collective agreements are staggering. Even in two countries like Holland and Belgium, where the proximity between Rotterdam and Antwerp has caused us to consolidate some management functions, the labor relations processes are totally independent of each other and the contracts bear little resemblance.

The conclusion of the Steuer and Gennard study that "nonrecognition of the manual worker trade unions by foreign-owned firms is not worse than among domestic firms in the United Kingdom" is certainly consistent with our experience. The Beckers et al. study of Belgium goes even further: "In Belgium the degree of unionization is higher in foreign firms than in the labor force as a whole. A 1971 survey of sixty-three foreign enterprises, employing 59,195 workers, showed unionization to be 82.4 percent, while the general degree of unionization in Belgium was, in 1970, slightly above 70 percent."

On the issue of membership in employer associations, Blanpain indicates that these associations play an important role in EEC countries. He then goes on to mention a number of American companies (including Esso) operating in the United Kingdom that are not association members. In 1969 I reviewed the various labor relations practices in each of our host countries and discovered that our major companies were all members of employer associations except in the United Kingdom and Germany. To figure out why they were different, our subsidiaries in these countries (each staffed entirely by nationals) ran separate studies, carefully weighing the pros and cons; both concluded that they were better off not to be members of employer associations. Here is a case of the American parent questioning nationally staffed affiliates as to why they were different from other national companies, with the affiliate confirming their decisions by careful analyses relating to their own business environments. Needless to say, we took no exception to their decisions.

Blanpain notes Shearer's comment that "The unique American casualness with respect to laying off workers, even when the company follows the rules, causes great difficulties." I certainly do not disagree with this statement; I think Americans are much more inclined to think of layoffs as a viable business decision than are Europeans. I cannot, however, resist commenting that the biggest rhubarb in recent times concerning layoffs in Europe was not with an American company: it was with Akzo Chemical Company in its home country, Holland. I mention this only to illustrate that companies other than American MNCs occasionally do make serious mistakes in judgment.

With respect to productivity bargaining, Blanpain says that its development "has been hailed as a major innovation in United Kingdom industrial relations, mainly due to the effects of foreign multinationals." He then quotes Allan Flanders on the 1960 agreements between Esso management at Fawley and the unions: "These agreements are without precedent or even proximate parallel in the history of collective bargaining in Great Britain." The statement that this innovation is a result of foreign multinational influence is incorrect. To begin with, Esso's problem was primarily a union fragmentation problem and the existence of an old, inefficient plant. Fawley was an old refinery with small, inefficient units trying to compete in the United Kingdom with new, large, modern refineries operated by competitors. The operations workers were represented by the Transport and General Workers' Union, the largest union in the United Kingdom. The maintenance workers were represented by seven separate craft unions. There were, of course, eight separate labor contracts, each bargained separately and at different times. Each union had, over time, negotiated specific practices for their members which, in total, were highly restrictive from an efficient operating point of view. At the same time, the U.K. government, in seeking to correct its balance-of-payments problem, was encouraging both unions and managements to achieve higher levels of productivity in British industry.

The Fawley management had a primary objective, which was to undertake a massive capital outlay to modernize the plant. To achieve this objective, they had to reduce manpower; otherwise, they could not justify the capital expenditure. If they did not make the capital expenditures, they would become noncompetitive and in time the plant would have to shut down.

Their strategy, worked out entirely by Esso Petroleum Company with no input from the parent (other than a lot of skepticism as to its feasibility), included the following ingredients: (1) to seek agreement by all the unions to joint discussions and the ultimate negotiation of identical contract provisions; (2) the identification and elimination of restrictive work practices which reduced efficiency; (3) the identification of actual and potential overstaffing and the need for manpower reduction; (4) the provision of liberal terms for early retirement to minimize the impact on displaced workers; and (5) the development of a scheme for workers to share in the improved productivity resulting from the introduced changes.

The productivity agreement at Fawley was a success; however, it was successful primarily because the existence of such gross inefficiencies and obsolete work practices meant that the savings resulting from changes in manning and work practices was of such a magnitude that there was "plenty for all." After modernization of the refinery and the introduction of efficient practices, the potential margin for additional improvement was small. As a result, productivity bargaining was discontinued at Fawley; there just was not enough pie left to share. It was never used effectively in our other operations in the United Kingdom, nor has it spread to any facility outside the United Kingdom.

Productivity bargaining was an innovative technique developed by Britishers to meet a very severe business problem in Britain. The impetus was not from the multinational nature of the company. Rather, its multinational nature probably impeded the process since the avowed skepticism by the parent had to be overcome.

In sum the experience of our company confirms Blanpain's general conclusions. First, that "findings on the United Kingdom and Belgium by and large do not support the conclusion that the multinationals, up to now, have really had a great impact." Second, in MNC approaches to industrial relations "there has been less change and innovation than adaptation to local patterns and attitudes."

Part IV. *The Response of Organized Labor to the Multinational Challenge*

BARGAINING WITH MULTINATIONALS: A TRADE UNION VIEW
A. M. Evans

In reviewing bargaining experiences with multinationals in the United Kingdom, it is important to distinguish between those that have built new plants and those that have taken over existing firms.

"Takeover" Multinationals

Among multinationals that were formed by takeovers of British firms, there have been few, if any, problems on the question of trade union recognition. The reason for this is obvious. Most of these companies were fairly well organized before the takeover and, therefore, the problem of trade union recognition was a moot point. In addition, because the old management structure was maintained and past relations with management continued, initially there were relatively few labor problems.

Many of these firms were originally members of employer associations, the majority belonging to the Engineering Employers' Federation (EEF), which was set up in the late 1800s as a countervailing force to the national unions that were being organized at the time. The employers were then relatively unorganized, and because of the unions' growing strength and adoption of national structures, they decided to establish their own associations. Unions are generally unenthusiastic about employer associations, and although they do not have any influence on the actual membership decisions of individual companies, they are quite happy if any

A. M. Evans is national organizer of the Transport and General Workers' Union, in the United Kingdom.

firm decides to disaffiliate. The main reason unions do not encourage employer associations is that they prefer substantial opportunities for plant and company bargaining.

In our negotiations with takeover multinationals in the United Kingdom, the Transport and General Workers' Union (TGWU) has, in fact, achieved some common companywide agreements on layoffs and pensions. In general, our relations with individual plant managers among takeover multinationals have been maintained on a good basis. Sometimes unions resent takeovers and the change in philosophy necessitated by the development of a corporate image, because some of their members may get lost in the large impersonal approach of the multinational firm. On occasion, there is also management resentment about the takeovers. There are a number of individual managers who do not like the look of the new corporate staff and are rather concerned that they may be sacrificed on the altar of efficiency. They are our allies in resistance to some of the changes. As a consequence, in many cases we have been able to retain our relationships with individual plant managers after a takeover.

The British Leyland Experience

The problems we experienced with British Leyland as a result of its takeover of a large number of small automobile companies are typical of those involving takeover multinationals. First of all, because of its need to integrate production capacity, the newly formed multinational seeks a corporate image. The practices existing in British Leyland's various plants were not compatible with each other; in its attempt to mesh practices in order to develop a corporate image, the firm tried to get help from national union officials. Normally British Leyland negotiated all its agreements at the plant level. Although they were party to national agreements reached by the Engineering Employers' Federation and the Confederation of Shipbuilding and Engineering Unions, these agreements provide only minima: the minimum time rate (which is the basis for overtime premiums and holiday pay), the length of the working week, and holiday periods. The take-home pay and the real conditions our members enjoy were negotiated at plant level, and there were differences among the various plants. British Leyland tried to involve national union officials in eradicating these differences.

In general, British unions strongly resist these sorts of changes. Because we desire an effective means of dealing with employers at plant level, we are reluctant to participate in the development of such a corporate image. Our union was pressured by British Leyland in a number of ways.

Initially the company proposed a change from a piecework wage structure to either an hourly rate or measured-day work system. At its annual meeting, when the chairman and the financial, marketing, and personnel directors meet with the senior national union officials to review the corporation's policies, the corporation's desire to change its wage structure from piecework to a measured-day work system was discussed. We welcomed this approach, and although we were officially prepared to support any opposition coming from our members, we did not put up any positive resistance to this change. Had our members in the individual plants felt that their current pay structure was preferable and resisted the proposed change, the union would have given its membership maximum support. This approach provided us with some strategic advantages, and, as a result, in every plant in which a change in the pay structure was negotiated, wages were consolidated at a fairly high level.

In its arguments for this change British Leyland used an unusual carrot-and-stick strategy. The firm argued that if it was to be competitive within the United Kingdom and worldwide, it needed to improve efficiency, which could be achieved partly by greater cost predictability. If an agreement could not be reached, the firm argued, it would lose its market position and would be in great difficulty because of foreign import penetration of the British auto market. The result would be plant closures. On the other hand, an agreement to consolidate piecework earnings at an hourly rate that was much higher than other rates operative in British manufacturing would increase take-home pay. In addition, they offered an improvement in the premium pay rate and holiday provisions and provided an opportunity to talk objectively about improving pensions and many other things. The result was that the firm was quite successful in establishing a corporate wage structure arrangement—almost 90 percent of its hourly paid workers are now paid under a measured-day work system.

Although the firm has been reasonably successful in this direction, however, it still has not established the corporate image it desires, because centralized bargaining arrangements have not been negotiated. We have a company procedure agreement, which is common to all of British Leyland's plants, but the final step of this grievance procedure is at plant level. This is a complete change from the old agreement with the EEF—the firm is still a member—which was recently abandoned by the unions because the employers were unwilling to agree to the unions' proposal for a modification in the status quo provision of the agreement. In general, our union is happy with the new procedure agreement.

The Chrysler Experience

Another multinational we have dealt with is Chrysler, which entered Britain in 1967 by taking over the Rootes group, then in serious economic trouble. Like British Leyland, Rootes had a number of diversified, geographically dispersed operations. Chrysler was interested in increasing efficiency. Although Rootes' diversity in local practices had been resolved somewhat before the Chrysler takeover, some major problems remained. Chrysler proposed a change from piecework to a measured-day work system, partly to resolve these diversification problems and partly, I think, to emulate the Ford Motor Company. The Ford Motor Company had centralized bargaining arrangements providing common wage rates, which produced relatively little local wage drift. (Although this negotiating structure did provide a fairly stable pay structure, its rigidity was something that Ford eventually paid for.)

I believe Chrysler also wants to establish some form of centralized bargaining structure. I cannot believe that they are happy that the Linwood, Coventry, Stoke, and Brighton agreements are negotiated separately. It would seem to be to their advantage, for example, for the engine plant in Stoke and the assembly plant in Brighton, which are within only a few miles of each other, to negotiate one agreement. My union believes that, although in the last few years the same pay increases have been negotiated at both plants, it can negotiate more substantial wage adjustments separately at the individual plants.

Let me explain. Naturally, our members who work for Chrysler in Scotland would like to achieve the higher level of earnings that exists in the midlands. Chrysler initially resisted such a proposal, but then agreed in principle to a philosophy of the parity of pay between plants, to be implemented on a phased basis because of the wide original differences. When Chrysler finally offered its parity approach, we were suspicious that the firm was trying to achieve a strategic advantage. If parity in pay was achieved between Linwood and Coventry, we reasoned, then Chrysler might propose a formal centralized bargaining arrangement. It would be logical for them to suggest that since we now negotiate a common pension scheme and layoff procedure, we should bargain nationally on wages.

Consequently, the agreement we reached with Chrysler in 1971 on the philosophy of parity was to achieve a similarity in pay levels, but to maintain pay structures with different classifications in Linwood as distinct from Coventry. This meant that even though the top classification workers earned the same at both plants, most laborers at Linwood earned more than those at Coventry. In this way, we were able to maintain both differences in the pay structure and individual plant identification and autonomy. As a result, we do not have parity in the pure sense of the word, and our union believes that it is a strategic advantage to maintain this sort of system.

The Massey-Ferguson Experience

In our negotiations with Massey-Ferguson, which bought out both Standards and Perkins, we have been able to retain the philosophy that national negotiation should provide only minima with room for bargaining at the plant level. We have cooperatively identified those matters that are appropriate for national bargaining and those that are appropriate for local bargaining. Nationally, we determine minimum wages and negotiate on pensions, the workweek, and holidays; pay structure issues are determined at plant level.

Massey-Ferguson is trying to develop the same sort of corporate image that other multinationals have tried to establish. Their plants in Coventry, however, are still known as Massey's, and the diesel and marine engine plant at Peterborough is known as Perkins of Peterborough. At Peterborough, earnings are well below those at Coventry, and we have had a lot of trouble persuading the company to develop a common policy for take-home pay. On this question, the unions are not concerned about pay structure, for the pay structure at Peterborough is an hourly measured-day work system, while the Coventry pay structure is an incentive piecework system. We feel that pay structure is an irrelevant point. What is important is what a worker gets in the pay packet at the end of the week, and in many cases, you cannot justify paying similar workers less in one location than in another.

"New Plant" Multinationals

The problems we have experienced with multinationals that have established new plants in the United Kingdom are largely different from those described above.

The Minnesota Mining and Manufacturing Company Experience

A typical problem arose with the Minnesota Mining and Manufacturing Company (3M), which built a new plant in Gorseinon, South Wales, and also took over an old plant in Birmingham. The firm did everything possible to avoid trade union organization being developed. Initially, it moved in and informed us that we could not have recognition, even though we had already established a membership base. The firm wanted to apply the American approach: an election on the issue of unionization in which a majority of workers deciding to become union members would resolve the recognition issue. The TGWU did not like this approach, particularly in South Wales, where the union already had a strong organization. Because the existing organization *was* strong and there was a great deal of community spirit, the union was afraid that some Welshmen might not want to join because they believed that membership carried with it a particular kind of political commitment and was not simply a means of improving pay and working conditions. The union's objection to such ballots is based on their potential negative impact on the community: if the union initially lost the recognition ballot, but some years later won representation rights, there might be recriminations against those who voted against the union in the first ballot and the community spirit might start to crack a bit. Consequently, our union opposes representation ballots, and it did so in this case, thus producing a very long strike at 3M. Eventually the TGWU won recognition.

Once we had achieved recognition, strange things began to happen. The union had been trying to organize workers at the firm's Birmingham plant. I had leafleted the factory but had signed up only one member. Out of the blue, the TGWU's regional secretary in the midlands got a letter from a 3M director in the United States requesting a meeting about the situation at the Birmingham plant. We were very puzzled, because at the time our membership campaign had been a failure. At our meeting with the firm's American managing director, we were informed that following the union's leaflet campaign, the company had surveyed its workers in the plant to determine whether they wanted to join a union. In this ballot, 90 percent of the workers had elected to become members of the TGWU. The firm then offered us the use of its canteen for recruitment activities and agreed to give its employees time off with pay during working hours to attend those meetings. Indeed, if all multinationals were as responsive as this, the TGWU would really be in business. Ultimately, we achieved our membership as a consequence of an invitation by the company, but I am sure that the earlier strike at Gorseinon had something to do with it. An underlying motive must have been to prevent a recurrence of conflict with the union on the issue of recognition and membership recruitment.

Another strange experience with 3M occurred when it decided to close down the old plant in Birmingham and to move its operations to a new location in Atherstone. The personnel director informed me of this decision and asked my advice concerning what should be done to ease the transition from the old to the new plant. Immediately I outlined all of the proposals our union would normally make in a situation in which a plant closure was inevitable. I stressed the importance of retention bonuses to hold on to the firm's labor force while the new plant was being built, and of transferring as many of the current employees as possible to Atherstone. I also urged assistance for workers in obtaining mortgages and housing, including consultations with local government officials in Atherstone about the availability of mortgages. I proposed settling-in grants and furniture allowances for workers who were going to make the move. Finally, I noted that those employees who were to be laid off as a result of the move should be paid at least two-thirds of their current earnings until they found a new job. The firm accepted and implemented all of these proposals. Their obvious concern was to maintain customer satisfaction by providing a smooth transition in the changeover from the old to the new plant, but in all fairness to the firm, they were very responsive to their employees' needs and concerns.

The Ford Motor Company Experience

The Ford Motor Company, a very important example of a "new plant" multinational, has also strongly resisted union organization. Initially we had substantial problems with victimization and militant shop stewards being fired or transferred from one department to another. Nevertheless, over the years as the unions increased their strength, we have been able to negotiate fairly effectively with the Ford Motor Company in the United Kingdom.

In 1969 the company went through a traumatic experience when, after a breakdown in national negotiations, it failed in its effort to win a high court ruling in support of its requested injunction against TGWU and the Amalgamated Union of Engineering Workers. From this experience the firm learned that it could not get an agreement to stick unless the workers and the executives of the unions involved were committed to it—that an agreement accepted by the union representatives on Ford's National Joint Negotiating Committee was simply not enough. In 1969, in addition to worker opposition, the executives of the major unions involved in the negotiations were not prepared to accept Ford's package deal proposal. The union representatives on the negotiating committee were told, before they put their signatures on the agreement, that "We are not going to have it (no matter how you might feel personally about the situation) and your job as representatives of our unions is to say that our executives have instructed us to oppose it." Unfortunately, the representatives did not follow these instructions; they went ahead and approved the agreement, and, as a result, Ford had lots of problems.

Since then, however, the firm's attitude toward collective bargaining has changed. One major problem Ford has in the United Kingdom is that the firm gets much more publicity than it deserves. The media seem to take a great deal of pride in publicizing the activities of the Ford Motor Company. Sometimes we seem to be negotiating in a circus rather than privately across the table. The publicity can often be used strategically to the unions' advantage, especially when they have a good case (of course you all know that we always have a good case).

In collective bargaining sessions at Ford, in addition to the full-time officials, a delegation of the principal lay representatives are also available for consultations (with time off with pay). Once a claim has been presented and there has been a joint dialogue and adjournment, we bring in the principal shop stewards and review with them what we have done. (We have persuaded the company to provide the union with facilities to meet their members in the plant when the negotiations are completed.) Because we are opposed to ballots, we do not ask the membership to vote formally on the proposed agreement. What we normally do is have a mass meeting of some two or three thousand workers, tell them what we have negotiated—the offer and our recommendations—and then simply take a vote informally.

Of course, we have continuing problems in bargaining with a multinational like the Ford Motor Company. Between 1971 and early 1974, for example, the British government introduced a series of counterinflationary measures. Ford, being very loyal to the host country government, accepted these policies. One pound per week plus 4 percent was the statutory norm for wage increases, and fines were to be imposed if this limit were breeched. The unions reluctantly acquiesced in this situation, but tried to improve pensions and other benefits that were not covered by the policy. The same thing happened in 1972, when there was a national three-month wage freeze, which the company endorsed. In 1974, however, we were able to bargain to a certain extent, because the norm was 7 percent plus a cost-of-living threshold adjustment possibility.

Our experience with an incomes policy is very informative. The unions like to have a situation in which there continues to be a degree of flexibility in wage negotiations. In the Ford Motor Company, because of its structure and very complete corporate image, the conclusion of the national negotiations is very important because an assembly line worker in Belfast is paid just exactly the same as a worker in Halewood or Dagenham. Ford has a tight central bargaining arrangement with a fairly sophisticated pay structure based on job evaluation; but because it has no room to maneuver, it often finds itself in a less competitive situation than small companies that remain competitive and are therefore able to recruit labor. The statutory incomes policy can thus be applied more effectively to multinational corporations with centralized pay structures than to small companies with maybe two or three hundred workers. One serious problem Ford faced because of its rigid pay structure was 3,000 unfilled vacancies at Dagenham in the southeast of England. The firm could not get skilled labor or anyone to work on the assembly line. Who would want to work on the assembly line if a less demanding job down the road paid just as much? People work on an assembly line because they get a good reward, not just for the love of it. Ford was forced to go as far as 300 miles away to Newcastle to persuade workers to come to work at Dagenham. The firm was prepared to pay them settling-in grants of twenty pounds and their board and lodging for two or three weeks. In addition, these workers were paid ten pounds a week above the negotiated rate for twenty weeks thereafter. Because Ford had no alternative, it made the unions a handsome offer, and we concluded a very good agreement.

Some Conclusions

In my experience, the TGWU has been able to bargain quite effectively with most of the multinationals in the United Kingdom. We have had some problems with MNCs in takeover situations where they have pressed for common pay structures and centralized negotiating arrangements, which normally do not exist in Britain's metalworking industries. In addition, several MNCs have gotten into difficulty when they tried to apply home-base industrial relations philosophies and practices in the quite different setting that exists in the United Kingdom. In time, however, most MNCs have adapted to the local environment and have become quite cooperative after being confronted by a strong union. As is true generally, good industrial relationships depend on the organizational density of the trade union movement, and the key to the TGWU's success in dealing with these MNCs has been its membership strength. I am quite sure that the MNCs in the United Kingdom would behave quite differently if they were able to deal with a weak or divided trade union movement.

Comment

James B. Long

Bekaert Steel Wire Corporation (N.V. Bekaert, S.A.) was founded in 1880 in Belgium by an iron articles dealer, Leon-Leander Bekaert, who wanted to expand sales. His customers were interested in purchasing barbed wire, and there was none available at the time; so Mr. Bekaert started hand twisting bent nails between three strands of wire, thus producing a commercially successful product. By 1885 hand production had increased enough to support a work force of fifty employees. In 1895 a wire drawing machine was purchased and an expansion of output began, which lasted until World War I when the factory was demolished. The initial factory was in Zwevegem, Belgium, about ninety kilometers from Brussels. After the war, Bekaert operations again expanded in Belgium and spread to France in 1922 and England in 1933. In 1927, the Zwevegem plant became the first plant in Europe to use the continuous wire-drawing process and hardened steel dies. Military action in World War II destroyed the plant a second time. It was rebuilt, and employment surpassed 1,600 by 1950. Following the Zwevegem plant's second rebuilding, international diversification began again with manufacturing facilities in various nations— Argentina in 1948, Chile in 1950, Spain in 1960, Italy in 1961, France and Venezuela in 1962, Honduras in 1969, the United States in 1970, Japan and the Netherlands in 1971, and Ecuador in 1972. The Bekaert group today consists of forty-one plants in fifteen nations. It has been a public shareholder corporation since 1969, with consolidated sales in 1973 of more than 16 billion Belgian francs or well over $400 million. The firm is not a basic steel company; its product line encompasses steel wire and related products in the broadest sense.

In turning to the topic of bargaining experience with multinationals, I must confess my very limited experience. We have had no transnational bargaining in the Bekaert North American group. As corporations and labor organizations move into an era of functional multinationalism and possible transnational bargaining, however, there are several significant factors to be considered. The development of industry and labor organizations has taken place among basic sociological and philosophical differences in Europe and North America, which may have had substantial effects on the transnational endeavors of both groups. As history is the foundation of tomorrow, attitudes and social implications developed dur-

James B. Long is personnel manager of the Bekaert Steel Wire Corporation, Rome, Georgia.

ing the formative years of any group have a direct influence on initiatives taken later. For example, European labor unions trace their formation to the early craft guilds, which played a very major part in the societal creation of their respective occupations, and thus enjoyed virtually instantaneous social acceptance. Contrast this experience with that of the North American labor movement, which was born in an environment of strikes and violence. Many observers suggest that even today the American labor movement has far less social and political acceptance than is enjoyed by European labor organizations. These attitudes, which were formed during the early days, obviously influence the mutual acceptance or rejection of various labor movement and management aims, goals, and objectives.

As a result of these attitudes, transnational bargaining with multinational corporations may as yet be fraught with unresolved philosophical differences within companies and unions, on a national and multinational basis. The powers of sovereign states, which are intensified by the existence of many direct and indirect variables, need to be transcended. Each nation has unique laws and regulations that structure activities of groups within that nation. Imagine the difficulty of applying the regulations and laws of a particular nation, word-for-word, to a situation in another country thousands of miles away. I maintain that no company or union has yet been able to surmount these cultural, legal, and philosophical variables on a multinational basis.

Although we have not had any transnational bargaining within the Bekaert group yet, some situations in Bekaert North American have led me to believe that if transnational bargaining efforts are made, there will be problem areas for both groups. One such area is the lack of understanding of why different fringe benefits are enjoyed by workers employed by the same company in different nations. Fringe benefits at Bekaert's Rome, Georgia, plant are considerably lower for comparable jobs on a percent-of-wage basis than at its Belgian plant. The jobs in Belgium have lower hourly wage rates than those in Georgia, but higher fringe benefits on a percentage basis. When the total wage-benefit package is costed out on a purely dollar basis, however, the two packages are virtually identical. In a transnational bargaining situation, human nature being what it is, it is likely that the employees in Belgium would be envious of the higher wage rates in Georgia, while the employees in Georgia would be envious of the higher percentage fringe benefit package in Belgium. As a result, through a lack of understanding or communication, there might be a pyramiding of demands which could be unfavorable to both groups.

In addition, from the standpoint of wages and fringe benefits some foreign expansion plants are treated significantly better (and some worse) than are the parent company's national operations. In the 1950s and the 1960s this was obvious in the operations of some North American multinationals. I would suggest, however, that it may be socially undesirable to equalize this treatment by exporting high wages and high productivity from an industrialized country to a multinational operation in a lesser developed country. In considering these problems and the repercussions of their solutions, we need to avoid casting aspersions against management and organized labor, and to get some convergence of views to develop a mandate on areas where there can be mutual trust and, thus, useful progress.

Comment

Walter Schlotfeldt

Practitioners, who have to deal with labor relations at the plant or company level, do not have the luxury of applying a highly scientific approach to the problems of bargaining with multinational corporations. Their approach must be to discover how to solve day-to-day labor relations problems at the plant level, and it does not make any difference whether the companies are multinational or not.

According to my bargaining experience, labor relations in all companies in West Germany are practically the same. Management faces the same problems whether the company is named Siemans, Hoechst, Volkswagen, Ford, or Opel. These problems may be quite different from those in Britain or in the United States, however, because of different labor relations tradition and development. Contrary to the situation in the United States and Britain, German labor relations are shaped significantly by law and every company in West Germany, whether German or foreign owned, is subject to national legislation.

A second distinctive feature is West Germany's dual negotiations system. At the first level, strong trade unions are responsible for collective bargaining on wages and other working conditions. These negotiations are normally done through employer organizations. For instance, Opel bargains through employer organizations in Hesse for its Rüsselsheim plant, in North Rhine-Westphalia for its Bochum plant, and in Rhineland-Palatinate for its Kaiserslautern plant. There is only one German automotive company that does not bargain through an employer

---

Walter Schlotfeldt is director of personnel of Adam Opel A.G., Rüsselsheim, Federal Republic of Germany.

organization—Volkswagen, the German-owned company. All other companies bargain on an industrial organization level. In this bargaining, whether the representatives come from German- or foreign-owned companies is of no importance, since all companies are affected the same way by the outcome of the negotiations. The critical differentiating factors are the size or the importance of the company and the quality of the personnel involved.

The second level of negotiations, or consultations, is with works councils. Anglo-American trade unionists have fought violently against the international recognition of works councils, because they were afraid that works councils would undermine the authority of trade unions. Yet Germany has had works councils since the nineteenth century, and I would argue that they have contributed greatly to the relative labor peace in Germany. The works councils are bodies of employee-elected representatives; all employees in the company participate in the elections, whether they are unionized or not. This has had little impact on the extent of unionization. In Opel's Rüsselsheim plant, 92 percent of the employees are unionized, although the average unionization rate in German industry is only 30 percent, and all works council members are also union members.

Multinational corporations have difficulty understanding the works council system. Many representatives of foreign firms that wish to invest in West Germany have come to see me to discuss what it means for a company to deal with a works council. In each instance it took hours to explain to them what the works council relationship means for a company like ours. The works councils in all German companies are organized the same way, but there are nuances in how various companies deal with their works councils. For instance, Opel takes great pains to inform its works councils about the economic and financial situation of the company, and discusses future investment, marketing, and production programs with them. Other German company managements take different positions.

Another subject of interest in multinational companies is labor standards. My experience has not revealed any difference of standards between German-owned or foreign-owned companies in Germany. Such differences exist between all kinds of companies. In the Rüsselsheim area, for example, Opel pays higher wages than Maschinenfabrik Augsburg-Nürnberg A.G. (MAN), which is situated nearby; lower wages than IBM, which is situated in Mainz; and about the same wages and salaries as Hoechst, which is a chemical concern very near the Rüsselsheim plant. Opel probably has a better old age and private insurance system than some of the neighboring companies. These conditions depend very much on the developments within each company and on priorities set by the various works councils and managements on different aspects of working conditions and fringe benefits.

My general conclusion is that it does not matter whether a company is foreign or nationally owned; what is important is that the firm approach labor relations problems in the same way as its neighbors. As long as there are reasonable, although militant and tough, partners on the other side, who are willing to accept that the outcome of labor negotiations has to benefit all concerned, I am not worried about the development of national or multinational companies, wherever they are.

TRADE UNION IDEOLOGIES
AND THE
MULTINATIONAL COMPANIES
Everett Kassalow

From a handful of union organizations I will attempt to illustrate the variety in union response to the growing importance of multinational corporations, concentrating on industrial relations positions in and implications of transnational (or international) union bargaining or meetings with multinational companies. In selecting statements and resolutions, as opposed to actions, I will doubtless give too great weight to ideology and to differences between unions. A full reading of all the experience would show many similarities, but I shall concentrate on differences. I shall deal primarily with the so-called free unions, those generally associated with the International Confederation of Free Trade Unions (ICFTU); the International Trade Secretariats (ITS) such as the International Metalworkers' Federation (IMF), which will be my prime example; the Communist World Federation of Trade Unions (WFTU); and to a lesser extent, the World Confederation of Labour (WCL), formerly the International Federation of Christian Trade Unions.[1]

Everett Kassalow is professor of economics at the University of Wisconsin.

1. The AFL-CIO is not currently a member of the ICFTU, though the AFL and the CIO were among its founders. The term *free unions* has, especially in the past, been used to distinguish these unions from Christian- and communist-oriented unions. In Europe with new mergers under way in the trans-European union sphere, this distinction is now less clear. Thus the European Trade Union Confederation, which was founded by unions affiliated to the ICFTU, has now accepted into membership the bulk of the Western European Christian national union confederations (from Belgium, Holland, etc.) as well as the Italian CGIL, which is communist controlled, although it does have a minority socialist faction.

IMF and ICFTU Views on Multinationals

Most union bargaining and industrial actions have a highly pragmatic basis. The International Metalworkers' Federation is a good example.[2] For over a decade it has analyzed what it sees as special characteristics and advantages enjoyed by multinational enterprises in dealing with their workers. The IMF has been concerned with the development of what it calls multinationals' "world-wide sourcing," whereby the multinational constantly seeks out the cheapest centers of production cost for particular products or subproducts, using its great world communication system to bind these together into a worldwide production system. The IMF cites the ability of the MNC to play off one country's workers against another's in this process and to threaten militant unions with transfers of production out of the country unless the unions fall in line. Virtually all of the major union groups referred to below, regardless of their general ideological orientation, make similar diagnoses of the multinationals' labor policies.

To counter these multinational company advantages and tactics, the IMF has established worldwide company councils or committees (for Ford, General Motors, Toyota, Volkswagen, General Electric, and others) made up of trade union leaders from different countries in which these multinationals operate. These councils are expected to provide an exchange of data, support strikes, and make "steps toward the coordination of collective bargaining." In addition, the IMF has been among those unions that have supported the concept of an international code of conduct to regulate the fiscal, investment, and other policies of multinational companies.[3]

This IMF position is not unique, of course. Several other trade union secretariats have taken steps to establish transnational company committees to cope with multinationals in their industries. The ICFTU has endorsed these efforts of its "International Trade Secretariats in working toward coordinated collective bargaining with these multinational companies."[4] The ICFTU also has endorsed the effort "to secure the adoption

---

2. I have traced IMF's evolving position on the multinational question in my study, "The International Metalworkers' Federation and the Multinational Automobile Companies: A Study in Transnational Unionism" (mimeo), 1973.

3. See, for example, IMF, *Minutes of the Twenty-first Congress of the IMF*, Zurich, May 27-31, 1968 (Berne: Uniondruckerei, 1968), pp. 156-57, and *Minutes of the Twenty-second Congress of the IMF*, Lausanne, October 26-30, 1971 (Berne: Uniondruckerei, 1971), pp. 141-45. In its 1974 Congress, the IMF seemed to draw back a bit from earlier positions. Its resolution on multinationals spoke of "Extend, when requested by the trade union, joint representation of workers from all countries at the multinational's top management. . . . joint or coordinated collective bargaining if requested by the separate national unions. . . . representation on the corporations' supervisory boards where the workers desire it . . . ." The change is not great, but seems to indicate more diversity among affiliates as to the desirability of some of these objectives. See IMF, *Resolutions Adopted at the Twenty-third Congress of the IMF*, Stockholm, 1974 (Geneva: IMF, 1974), p. 23.

4. The secretariats associated with the ICFTU, it is generally conceded, are the more important ones on the international labor scene, particularly in those parts of the world where most

of an international agreement, laying down a code of conduct (to regulate objectionable practices) for multinational companies and containing provision for trade union participation in its enforcement."[5]

Although the ICFTU is critical of the multinationals, it does not express general ideological opposition to them in the sense of supporting their *general* replacement by nationalization. A 1969 resolution, reaffirmed by ICFTU and most international trade secretariats in a meeting at Tokyo, October 4-5, 1973, noted that "the international organisation of production can play an important role in spreading new technical know-how and in giving an impetus to economic growth and social progress, provided that trade union action in all its aspects is brought to bear upon multinational companies, so as to safeguard the interests of the workers and the public as a whole. . . ." The same statement does list serious criticisms, however, about MNC actions that "impinge on national economic policies . . . [such as] the arbitrary transfer of production and research from one country to another; tax evasion by means of internal transfers at artificial prices . . . the circumvention of exchange control regulations . . . ."[6]

The AFL-CIO also lends general support to the activities of the trade union secretariats, and the idea of international regulation of multinational company conduct. Its disappointment, however, with progress in both these efforts leads it to emphasize programs for the national regulation of such companies.[7] It is important to recall that the United States is the principal exporter of multinational plants (it has been variously estimated that from 60 to 70 percent of MNC manufacturing plants in host countries are U.S.-owned firms), and thus it is not surprising that the American labor movement has been most concerned with the job-export problem and has sought more direct national controls over the MNC.

---

multinational subsidiary plants operate. France and Italy, where communist-oriented labor federations are the largest, would be exceptions, since the secretariat-affiliated unions in these countries are in a minority position. See, for example, the analysis of the French Confédération Française Démocratique du Travail, *Document de travail: Les Problèmes internationaux* (Paris: CFDT, 1973). The CFDT is itself a member of the World Confederation of Labour, though a few of its affiliates belong to trade union secretariats associated with the ICFTU. In the case of both the WCL and WFTU, the trade union internationals, as they are usually called, which group category (industrial or occupational) unions transnationally on a vocational basis, seem to have less importance and are less autonomous than is the case with the ITS associated with ICFTU.

5. For ICFTU statement on the multinational challenge, see ICFTU, *Report of the Tenth World Congress*, London, July 10-14, 1972 (Brussels: ICFTU, 1973), pp. 580-81. Not all ICFTU secretariats interested in the multinational question have adopted this policy, which calls for a "code of conduct."

6. ICFTU, *Economic and Social Bulletin*, no. 1 (January-February 1974): 18-19.

7. See the statement and response to questions by Nathaniel Goldfinger, director of research, AFL-CIO, in United Nations, Department of Economic and Social Affairs, *Summary of the Hearings before the Group of Eminent Persons to Study the Impact of Multinational Corporations on Development and on International Relations*, ST/ESA/15 (New York: United Nations, 1974), pp. 43-52.

Unionists in Sweden have also taken steps to regulate the export of capital in order to protect employment at home. At their 1973 Congress the Swedish metalworkers set forth a program that included the statement: "Investment shall first and foremost be considered in view of the consequences for employment in Sweden."[8] This has been followed by the extension of government controls over investment.

German union representatives on the supervisory board of the Volkswagen Company are said to have used their votes to help block, or at least delay until recently, that company's plans to construct a plant in the United States—for fear this would endanger employment at Volkswagen plants in Germany.

Generally, these free Western unions are extrapolating from their past national experience in trying to cope with multinational corporations. They are seeking to find instruments that will enable them to offset the power of these companies, and in this effort they look to international (and national) bargaining devices, on the one hand, and legislative types of control, on the other. This is in the same reformist tradition whereby they also have sought to regulate the activities of corporations by collective bargaining, legislation, and administrative devices in their own countries in the past. The new ingredient is the emphasis on international measures.

The attention that the free unions have given to the multinational question indicates that to them it poses new and fairly distinct social and economic issues. It is not that they would claim there were no multinational companies earlier, but in the aggregate sense this is a new phenomenon. Not much emphasis is given to proposals for nationalization of these companies, and there is little or no reference to the concept of "international monopoly capitalism," which was more characteristic of the declarations by international trade secretariats before World War II. The more modern concept of oligopoly is referred to on occasion.

Multinationals and the World Federation of Trade Unions

What are the views of other union groups, with different philosophies, on the issue of multinationals? The communist-led World Federation of Trade Unions has a somewhat different position. In the first place, its officials generally take pains to emphasize that multinational companies are basically just another manifestation of the contradictions of world monopoly capitalism. *"Contrary to what all these bourgeois theories claim, the character of capitalism has not changed.* The multinational companies it has created are the increasingly acute expressions of contradictions between capital and labor, as is confirmed by the persistent un-

---

8. Swedish Metalworkers Union, *A Program for Action*, 29th Congress, August 26-September 1, 1973, p. 18.

precedented struggles being waged by all categories of workers. . . ."[9]

What of the proposed international codes of conduct? The WFTU criticizes them as an "illusion" about "changing the nature of capitalism":

> Some trade union leaders in the reformist tradition . . . are expressing views supporting the multinational companies and . . . are trying to bring the trade unions to seek international norms and institutions which would compel the multinational companies to make their social policy more progressive. To hope that the multinational companies will allow themselves to be liberalised by the monopolies' State, or by a supra-national body set up by the monopolies is an illusion about changing the nature of capitalism.[10]

Although the WFTU does argue that the multinational companies basically represent "the expansion and domination . . . which are characteristic of the development of contemporary capitalism," this expansion, in the WFTU view, makes it more than ever necessary for various trade union forces in the world (communist and noncommunist) "to raise the level of joint international action."[11]

More to the point, what about the programs of the IMF, the IUF, and other trade union secretariats, supported by the ICFTU, to establish world company councils or committees to act as a counterforce (consulting, bargaining, for example) vis-à-vis the MNCs? How are these proposals viewed by the WFTU? Here the differences appear to be significant, if somewhat subtle. In his statement to the UN inquiry on multinationals in 1973, WFTU Secretary Albertino Masetti declared that they could not "agree to any limitation on trade union action at the national level through agreements between so-called 'multinational trade unions' and the multinational corporations."[12] On the contrary, he stressed "the need to strengthen trade union action at the country level (whether host or home), in order to create the conditions which will allow freely coordinated action by the unions at the international level." Masetti argued that "there can be no question of retaining the [UN] Report's ambiguous formulation regarding the so-called 'multinational trade unions.'"[13]

---

9. "The Trade Unions against the Multinational Companies," *World Trade Union Movement*, nos. 5-6 (May-June 1971): v.

10. Ibid., p. vi. Testifying before the UN Group of Eminent Persons, Albertino Masetti, secretary of the WFTU declared: "In no case can the adoption of an 'international code of conduct' be turned into an instrument for legitimizing and supporting the multinational corporations . . . ." UN, *Summary of Hearings*, p. 317.

11. "Opening Report" by General Secretary Pierre Gensous to the 1973 Congress of the World Federation of Trade Unions, in *World Trade Union Movement*, nos. 11-12 (November-December 1973): 11.

12. UN, *Summary of Hearings*, p. 315.

13. Ibid., p. 316. He was doubtless referring to the preparatory document issued by the UN prior to these hearings, *Multinational Corporations in World Development*, ST/ECA/190 (New York: United Nations, 1973). In its section on "Programmes of Organized Labour," this report stressed the work of those secretariats covering the chemical workers, the metal workers,

In response to the question of "WFTU's opinion on international labor unions vis-à-vis multinational corporations," Masetti stressed the need for more international cooperation by the labor movement. But "the notion referred to in the report of a so-called 'international trade union' with institutionalized power of negotiation, is something else." The exchange of data between national unions should be stressed, "but the possibility of combining for possible joint bargaining and action must be sought for in the development of national norms and not in a permanent reduction of their functions and their power of negotiation in favor of a so-called multinational union."[14]

It is instructive to compare this position with the resolution of the IMF at its 1971 Congress, when it declared, "As the international corporations become less dependent upon the profits drawn from any single country, the power of each national union acting alone will be correspondingly weakened." The IMF concluded that it "must prepare for joint action across national borders," stating, "Effective joint action will require also the yielding of some measure of autonomy by each national affiliate of the IMF."[15] I do not suggest that all IMF affiliates that voted for this statement are necessarily prepared to make grants of bargaining power to the IMF, but the differences between this position and that expressed by a number of communist-oriented labor organizations seem significant.

I concede that these differences are not gigantic, but they do seem to be consistent and to have an ideological basis, namely a rejection by the communist-oriented unions of the "reform" or "control" or "countervailing" concepts central to the approach of the ICFTU and the secretariats.

Support for a position like that of the WFTU can also be found in some other communist-led union groups. Scorning the possibility of an inter-

---

and the food workers—all loosely associated with ICFTU—to conduct multinational action vis-à-vis the multinational companies. The report (pp. 79-80) also spoke of the possibility that such action might "act as a counteracting force," and noted that "Most labor groups also favor the establishment of a code of conduct at the international level." It is not surprising that WFTU took exception to these aspects of the report. On the other hand, leaders of the metal, food, and chemical secretariats have argued that WFTU and some communist union opposition to world councils springs from their general weakness in most parts of the world where MNCs are active, as well as from ideology. The ICFTU also was critical of this UN report on the grounds that very little of it was devoted to union interests and problems with multinational companies. See ICFTU, *Economic and Social Bulletin* 22, no. 1 (January-February 1974): 23.

14. UN, *Summary of Hearings*, p. 321.

15. IMF, *Minutes of the Twenty-second Congress* (1971), p. 143. At its 1974 Congress the IMF resolution on multinationals was more refined and cautious. It supported efforts of its unions to achieve "representation of workers from all countries at the multinational's top management," and "joint or coordinated bargaining" with multinationals where these were "requested" or "desired," by the unions. IMF, *Proceedings of the Twenty-third Congress*, Stockholm, July 2-6, 1974 (Geneva: IMF, 1974), p. 165.

national "trade union counter-power" to multinationals, the French Con-fédération Générale du Travail (CGT) adds, that it "has always considered the idea of trade union power in a social system subjected to the domina-tion of big business as illusory." This confuses "economic and political power." Programs such as codes of conduct and international bargaining merely "make acceptable the capitalist relations of production and the new forms of exploitation."[16]

To indicate further that the positions of the CGT and the WFTU have a common ideological basis, let me cite the comments attributed to an allegedly communist-influenced group of shop stewards from England and Italy set up a few years ago to deal with some issues in Dunlop-Pirelli, the Italian-British rubber manufacturing group. These unionists opposed multinational company bargaining, declaring that they "must avoid any moves in the direction of creating international 'company unions', with the workers seen as no more than members of some vast international cor-poration, in which their only hope of improvement comes from what they can win from the company."[17]

The CGT position is similar to its stand on enterprise agreements following World War II. The noncommunist union centers broke away from what had been an almost exclusive emphasis on industrywide agree-ments and began to sign individual enterprise agreements in the mid-fifties—the agreement with the Renault Company was the significant pathbreaker. The communist labor unions at first refused to follow this trend, presumably on the grounds that it involved a weakening of broad class lines. Within a few years this CGT opposition disappeared, as it became clear that important gains could be made through enterprise agreements. When and if negotiations between unions and multinationals make some headway, there may well be a change in position among com-munist unions outside of the communist countries.

British Trades Union Congress:
Cautious Support for International Bargaining

It is helpful to compare the positions of the WFTU and the CGT with that expressed by the British Trades Union Congress (TUC), an affiliate of the ICFTU. In a special 1970 meeting on "international companies" the TUC recognized many obstacles in the path of international collective bargaining, including "the very proper jealousy with which national trade union leaders guard their own sphere of influence, and the quite natural

---

16. CGT, *The CGT and the Multinational Companies* (Paris: CGT, 1973), leaves 23-24.
17. As quoted by Herbert R. Northrup and Richard L. Rowan, "Multinational Collective Bargaining Activity: The Factual Record in Chemicals, Glass and Rubber Tires," *Columbia Journal of World Business* 9, no. 1 (Spring 1974): 121.

reluctance of the average trade union member to become involved in the problems of people beyond his own frontiers." But the TUC urged "a long term educative process" whereby "a real and co-ordinated countervailing force" of union power vis-à-vis multinationals could "gradually be created." The TUC also supported ICFTU calls for greater international regulation of such companies.[18]

In a report to its 1974 Congress, the TUC again lent cautious support to international union efforts to "counter and ultimately perhaps to bargain" with multinationals:

> In certain sectors and companies, this will also involve the establishment of effective communications on the *international level* to counter and ultimately perhaps to bargain with the managements of multinational companies, whose ability to deploy large-scale resources across frontiers and potentially to play one group of employees in one country off against workers in another calls for a new kind of response from the international trade union movement.[19]

This is by no means a total commitment to transnational bargaining. That, in any case, would be a matter for decision by the TUC's respective affiliates, many of which, of course, belong to the various international secretariats.[20] It does, however, indicate a fairly clear difference from the WFTU and CGT positions outlined above.

Unions, Multinationals, and Worker Participation

One other area of policy difference between many of the ICFTU affiliates and the communist-led unions is worth mentioning. Increasingly, many Western European unions have been advocating forms of worker (and union) participation in the management of large capitalist enterprises. Such rights of participation have been achieved in recent years by several Scandinavian unions, have long been enjoyed by the German unions, and seem

---

18. Trades Union Congress, *Report on a Conference on International Companies*, London, October 21, 1970 (London: TUC, 1970), pp. 21-22.

19. Trades Union Congress, *Industrial Democracy*, Report by the TUC General Council to the 1974 Trades Union Congress, Supplementary Report B (London: TUC, 1974), p. 28. This was, of course, a report devoted to the wider issue of industrial democracy and worker participation in management.

20. Some of its affiliates might not go even as far as this statement by the TUC. See, for example, "Multinational Power," *Industrial Society* 56 (January-February 1974): 6-8, by Jack Jones, general secretary of the giant Transport and General Workers' Union. Jones accepts the need for "occasions when a specific problem demands talks at an international level with employers," but feels collective bargaining "sovereignty" must "remain in the plants." The TGWU has, on the other hand, participated extensively in and supported the work of the IMF in the automobile companies' council, which has included proposals for some aspects of transnational bargaining with major auto companies. It also is very active in the International Transport Workers Federation (ITF), the ITS that covers transport. The ITF has a long experience with joint international union action to achieve bargaining and related objectives.

to be on the agenda of other ICFTU affiliates. It appears likely that these same unions will look to similar forms of participation with multinational companies, on at least a trans-European basis. In some respects these union movements see worker participation on managerial boards as an additional device to influence multinational companies.

For the communist unions there is a principled opposition to such proposals, and they have made clear their position in the context of the multinational company issue. Here is the reply of Masetti of the WFTU, in the UN multinational inquiry, to the question: "Does the WFTU think the unions should share in the management of enterprises?"

> The opening of the boards of directors of capitalist enterprises to union representatives is dust in the eyes of the workers and an attempt to make the unions responsible for decisions which in important and controversial cases are in one way or another imposed by the owners of enterprises in the light of their exclusive preoccupation with profits. It is not a way whereby workers can influence the decisions of owners regarding the management of enterprises.

Masetti went on to defend the union's *right* for information, but he reiterated opposition to devices "seeking to integrate unions into the managing bodies of enterprises."[21]

Having indicated some differences between the ICFTU and the WFTU, let me finally note that at its October 1973 Congress, the WFTU took a position closer to that of the noncommunist unions on this matter of approaching and possibly negotiating with multinational companies in the capitalist world. In its "Policy Document" it called for "clear plans" by unions to meet "the multinationals' international strategy," and it advocated such measures as: "a systematic exchange of information between trade union organizations on all living and working conditions within the same company operating in different countries; the drafting of a joint platform of demands from workers within the same multinational company; the creation of a coordinating committee made up of trade union delegates and representatives from factories within the same multinational company."[22]

---

21. UN, *Summary of Hearings*, pp. 321-22. Similar opposition to forms of worker participation in the management of multinational enterprise was expressed by Henri Krasucki, secretary of the French CGT, in addressing the trade union conference called on multinationals in Chile in 1973, before the fall of the Allende government. See "Intervention de Henri Krasucki," *Le Peuple* (CGT, Paris), no. 920 (June 15-30, 1973): 19-20. According to the *Financial Times*, September 3, 1974, in the debate at the British Trades Union Congress 1974 annual meeting, which adopted a resolution favoring the principle of union-elected directors in top company supervisory boards, most communist union leaders were in opposition. They were joined in this opposition by a few of the large "moderate" unions, and together they succeeded in modifying the original proposal so that workers are to be given their choice as to whether they prefer the worker-director or other types of industrial democracy.

22. World Federation of Trade Unions, *Proceedings of the 8th World Trade Union Congress*, Varna, Bulgaria, October 15-22, 1973, p. 42. CGT Secretary Mascarello states that the European company law (in the EEC) "should expressly provide for: The obligation to inform

This does not accept transnational bargaining, but it comes closer to what the trade secretariats and the ICFTU are demanding.

The World Confederation of Labour and the Multinationals

To understand the position of the WCL, one must know that it also has clearly opted for the replacement of capitalism by a socialist order.[23] It notes, for instance, that although conflicts exist "between governments and multinational companies" in the capitalist world, "the philosophy and interests" of the two "coincide on the problems which are essential." For the WCL, the multinational companies are the "channel of imperialism." Because of them, "No planification is possible. This is in fact a new colonialist situation."[24]

Nevertheless, the WCL supports the call for a "minimum code" at the level of the United Nations to regulate various economic aspects of MNC conduct. This code also would include "social" provisions such as "trade union representation at the corporate level in each sister company" and "the obligation of holding a yearly meeting (at the company's costs) of all the trade union delegates of the group." For labor questions the enforcement of this code "would be ensured by a body of (international) labor inspectors (comprising trade union controllers)."[25]

Although the trade union secretariats were seen as having some value, WCL expressed reservations because these "structures have come down to us from a certain type of economic organization (professions, industries), or from a certain type of political organization (regions, nations, ideologies)." Today, "the full and real taking in hand can only be done but by the entirety of the trade union movement" because of the pervasive power of the multinational companies. To do this, there is need in each continent and globally, for a fusion of the "trade union, independent, anticapitalist forces."[26]

WCL also has a reserved position on multinational collective bargaining, believing it "may not be desirable" unless it results from a real

---

and consult representatives of the workers, with the management of the company accepting full responsibility for its decisions." *World Trade Union Movement,* no. 1 (January 1971): 15. The distinction here is in the willingness to be consulted without participating in or being in any way responsible for the decisions. In most instances ICFTU unions are prepared to share in that responsibility, if it is genuinely provided.

23. It is also critical of Soviet-style socialism.

24. WCL, *Sociétés Multinationales* (Brussels: WCL, 1973), pp. 3-5. This consists of extracts from documents prepared for the WCL Congress of September 1973. WCL also submitted a document to the UN Economic and Social Council, but the one used here is more extensive. All quotations from this collection have been translated by Kassalow.

25. Ibid., pp. 8 and 9.

26. Ibid., p. 12.

"balance of [union and company] forces," and does not take place in a "vacuum."[27]

In the case of a number of ICFTU, WCL, and one or two WFTU affiliates, the new realignment of European trade union forces that seems to be under way may lead to reconciliation of some of these divergent approaches to multinational company bargaining.[28]

Geographical Variations in Union Policy: Asia

Each of the foregoing global labor bodies, such as the ICFTU, WFTU, WCL, and IMF, has been sharply critical, if not fundamentally antagonistic, to the MNC, calling for new laws to tax them and impose restrictions on their capital export. There are important variations in Asian union policies toward these companies.

C. Devan Nair, secretary general of the Singapore National Trades Union Congress and a prominent leader in the Asian section of ICFTU, has been among those who have warned the ICFTU and its leading Western affiliates not to be too "protectionist" (in the sense of overinhibiting capital export) toward multinational corporations. He sees the multinational corporation, effectively controlled, as a source of investment and a vehicle for the transfer of technology to the third world.[29] (Singapore is unusual among third world nations in Asia in that it has a strong, socialist-oriented government and probably a greater sense of its ability to deal with multinationals. It also has no rural hinterland and has felt the need for Western investment most keenly.)

The Asian ICFTU as a whole has tended to find its own policy variations on multinationals. In the light of the "ever-widening development gap between the developed and developing sectors of the world," it seeks an approach that would direct more of the multinationals' investments to the less developed countries. At the same time, the Asian ICFTU would control "the dangers posed by operations of multinational corporations" through a code of conduct that would compel MNCs "to ensure that foreign private

27. Ibid., p. 11. The language here is a bit difficult to translate as the WCL statement declares such bargaining "n'est pas souhaitable à froid mais doit aussi resulter d'un rapport des forces." (We have translated "à froid" as a "vacuum.") The balance of forces seems to refer to a conception of the collective agreement which is not to be construed as "integration" or "social peace" with capitalism. I have dealt with this distinction from the way in which the collective agreement and negotiations are usually viewed in the United States or by the more reformist unions of Western Europe in an article on the left-tending CFDT, WCL's affiliate in France. See Everett M. Kassalow, "The Transformation of Christian Trade Unionism in France," *Journal of Economic Issues* 8, no. 1 (March 1974): 24-27.

28. I refer especially to the formation of the European Trade Union Confederation (ETUC), which embraces ICFTU, WCL affiliates, and, as of 1974, one WFTU affiliate (the Italian CGIL) in Western Europe.

29. C. Devan Nair, "The ICFTU and Multinationals," *Asian Labour* 21, no. 102 (September 1973): 2-4.

investments contribute to the realisation of carefully worked out economic and social national goals." It also speaks of the obligation of MNCs to adapt their technologies "to maximize employment."[30]

In labor-management relations, the Asian ICFTU has called for "the strict observance by all multinational corporations of minimum international standards as laid down in conventions and recommendations of the ILO, in particular full observance of conventions relating to freedom of association and the right to collective bargaining."[31]

In Japan several unions formed a combined union-government-management committee to look into the labor policies and practices of multinational companies, particularly of Japanese companies operating abroad. This committee, which is interconfederal since it embraces unions from different general labor confederations, is called the Liaison Council for the Study of the Industrial Relations and the Multinational Enterprises. Its objective is the establishment of a "code of behavior for Japanese enterprises operating overseas."[32]

This represents, in some respects, one of the largest advances unions in industrialized countries have made toward regulating or influencing multinational labor conduct. It seems to reveal some special aspects of union management and government structures in Japan.[33] Most of the leading Japanese metal unions are firm adherents to the IMF, and have supported its various programs in the multinational field. This Liaison Council is obviously, however, a new and additional departure to strengthen union organization and sources of data on Japanese multinational companies.[34]

Union Policy Variations within a Sector: IMF Auto Councils

Another interesting variation in union policies or practices can be illustrated by reference to the oldest effort on the union side to counter multinational companies: the IMF world auto councils, whose efforts go back to 1953 or 1956, though they are sometimes dated only to 1964.

---

30. "General Conclusions of Asian Seminar on Multinational Corporations," *Asian Labour* 21, no. 103 (October-November 1973): 6-7, 12.

31. Ibid., p. 7. The global international union bodies, of course, also strongly support this call for international labor standards to be applied to MNCs. Indeed, none of this Asian "gloss" on ICFTU policy is in much conflict with the latter, but the attitudes toward the uses and potential value of MNC investments vary. In accepting or even encouraging multinational company investment, some Asian unions are reflecting their close attachment to their countries' development programs.

32. *Japan Labour Bulletin* 13, no. 6 (June 1974): 5.

33. One should also mention the successes of the Swedish unions in persuading that country's Social Democratic government to enact several regulatory measures vis-à-vis multinationals operating abroad.

34. See "Brief Introduction of International Metalworkers' Federation in Japan Council," May 1974, Tokyo, Japan, pp. 5-6 (mimeographed).

The UAW was originally the principal force behind the program to establish world auto company councils. The obstacles the UAW and the IMF have encountered in this work illustrate the policy difficulties that can arise between unions from different countries, even when relatively likeminded, as they try to come to grips with the multinational issue.

For example, in the 1950s the UAW made a strong effort to persuade European IMF affiliates of the desirability of developing company-level bargaining in their national approaches. This was related to the effort to build worldwide councils of unions of workers covering particular multinational auto companies operating across the world. The German metalworkers union (IGM), for instance, then (and now) pursued a general policy of bargaining in Germany with the great bulk of the metal fabricating industry (usually described in Europe as the engineering industry) on an industry-by-region basis. The prospect of splintering this industry-region approach in order to concentrate on particular large companies, in this case the automobile companies, was not readily acceptable to the IGM.

The IMF has managed to transcend difficulties of this sort with its auto company councils. It has developed regional strength (witness its European, Latin American, and Asian auto meetings), and indeed since the early seventies Japanese IMF world auto company councils have begun to make a significant mark.

But some of the policy differences arising out of differing national union approaches continue to be troublesome. At a meeting of its IMF Chrysler World Auto Council on May 10-11, 1973, when the chairman tried to promote a policy of common expiration dates for all collective agreements entered into with Chrysler and IMF affiliates throughout the world, several contrary interventions occurred. Representatives of the IGM noted that in West Germany the basis of agreements in all metal bargaining was regional and "could not be changed without changing the whole structure of collective bargaining." A British trade union representative expressed fear that common expiration dates "could put a tremendous financial pressure on the union if a strike should occur." Another British delegate felt that the related matter of a coordinated strike strategy, of which common expiration dates were one part, might be "utopian," especially in face of legal barriers that might exist with regard to sympathetic strikes. On the other hand, delegates from several countries indicated no great barriers even to sympathetic strike action. In this meeting the issue seems finally to have been deferred.[35]

The incident points up the sometimes tortuous path of policy making in a multinational democratic union body. But even in national negotiations,

35. IMF, World Automotive Councils, "Meeting of the IMF Chrysler World Auto Council," May 10-11, 1973, Geneva, pp. 8-11 (mimeographed).

union officers often must reconcile diverging geographical, occupational, or departmental interests and needs.

One more example of the kinds of difficulties IMF faces in its work concerns its Swedish metalworkers' union affiliate. The union is part of the general bargaining framework for wages and related benefits of the Swedish general confederation of unions (LO) and the Swedish employers' confederation (SAF). In that framework the metalworkers and the LO have supported the concept of a solidarity wage, based on the principle that workers should be paid the same wage for comparable work, regardless of the industry. In other words, a skilled mechanic should receive approximately the same wage regardless of the manufacturing industry or company in which he or she is employed.[36]

It is difficult in some ways to reconcile this solidarity wage policy with the call from time to time in IMF world auto councils that wages in the auto plants of the world should be harmonized on the basis of *relative* productivity factors—in other words, that wages should reflect the productivity of auto workers in the particular companies in the countries in which they work.

These instances of difficulty show some of the differences in national union policies that have to be reconciled in transnational union work. Considering how new this effort is, its progress has been noteworthy.

Indeed, the international director of the Swedish metalworkers' union, Jan Olsson, has argued strongly that the "Swedish trade union movement of today feels nothing strange in participating in discussions on international agreements which exceed Swedish law and agreements." The LO supports the solidarity wage policy, but Olsson feels it might "even land up in a situation where it may be considered that international bargaining on wage conditions in multinational enterprises could be the best possible way."[37]

Olsson himself has perhaps best expressed what really has kept the multiplicity of unions together, moving forward vis-à-vis the multinationals. Both the national unions, such as his own, and others such as the IMF work together "on a jointly held concept of changing the power structure of society so that the influence of a wage-earner increases both in the general economy and in the companies."[38]

---

36. The policy generally is aimed at "narrowing the range of wages, first among unions, thereafter among groups, finally among individuals within groups." See Rudolf Meidner and Berndt Ohman, *Fifteen Years of Wage-Policy* (Stockholm: LO, 1972). Philosophically, the policy also reflects some LO desire to prevent elite wage groups from developing.

37. See the interesting exchange between Hans-Goran Myrdal of the Swedish employers' confederation and Jan Olsson of the Swedish metalworkers' union in *The Multinationals and the Swedish Labor Market* (Stockholm: Svenska Dagbladet, 1973).

38. Ibid., p. 22.

Some Conclusions

One cannot but be impressed with how deeply unions feel challenged by the power issue. This sense of loss or a threat to their power arising from the growth of multinational companies—power the unions have spent many decades building up—steers these same unions toward international channels. Also impressive are the literally millions of dollars that have been expended on transnational union meetings called to deal primarily with multinational company issues in the past decade.

The search for ways and means of redressing this sense of power loss is likely to keep the unions driving forward to find mechanisms and devices for coping with multinational companies, even in the face of policy differences. The very existence of large numbers of multinational companies and their economic importance assists the unions in this process. The size and character of these companies make them an element around which many unions find an important new point of transnational identification.[39]

One can hardly forecast the future forms of transnational industrial relations. For the years immediately ahead, however, it would seem that where transnational meetings between unions and multinational companies are accepted, these are likely to be of a consultative character, rather than in the form of transnational collective bargaining.

---

39. Sustained interest in transnational or international unionism has, in the past, been confined largely to top officials of the various union movements. The MNC as a new source of transnational unionism may conceivably produce newer forms of transnational interest and solidarity, particularly at the level of the union at the plant and enterprise. The many spontaneous, unofficial meetings, in recent years in Western Europe, of shop stewards from particular MNC plants in different host countries, suggest the latent force to be found at that level.

Comment
Emilio Gabaglio

When the number and variety of trade union organizations at world, regional, and national levels are considered, it is not easy to sketch a comprehensive picture of their various attitudes toward multinational companies. Basically, however, I agree with Everett Kassalow's evaluations. My contribution will supplement the Kassalow paper with additional information regarding the experience of the Western European trade union movements, particularly the European Trade Union Congress (ETUC) policy on multinational companies.

It is a fact that when the International Confederation of Free Trade Unions (ICFTU), the World Federation of Labour (WCL), and the World Federation of Trade Unions (WFTU) official points of view on the problem of multinational companies are studied, there is a natural impulse to analyze the political and ideological differences among these organizations. Differences identified in such an analysis, however, do not help significantly in understanding the specific actions of individual ICFTU, WCL, and WFTU national affiliates. I do not maintain that official statements are completely irrelevant as far as the attitudes and actual policies of affiliated unions are concerned, but I think it is generally true that the international trade union movement has never been less monolithic than at this moment. This is particularly true in Western Europe, where political and ideological differences no longer prevent national trade union centers from participating in initiatives concerning individual multinational companies. Recently in most European countries in which trade union pluralism exists, unity of action has developed at some level and in some degree. In Italy, a federation of the three national trade union organizations has been set up, representing an institutionalized unity of action, even if not a real organic unity; permanent consultative relations between the labor federations exist in Holland; and unions readily unite in collective bargaining when initiatives are taken by the main labor organizations in France and Belgium.

A very important development was the 1973 establishment of the European Trade Union Congress in which practically all significant national trade union centers of Western Europe are enrolled. The single exception is the communist-led French General Confederation of Labor (CGT), whose formal request for dialogue regarding its eventual affiliation has already been presented to the ETUC executive committee. The ETUC, initially

Emilio Gabaglio, Italian General Confederation of Labor (CGIL), Department of Research.

formed by the European organizations affiliated to the ICFTU, was enlarged at its Copenhagen Congress in May 1974 by the simultaneous affiliation of those organizations formerly affiliated with the WCL European organization and other formerly autonomous national centers. Moreover, in July 1974 the ETUC executive committee, mandated by the Copenhagen Congress for such a purpose, ratified the affiliation of the communist-socialist-led Italian General Confederation of Labor (CGIL). The impact of such a comprehensive unitary trend, at both national and European levels, naturally strengthens the trade unions' response to the multinational companies. This trend also creates a strength that is equal, if not superior, to the centrifugal forces of the persisting political and ideological differences of the different international labor movement affiliations of the various national trade union centers. In view of the emergence of this new European reality, one might be tempted to argue, and rightly so, that the need trade unions feel for adequate, updated policies to cope with the growth of economic interdependence and with their relations with multinational companies is a powerful factor encouraging an eradication of those divisive elements that still exist in the international trade union movement. In short, this trend toward unity may lead to a more realistic and more pragmatic consideration of problems.

From a practical point of view, as Kassalow has suggested, two different approaches to the problem of multinational companies have been typical of the European trade union movement. The first approach sees initiatives leading to the development of a gradual coordination of trade union activities inside one single multinational company, a kind of approach that has been developed mainly at the national union level. The second approach has supported actions seeking public control of multinational companies, at both the national and the international level. These two different approaches are not at all contradictory; in fact, they are complementary, although the first approach is of greater interest to the more militant trade union organizations.

As the Kassalow paper indicates, coordination of trade union action inside a single multinational company has principally been the task of the international trade union secretariats associated with the ICFTU. In a number of European cases, however, such action developed outside the international trade union secretariats through multilateral contacts among individual unions linked with national organizations of different international labor groups. This has happened in the chemical sector, for instance, and is now happening at Fiat of Italy and Seat of Spain, on initiatives taken by the Italian trade union movement and the unofficial Spanish democratic trade union group. In both these cases, the goals have been the exchange of information among the different unions concerned, the organization of permanent consultative relations, and international solidarity in case of strikes in either country. In neither case, however, have developments reached the point of real transnational collective bargaining.

Public control of the multinational companies has recently had a boost through the European Community, which now includes nine countries. In January 1974 the ETUC Executive Committee passed a resolution on the issue of multinational companies substantially parallel to the well-known position of the ICFTU. There was a significant addition, however. The resolution singled out the European Community as a supranational body with sufficient power to impose regulations on multinationals if appropriate legal instruments were provided as the Rome and Paris treaties allowed. In 1974, on the basis of this resolution, the ETUC governing body started discussions on the possibility of beginning action on one specific point, the issue of worker representation in the multinational companies based in the European Community countries.

As is well known, different forms of worker representation currently coexist in Europe. At one extreme there is the German codetermination model, while on the other there is the opposition by all Italian trade unions to any representation that may involve the workers in industrial management decisions. Of course, there are a variety of positions in between these two. Such different national viewpoints are also reflected within the trade union movement at the community level, although a common position has been agreed upon in ETUC as far as the proposed statutes for the European company and the so-called fifth directive on company law are concerned. Both these proposals involve worker participation models.

The ETUC currently intends to formulate a proposal of its own generally seeking the institution of worker representative councils in the multinational companies operating in the EEC countries for the purpose of providing information to and consultation with employees. These councils will operate at the corporate level when the head office of a multinational is in an EEC country and at subsidiary level when the head office is outside the community. Such councils, whose actual compositions are to be negotiated with management but are expected to be composed of delegates designated by the trade union organizations concerned, must be empowered to meet several times a year. It is understood that members of this council will be empowered to execute their mandate during working hours under the same guarantees unions have obtained in the plants from which the delegates are selected. According to the ETUC proposal, a council, first, should regularly receive verbal and written information on the general development of the economic sectors in which the multinational company operates and information on the operations of the multinational company itself from economic, financial, and structural points of view. Second, a council should be consulted before the implementation of any management decision that could directly affect employees' interests, such as investment changes, rationalization plans, the closing down and transfer of firms or parts of firms, mergers or collaborations with other firms, modification in working methods, and so on. Third, a council should be empowered to know in detail and to discuss with management the annual consolidated budgets of the multinational company.

As Kassalow stated, trade unions see the multinational company as something that erodes and endangers the bargaining power unions and workers have built up in the past on a national basis. Although well established by different formulas across Europe and having won representation rights within national boundaries, trade unions are now confronted with the risk of being at least partially deprived of these rights since multinational companies operate across national borders. This is the problem the ETUC, in the initiative described above, is trying to deal with, at least for the nine EEC countries. In collective bargaining and on the issue of employee representation, the trade union movement cannot and will not accept that it should be deprived by multinational corporations of anything for which workers have been struggling so much and so long.

WORLD AUTOMOTIVE COUNCILS: A UNION RESPONSE TO TRANSNATIONAL BARGAINING

Burton Bendiner

We, as representatives of labor, welcome the plethora of written and oral discussion on the subject of multinational corporations; the more the issues are aired and the general public is made aware of the problems, the greater the chance of some solution. There is an urgent need for solutions to some of the problems raised by this worldwide development, not only for trade unions organized in the plants of these multinational companies, but also for the citizens living and working in the economies affected by the operations of these international giants.

Because labor's point of view on the development of multinationals is often not made clear, I would like to describe one labor response to the development of multinational companies—the position and the work of the World Automotive Councils of the International Metalworkers' Federation (IMF).

The IMF is an organization based in Geneva representing more than 130 trade unions in sixty-eight countries, including some of the largest unions in the metal industries throughout the world. The federation has a total membership of approximately 12 million.

The establishment of IMF World Automotive Councils in 1966 constituted a major response by labor to the global development of the multinational automotive companies. Originally a communication or nerve center, the Auto Councils' Office has since undertaken a more positive role in striving for coordinated collective bargaining among the unions in the

---

Burton Bendiner is coordinator for the World Automotive Councils, International Metalworkers' Federation, Geneva, Switzerland.

186

world automotive industry.

There has been an expansion of the councils themselves. In 1966, there were but four: General Motors, Ford, Volkswagen-Daimler-Benz, and Chrysler teamed with Fiat. Today there are ten councils, including representatives of unions organized in the world plants of most of the major automotive producers: British Leyland Motor Corporation, Renault-Peugeot, Citroën, Toyota, Nissan, and Volvo-Daf have been added.

Functions of the World Automotive Councils

Basically, the function of the councils is to provide communication channels, solidarity action, and periodic company council meetings, all of which can involve coordinated collective bargaining.

Communication Channels. The maintenance of communication channels among the unions organized in different plants of the same company in different countries involves the routine notification to all members of a council that collective bargaining negotiations are opening on a specific date, what the union's demands are, and management's response, if any. The course of the negotiations is followed closely. If there is a speedy settlement, the terms of the new contract are circulated among all council members. If there is a conflict—impasse or strike—as is frequently the case in developing countries where the union may be weak, the Auto Council coordinator can take a hand.

The 1974 Nissan-Mexicana strike at the Cuernavacos, Mexico, plant of the Japanese company's subsidiary is a case in point—an example of coordinated collective bargaining in a multinational company on a global scale.[1] The Coordinator's Office in Geneva was informed by cable by the IMF representative in Mexico City that the union at the Cuernavacos plant was on strike, involving about 13,000 workers. A wage increase was the chief issue; the union and management were far apart and an impasse had developed. In addition, there were complicating factors in the local situation: a group of dissidents was determined to embarrass the local union leadership.

A first step was to inform Ichiro Shioji, president of the Confederation of Japanese Auto Workers and head of the Nissan Auto Workers' Union in Japan. Shioji helped the IMF inform the Nissan and Toyota councils. When the issues were made clear to him, Shioji discussed the Mexican union's demands with the parent company's industrial relations department and with the top management dealing with the company's Mexican subsidiary. Shioji had the backing of his own union and of the confederation,

---

1. IMF World Automotive Councils Correspondence, File, April 1-15, 1974, and *Metal*, July 1974.

but he also had to listen to the Tokyo office's side of the story and to the version that it had received from the local management in Mexico City. This information was sent to the Geneva office and relayed to Cuernavacos. After denials, further explanations, clarifications, and eventual concessions on both sides, a final settlement was made 7 percent above the local management's original offer.

Although it was not global union agreement, it was coordinated collective bargaining—Mexico City, Geneva, and Tokyo. A settlement would have been possible without the IMF Nissan World Auto Council, but undeniably it would have been a lot more difficult for the weaker Mexican affiliate of the IMF to reach satisfactory terms with the company. Also, it would have taken a good deal longer were it not for the assistance of the stronger Japanese union.

Solidarity Action. In cases of actual strikes or work stoppages, the Coordinator's Office has been following the course set in the Joint Meeting of the IMF World Automotive Councils in 1971 where, in the course of the Ford (United Kingdom) strike, a private meeting was arranged between the stewards at the struck plant at Dagenham, England, and their counterparts at Cologne, West Germany, to discuss strike strategy.[2] At that particular meeting the German works council members agreed to desist from overtime on work that ordinarily would have been done at Dagenham.

There are other examples, but one must be careful not to romanticize in matters of solidarity action. There are those who talk of widespread work stoppages in different countries to support a strike in one of the plants of a multinational company. The Coordinator's Office in Geneva has not as yet asked one union to sacrifice even an hour's pay on behalf of workers of a subsidiary of the same company in a foreign land. Such action would never be taken lightly. There have been, however, incidents of spontaneous action, such as the French Peugeot workers' token strike in support of their counterparts in Peugeot of Argentina.[3] The union in Ford's Broadmeadow plant in Australia declined with gratitude an offer by the Ford workers in Venezuela to make a similar symbolic gesture.

Company Council Meetings. Practical methods of solidarity action are a prime topic on the agenda of each periodic meeting of the individual company auto councils. At these work sessions, basic plant problems, priorities in bargaining demands, and the creation or loss of jobs due to the company's transfer of operations are discussed thoroughly. An autumn 1974 session of the IMF Ford Auto Council in London decided, for example, that approaches should be made to individual Ford companies in each Euro-

---

2. IMF World Automotive Councils Release, March 30, 1971.

3. IMF European Automotive Conference Proceedings, Paris, December 1969; IMF Latin American Automotive Conference Proceedings, Buenos Aires, January 1970.

pean country for disclosure of financial information and investment policy. This data will then provide the basis for more coordinated action by the unions in the Ford Council.

Third World Problems

Another important function of the councils should not be overlooked. Unions in the third world, generally struggling for recognition with limited resources for organization, particularly where there is a repressive government, are enormously heartened by any assistance from a stronger labor organization, especially in the parent company, even if in a foreign land, or from an international body such as the World Automotive Council Office. Even a simple message of solidarity support has an encouraging impact on the morale of the workers involved.

There have been many cases of flagrant antilabor or antiunion practices in subsidiaries of multinational automotive companies operating in developing countries, particularly in Latin America. Militant unionists have been discharged, jailed, and treated even in a worse manner with the connivance of the local management of great multinational corporations based not only in the United States, but in Europe as well.

What does the Coordinator's Office do about cases of this kind? Our approach has been to exert as much pressure as possible on the administration of the parent company at its home base through the dominant union, providing it is strong enough to add weight to its protests to management, to change the subsidiary's policy. The typical, pious rejoinder from the parent company is that it cannot interfere in the labor policy of a subsidiary in a foreign country with different labor laws, customs, and practices. Of course, this is not true; real decision making is performed at the home base and at the very least, substantial influence can be effected as it has been in some cases where pressure has been exerted.

The IMF and its World Automotive Councils do not themselves engage in collective bargaining. We would not presume to instruct or give advice to our affiliates who already have long experience in bargaining tactics. We do, however, give assistance to unions in the developing countries in preparation for collective bargaining.

For example, in October 1974 the auto councils completed a series of seminars in South American automobile manufacturing centers in Argentina, Brazil, Venezuela, and Colombia, and in Mexico. Auto union representatives came from France, West Germany, and the United States. Discussions centered around "beefs" relating to the speed of the assembly line and the forty-eight-hour week plus compulsory overtime at San Bernardo de Campo in Brazil, where there is no formal collective bargaining contract with the union. The visiting representatives discussed how similar problems were handled in their countries.

There are management officials who claim that the multinational corporations have brought great blessings to the third world in the form of greater employment and opportunities for technological training; I take issue with this claim. I have seen automotive production divisions in India and other areas in Asia (for example, Ashok-Leyland near Madras) constructed on a capital-intensive rather than labor-intensive basis and equipped with surprisingly sophisticated machinery. In other industries, there are regions of Latin America, Indonesia, Malaysia, and Singapore where lower labor costs were obviously the primary motive for industrial plant establishment and accompanying this, in some cases, there has occurred a depletion of the country's natural resources, such as ores, timber, and fish.

There are obvious differences among unions in industrialized and developing nations in their attitudes toward multinational enterprises. We, at the IMF, have sometimes been asked by unions in the developing countries why we are fighting the multinational companies. I would like to clarify this point. First of all, we are not against multinational corporations simply because they are establishing networks of plants all over the world. This is a natural development of our economic societies, against which it would be fruitless to rail. What the unions are striving for is some regulation of these multinational giants. We believe that when a government, whether in a developing country or in an industrialized one, invites a world corporation to set up operations on its soil and gives it enormous advantages in the form of tax grants, real estate options, exemption from certain currency regulations, and assistance in manpower recruitment, the company should be required to fulfill certain obligations. Among these obligations are free collective bargaining, the guarantee of trade union rights, and adequate wages and working conditions.

Specific Collective Bargaining Goals

Common Expiration Dates. One of the specific collective bargaining goals, held by the auto councils since their formation, is more common contract expiration dates. Although progress has been slow, because of the natural obstacles inherent in diverse collective bargaining procedures in different countries, we may gain momentum now that there is a trend in some nations for shorter term agreements due to unstable inflationary conditions. The fact that in many countries there are national, regional, and local agreements (West Germany, Italy, and Great Britain to some extent), all with different expiration dates, is undeniably an obstacle but certainly not insurmountable. Open-end agreements, such as those in France, negotiable on sixty days' notice by either side, are flexible enough to fit into the dates of contracts in the parent company and its subsidiaries in other countries. Not all labor people agree, however, that common expiration dates are a valuable bargaining technique. This is one of the issues we are thrashing out in the round-table discussions among union representatives from different countries at our World Automotive Council work sessions that we have been conducting on a company basis.

Harmonization. Since 1971, a portion of each council meeting has been set aside for separate meetings of each company council in which priorities in collective bargaining demands are recommended. The pay envelope has unquestionable top priority. The battle for some harmonization of wages on a regional basis, such as the European Economic Community, continues, but there are obvious problems. There is not always wage parity in the industry between national regions, let alone across national boundaries. In addition, it is nearly impossible to define unit labor costs and differences in living costs in different countries in this inflationary era.

Harmonization of the number of paid holidays, periods of annual leave, health and retirement benefits, and control of the speed of the production or assembly lines is having more success. Our council releases on settlements have helped set up target gains. For example, publicizing the achievement of eight minutes of relief time in each work hour won by the West German Metalworkers' Union (IGM) in its regional Baden-Würtemberg agreement, covering Daimler-Benz and the Robert Bosch parts factories there, sparked the automotive unions in Argentina to demand improved rest period conditions in their coming contractual negotiations. Another IMF report showed that British automobile workers were behind auto workers on the continent in days of annual leave and paid holidays, sparking the British unions to attempt uniformity.[4]

There can be no doubt that the relationship among the unions in the different company councils represents a continuing operation with significant potential. Coordinated collective bargaining is present in varying degrees. Whether or not this leads to international collective bargaining does not, in our opinion, affect the great value of the present cooperation and coordination among unions in the automotive industry on a global scale.

---

4. IMF Chrysler World Automotive Council Meeting, Proceedings, May 1973; *Labour Tribune*, April 4, 1973.

A MANAGEMENT VIEW OF TRANSNATIONAL BARGAINING

John Alan James

In addition to being a highly controversial subject, transnational bargaining is also a vague and misunderstood concept. Let us suppose that transnational bargaining is defined to include all the following circumstances:

1. a collective bargaining relationship that takes place between responsible representatives of a company and legally recognized representatives of employees of that company in several different countries;

2. a bargaining relationship involving economic issues such as base pay, overtime, and fringe benefits in the several countries; and

3. a situation in which any agreements reached will be recognized as legally binding by the unions in each appropriate country.

If this definition of transnational bargaining is accepted, then to my knowledge it has never occurred. Furthermore, I believe that, unless major modifications are made in the labor laws and regulations of most European countries, such relationships will be very difficult to achieve.

This is, however, only one of many possible definitions. We could take a much broader approach and define transnational bargaining to include discussions by unions and one employer or with a group of employer associations within, for example, the European Economic Community. These discussions could cover such issues as job security, minimum and maximum working hours, transfers of production, and investment policy. The regional agreement could be sent to the individual parties in the

John Alan James is president of Management Counsellors International S.A., Brussels, Belgium.

several countries as a nonbinding recommendation. All of the national parties could agree to incorporate all of the items of the regional agreement into the national agreements. I do not believe such a procedure has taken place, but it could and would be considered by some as transnational bargaining.

Another aspect of industrial relations at the transnational level are those discussions which have occurred between the management of major multinational companies and union representatives from a number of countries. Philips has held four such meetings covering the countries of the original Common Market. Nestlé has held one meeting with union representatives from throughout the world. There have been other such meetings. To my knowledge, however, none of these discussions has ever been viewed as part of a collective bargaining process. No regional or international agreement has been passed on to national unions, national managements, or employer associations as a recommended framework for national agreements.

In Europe, the Treaty of Rome does not include provisions relating to collective agreements. It defines only broad social policy goals. The laws of the EEC member states do not contain provisions that allow for collective agreements across borders nor do they preclude such agreements.

If transnational bargaining were to take place, Europe would seem a likely place for it to develop, especially within the EEC. Until the proposed European company law is adopted, however, the legal situation will remain vague and complex.[1] Any moves toward legally binding collective agreements will be inhibited until national laws are modified to achieve conformity. This will take time and will be resisted by those parties with vested interests in retaining present national structures.

One approach might be for a group of employer associations and unions to form a European bargaining commission for their industry. The en-

---

1. Since 1970 the Statute for European Companies, proposed by the Commission of the European Communites, has been debated and amended in reviews by the European Parliament, the Economic and Social Committee, and the Council of Ministers. The statute provides transnational companies ("Societas Europea") within the European Community a voluntary opportunity to obtain certain legal economic benefits. In return these companies must establish a separate supervisory board on which employees are to be represented and which has the authority to give prior approval to Board of Management decisions on important economic and organizational issues. In addition, in each "Societas Europea" a European Works Council is to be established with the following powers: (1) to codetermine decisions proposed by the Board of Management (decisions on rules concerning recruitment, promotions, employee dismissals, and the like may be made only with the approval of the works council); (2) to be consulted before decisions are made on important economic and organizational matters; and (3) to be informed on a variety of issues on a regular basis. In November 1976 the latest draft of the proposed statute was being debated by an ad hoc working party of the Council of Ministers, whose deliberations will be considered at future formal Council of Ministers meetings. See *European Industrial Relations Review*, no. 17 (May 1975): 2-4, 15-23, and no. 35 (November 1976): 6-8.—editors

suing international agreement would consist of several national agreements that conformed to the legal requirements in the individual countries. This procedure would overcome the current legal restrictions of the several nations. It would not be binding, however, and individual bargaining parties at the national level could refuse to accept it. With the differences in organizational strength and political outlook of the parties in some European countries, such as France and Italy, it is easy to visualize the difficulties that might occur.

A more formal approach might be to form a European bargaining commission whose members would be authorized by the appropriate national organizations to negotiate collective agreements binding on the national bargaining parties.

All these approaches are complex and the achievement of each would require considerable cooperation between labor, management, and government. Whether transnational bargaining is possible and whether it is worth it are questions that must be answered.

My task is to present a management view of transnational bargaining. What I say represents my own opinions; I represent no management group or body of thought. I do not believe that there is or could be consensus within the management of multinational companies on a subject as complex as industrial relations. I do not believe that there is general agreement within the American business community on what makes for successful employee relations. My experience also has shown that there is a considerable difference in outlook on this subject between American and European management. Therefore, it is impossible to present a management view that covers more than one's own opinions.

I do not believe that transnational collective bargaining has occurred, and I do believe that it will be difficult to achieve within the present legal bargaining frameworks of the several national states. I also am of the opinion that there are really very few people in either management or labor who truly wish to see the bargaining process extended beyond the present regional or national scope. We can expect resistance within all sectors: local, regional, and national labor officials; nonunion works council members; nonunion employees; company directors; employer association staff; and government officials involved in national mediation and arbitration duties. All of these people would see their roles changed and probably diminished if national bargaining were extended across national borders. Therefore, I believe that they will resist any such moves, both overtly and covertly.

The vast majority of multinational companies, both American and European, with which I have been in contact operate with a highly polycentric organizational philosophy when it comes to employee relations. This means that local managers are given the full responsibility and authority to conduct their relations with employees within the national structure. In the past eighteen months I have conducted seminars on this subject with over 2,500 managers representing over 300 multinational companies throughout Europe and the United States. I know of no company that has centralized its employee relations decision making or tactical planning at either corporate headquarters or a regional office. The situation is quite the opposite. Most companies are spending considerable time in educating key managers about employee relations in various countries so that they will appreciate the great differences and will not, therefore, interfere inadvertently in local matters by applying a "that's the way we do it at home" approach.

The large majority of multinational companies allow and encourage their local units to join employer associations. Only a very few attempt to bargain alone. As a result, their conditions of employment are minima established by the local collective bargaining process. If the conditions of employment vary at all, it is to provide supplements above these local agreement minima. Personally, I believe that it is best to leave the definition of the basic conditions of employment at the lowest possible level. Only then can we hope to keep individual plants and companies responsive to local conditions and their abilities to pay. As a matter of fact, I now find great fault with national bargaining patterns. Bargaining with two or three hundred companies at a time is bound to result in agreements which are uneconomical for some companies. In addition, breakdowns in negotiations which threaten economic sanctions against an entire industry or region can lead to inflationary agreements.

In recent years in Europe wages and salaries have been rising as much as 15 to 20 percent per year. In Belgium, West Germany, and Holland labor costs are 15 to 30 cents per hour higher than in Philadelphia, Los Angeles, and Chicago. Pressures are developing for 10 to 20 percent increases in 1975, indexation, and fourteen monthly payments, following the agreements which provided for thirteen monthly paychecks. This is all very well if by paying higher wages and salaries companies remain competitive, but this is not the case. Unemployment levels in most European countries have risen sharply as a result of continuing wage inflation. Demand for goods has dropped as customers refuse to accept higher prices. Unless individual plants and companies can develop workable plans to maintain costs, production levels, and employment, economic crises will develop in some countries.

I will not argue for cooperation between labor and management at the local level and at the same time encourage the continuation of national bargaining. As a result, I cannot conceive of moving the process even further from the workplace through transnational bargaining. There is only one sound basis for doing so and that is if by discussing issues with one company at a regional or international level, the unions can develop special arrangements for certain units of the company to keep them competitive. Such agreements, as I stated earlier, would not necessarily be binding on the national unions, so effective cooperation between them would be important.

I do not want to be wholly negative on this subject, however. I can see great potential value in the type of meetings that the Philips Company has held with the European Metalworkers Federation. I say potential value because first we must drop the term "bargaining" and talk about discussions. Management must be assured that entering into such meetings will not result in bargaining per se or in undue interference with the rights of local management and national labor relations institutions. Without these assurances, I believe that most companies will continue to resist discussions at the regional and international levels. This is unfortunate, for cooperation is definitely needed at all levels and between all parties if the world is to survive an economic crisis. Many company managers believe in creative approaches to employee relations and might be willing to sit down and discuss their long-range plans, including the implications for manpower planning and methods for avoiding or alleviating hardship. But they are likely to do so only if they are assured that all parties will enter into such discussions with a spirit of cooperation, an agreed agenda, and an agreement to limit the discussions to those items that will not interfere with the autonomy of local managers and local institutions.

I would, therefore, strongly recommend that the term "transnational bargaining" be dropped from our vocabulary. Instead, methods should be sought to encourage cooperation in creative employee relations at local, regional, and international levels.

Conference Participants

Angle, Frank W., Director of Labor Relations, General Motors Overseas Operations, New York, U.S.A.

Annibaldi, Paolo, Central Personnel Division, Fiat, Torino, Italy

Banks, Robert F., Dean, James Madison College, Michigan State University, East Lansing, Michigan, U.S.A.

Belford, John A., Vice-president, Personnel and Industrial Relations, Massey-Ferguson, Ltd., Toronto, Ontario, Canada

Bell, Russell, Director of Research, Canadian Labour Congress, Ottawa, Ontario, Canada

Bendiner, Burton, Coordinator, World Automotive Councils, International Metalworkers' Federation, Geneva, Switzerland

Blackman, Herbert N., Deputy Assistant Secretary for Trade and Adjustment Policy, Bureau of International Labor Affairs, U.S. Department of Labor, Washington, D.C., U.S.A.

Blake, David H., Professor, Department of Political Science, University of Pittsburgh, Pittsburgh, Pennsylvania, U.S.A.

Blanpain, Roger, Professor of Law and Director of the Institute for Labor Relations, University of Leuven, Leuven, Belgium

Bowie, Thomas, Deputy Coordinator, International Labor Affairs, U.S. Department of State, Washington, D.C., U.S.A.

Clack, Garfield, Chief, Industrial Relations Research Division, Canadian Department of Labour, Ottawa, Ontario, Canada

Clarke, Oliver, Principal Administrator, Organization for Economic Cooperation and Development, Paris, France

Cole, Robert E., Director, Center for Japanese Studies, University of Michigan, Ann Arbor, Michigan, U.S.A.

Copp, Robert, Overseas Liaison Manager, Labor Relations Staff, Ford Motor Company, Detroit, Michigan, U.S.A.

Danielian, Ronald L., Director, Center for Multinational Studies, Washington, D.C., U.S.A.

Dilles, Marcel, Industrial Relations Manager, Ford-Werke A.G., Genk, Belgium

Enckell, Laurent C., Representative, International Union of Food and Allied Workers' Association, New York, New York, U.S.A.

Estep, Richard, Research Director, United Paperworkers International Union, Flushing, New York, U.S.A.

197

Evans, A. M., National Organiser, Transport and General Workers' Union, London, England

Flanagan, Robert, Associate Professor of Labor Economics, Graduate School of Business, University of Chicago, Chicago, Illinois, U.S.A.

Ford, Charles, General Secretary, International Textile Garment and Leather Workers' Federation, Brussels, Belgium

Gabaglio, Emilio, Research Department, General Confederation of Labor (CGIL), Rome, Italy

Gladstone, Alan, International Labour Office, Geneva, Switzerland

Heise, Paul A., International Economist, Bureau of International Labor Affairs, U.S. Department of Labor, Washington, D.C., U.S.A.

James, John Alan, President, Management Counsellors International S.A., Brussels, Belgium

Jedel, Michael J., Associate Professor, Department of Management and Institute of International Business, Georgia State University, Atlanta, Georgia, U.S.A.

Jones, Dallas, Professor, Department of Business Administration, University of Michigan, Ann Arbor, Michigan, U.S.A.

Kassalow, Everett, Professor, Department of Economics, University of Wisconsin, Madison, Wisconsin, U.S.A.

Kirk, Joseph, Jr., Sub District Director, United Steelworkers of America, Charlotte, North Carolina, U.S.A.

Koshiro, Kazutoshi, Professor of Economics, Yokohama National University, and Research Associate, Japan Institute of Labor, Tokyo, Japan

Kujawa, Duane, Professor of International Business, School of Business and Organizational Sciences, Florida International University, Miami, Florida, U.S.A.

Kuroiwa, Mokoto, President, Mitsubishi Aircraft International, Inc., San Angelo, Texas, U.S.A.

Levine, Solomon B., Chairman, East Asian Studies Program, University of Wisconsin, Madison, Wisconsin, U.S.A.

Long, James B., Personnel Manager, Bekaert Steel Wire Corporation, Rome, Georgia, U.S.A.

Malles, Paul, Economic Council of Canada, Ottawa, Ontario, Canada

McCullough, George B., Manager, Employee Relations Department, Exxon Corporation, New York, New York, U.S.A.

McPherson, James A., Vice-president, Industrial Relations, Hitachi Magnetics Corporation, Edmore, Michigan, U.S.A.

Neumann, Imgard, Economist, Investment Policy Division, U.S. Department of Commerce, Washington, D.C., U.S.A.

Nulty, Timothy E., Director, Research Department, United Automobile Workers of America, Detroit, Michigan, U.S.A.

Ollenhauer, Herman, Head, Industrial Relations Division, Commission of the European Communities, Brussels, Belgium

Olsson, Jan, International Secretary, LO Metal Workers, Stockholm, Sweden

Pierce, Marshall, President, Local 190, International Union of Electrical, Radio and Machine Workers, Rome, Georgia, U.S.A.

Reiser, Ralph, President Emeritus, United Glass and Ceramic Workers of North America, Columbus, Ohio, U.S.A.

Reynolds, Calvin, Vice-president, Human Resource Services, Inc., New York, New York, U.S.A.

Reynolds, Warren, Senior Program Officer for Economic Studies, Bureau of Intelligence and Research, U.S. Department of State, Washington, D.C., U.S.A.

Roberts, B. C., Professor of Industrial Relations, London School of Economics and Political Science, University of London, London, England

Rowan, Richard L., Professor, Department of Management, Wharton School, University of Pennsylvania, Philadelphia, Pennsylvania, U.S.A.

Schlotfeldt, Walter, Director of Personnel, Adam Opel A.G., Rüsselsheim, Federal Republic of Germany

Sharman, Ben A., International Representative, International Association of Machinists and Aerospace Workers, Washington, D.C., U.S.A.

Slezak, Labor Attaché, U.S. Department of State, Washington, D.C., U.S.A.

Smith, Charles H., Jr., Chairman, Chamber of Commerce of the United States, President of SIFCO Industries, and U.S. Employer Representative to the International Labor Organization, Washington, D.C., U.S.A.

Stieber, Jack, Director, School of Labor and Industrial Relations, Michigan State University, East Lansing, Michigan, U.S.A.

Sturmthal, Adolf, Professor, Institute of Labor and Industrial Relations, University of Illinois, Champaign, Illinois, U.S.A.

Sullivan, J. W., Grand Lodge Representative, International Association of Machinists and Aerospace Workers, Washington, D.C., U.S.A.

Taira, Koji, Professor, Institute of Labor and Industrial Relations, University of Illinois, Champaign, Illinois, U.S.A.

Tudyka, Kurt P., Professor, Peace Research Centre, Institute of Political Science, University of Nijmegen, Nijmegen, Netherlands

Valcavi, Domenico, Research Director, General Confederation of Labor, Rome, Italy

Wayland, William, Overseas Labor Relations Administrator, Chrysler Corporation, Highland Park, Michigan, U.S.A.

Weinberg, Nat, Economic Consultant, Sumner, Maryland, U.S.A.

Weintraub, Norman, Director of Research, International Brotherhood of Teamsters, Chauffeurs, Warehousemen and Helpers of America, Washington, D.C., U.S.A.

Woodcock, Leonard, President, International Union of United Automobile, Aerospace and Agricultural Implement Workers of America, Detroit, Michigan, U.S.A.